AP 生物

导学与应考指南

主　编　安生AP课程专家组
编　者　金　菁　王晓婷

东南大学出版社
·南京·

内 容 提 要

本书针对广大学习者学习 AP 生物的现状，在总结多年教学经验的基础上，以准确、贴切的中文注解，对生物中的基本概念进行讲解，并详析了难点、易错点，以批注的形式列出中国学生最感到困难的地方。本书还有适当的练习，供巩固强化之用。本书适用于有志参加 AP 考试的学生作为课程辅导及应试前总结知识点、应考冲刺之用。

图书在版编目（CIP）数据

AP 生物导学与应考指南/安生 AP 课程专家组主编．—南京：东南大学出版社，2013.9
　美国 AP 课程
　ISBN 978-7-5641-4478-4

Ⅰ.①A… Ⅱ.①安… Ⅲ.①生物课-高中-教学参考资料 Ⅳ.①G634.93

中国版本图书馆CIP数据核字(2013)第207605号

AP 生物导学与应考指南

主　　编	安生 AP 课程专家组	责任编辑	刘　坚
电　　话	(025)83793329/83790577(传真)	电子邮件	liu-jian@seu.edu.cn
出版发行	东南大学出版社	出 版 人	江建中
地　　址	南京市四牌楼2号	邮　　编	210096
销售电话	(025)83793191/83794561/83794174/83794121/83795801/83792174 83795802/57711295(传真)		
网　　址	http://www.seupress.com	电子邮件	press@seupress.com
经　　销	全国各地新华书店	印　　刷	南京新洲印刷有限公司
开　　本	787mm×1092mm　1/16	印　　张	15
字　　数	381 千字	印　　数	1—3500 册
版　　次	2013 年 9 月第 1 版	印　　次	2013 年 9 月第 1 次印刷
书　　号	ISBN 978-7-5641-4478-4		
定　　价	32.00 元		

＊ 未经许可，本书内文字不得以任何方式转载、演绎，违者必究。
＊ 本社图书若有印装质量问题，请直接与营销部联系。电话：025-83791830。

安生国际教育科学研究院图书策划委员会

主　　任　张梧华
委员会成员　张梧华　曹亚民　李　容
　　　　　　　王　健　卫　欣　张　莉
　　　　　　　刘　航　张　涛　林　猛

Preface 前言

AP 是 Advanced Placement 的缩写，中文一般翻译为美国大学先修课程、美国大学预修课程，指由美国大学理事会(The College Board)提供的在高中授课的大学课程。美国高中生可以选修这些课程，在完成课业后参加 AP 考试，得到一定的成绩后可以获得大学学分。美国高中 AP 课程有 22 个门类、37 个学科，已在美国 15 000 多所高中里普遍开设。它可以使高中学生提前接触大学课程，避免了高中和大学初级阶段课程的重复。目前，已有 50 多个国家的 4 000 多所大学承认 AP 学分为其入学参考标准和该项考试为考生增添的大学学分，其中包括哈佛、耶鲁、牛津、剑桥等世界名牌大学。

AP 考试每年 5 月举行，目前已经在全球 80 多个国家开设。

考试通过的 AP 课程可以折抵大学学分，减免大学课程，帮助学生缩短大学学时、跳级，更可节省高昂的大学学费。更重要的是，据统计，拥有优异 AP 考试成绩的高中生在未来的大学学习中有更加出色的表现和发展，美国各大学已将 AP 成绩看作衡量学生学习和研究能力以及应付高难度大学课程能力的重要指标。参加 AP 考试科目多、考分高的学生被美国名校另眼相看。英国、加拿大、澳大利亚等国也将此作为发放奖学金的主要条件之一。

随着中国出国留学的人数越来越多、越来越低龄化，很多学生和家长开始选择 AP 课程考试并将之作为跨入欧美著名高校的重要加分手段，因此 AP 课程在中国越来越热，报考人数逐年上升。

安生基金会是国内较早接触 AP 并从事 AP 课程教学的机构。近年来，安生和国内诸多知名高中签约，联办美国高中课程并 AP 课程国际班/部，并成功地在安生的专业升学队伍的帮助和指导下为欧美名校如哈佛、MIT 等输送了大批优秀学子，成为国内在 AP 教学领域异军突起的重要力量，受到了欧美名校、联办高中和诸多家长、学子的一致好评。

针对广大学习者学习 AP 课程的现状，在总结过去八年多在中国的 AP 教学和教研的经验基础上，结合 AP 课程最近的发展特点和命题的变化及趋势，我们组织了一线的优秀教学和教研团队编写了这套"导学与应考指南"丛书，主要科目是报考人数最多且我国考生感觉比较困难或希望得到高分的生物、化学、数学、经济学（宏观和微观）、物理等 5 门课程。在编写过程中，编者在总结过去若干年教学和教研经验的基础上，在详细分析历年 AP 考试题目的基础上，针对我国为非英语母语国家的特点，重点归纳了各门课程的重点、难点，并就如何在考试中解决实际问题以边栏批注的形式提出了可行的方法。应该说，本套丛书基本达到了简练、实用、清晰、易懂的初衷，不失为广大学子备考 AP 和谋求高分的良好参考用书。

本册为丛书中的生物学分册。AP 生物学是很多参加 AP 考试的同学有意报考但又畏惧其难度的一门课程，其知识难度和覆盖范围相当于美国大学一年级的生物学通论。自 2011 年美国大学理事会开始修改 AP 生物学课程及大纲以来，2013 年是改革后的第一次考试。本次修改对原有知识的覆盖范围、考查重点、考核方式均有重大调整。改革后的 AP 生物学旨在改变学生单纯依靠记忆知识的学习方法，帮助学生完善进行科学实践的逻辑思考能力。本书根据调整后的新大纲及考试方式，确定复习内容及课后练习，以顺应新 AP 生物学考试的要求。

新 AP 生物学考试仍由客观题和主观题组成，二者分别占总分值的 50%，考试时间 3 小时。主要考查学生对核心知识的系统理解以及进行科学实践的能力，包括通过建模手段解释生物学原理；运用数学方法解释生物学概念；对某一生物现象进行预测及判断；实验设计及对实验数据的分析。成绩使用 5 分制，3 分为有效分。AP 生物学考试的 5 分相当于大学成绩的 A 等；4 分相当于 A^-，B^+ 和 B 等；3 分相当于 B^-，C^+ 和 C 等。与之前的考试相比，虽考查范围有所缩减，但对于大多数仅有国内高中生物学的学生来说，知识的深度及广度均有所增加，尤其是主观题部分，对于英语为非母语地区的学生来说，如何用准确、清晰的语言阐述观点是一大难点，这也是本书采用以英文叙述为主并辅助中文解释的原因。

本书总共包括 10 章。第一章为新 AP 生物学考试的介绍，第二章到第九章根据修改后的大纲讲解了 AP 生物学考试的核心知识点，按生物化学、细胞学、遗传学、进化、分类学、内稳态、免疫和生态学的顺序进行编排。第十章对考试中会涉及的实验、公式及应用进行说明。为降低学习者学习 AP 生物学的难度和负担，每章节对重难点、易混淆概念都有详细解释，并且根据以往同学的反馈，对难以理解的知识精心绘制、总结了近百余张图片及表格进行说明。同时针对生物学专业词汇量大的特点，除每章结束后总结的词汇外，书后还配有单词自测部分供复习使用。

限于编者水平，书中难免存在不当之处，希望读者不吝指正，以便能在教学运用过程中得以不断改进、提高。

编者
2013 年 9 月

Contents 目录

Chapter 1 Things You Should Know about the AP Biology Exams 1

Chapter 2 Chemistry of Life 5

Chapter 3 Cell 25

Chapter 4 Genetics 55

Chapter 5 Evolution 95

Chapter 6 Biological Diversity and Classification 121

Chapter 7 Responding to Environment and Maintaining Homeostasis 145

Chapter 8 Defense against Disease 175

Chapter 9 Ecology 189

Chapter 10 Labs, Equations and Formulas 211

Vocabulary 219

Answers for Practices 229

CHAPTER 1
Things You Should Know about the AP Biology Exams

一、考试内容

根据美国大学理事会最新公布的课程修改方案,考试中涉及的主要知识点划分为四个主题(Big Idea),分别为:

Ⅰ. The process of evolution drives the diversity and unity of life.

Ⅱ. Biological systems utilize free energy and molecular building blocks to grow, to reproduce and to maintain dynamic homeostasis.

Ⅲ. Living systems store, retrieve, transmit and respond to information essential to life processes.

Ⅳ. Biological systems interact, and these systems and their interactions possess complex properties.

这样的划分打破原有纵向知识结构,强调知识点之间的联系,帮助同学建立一个系统的生物学框架。为方便叙述,以上四个主题简述为进化(Evolution)、能量与交流(Cellular Processes: Energy and Communication)、遗传与信息(Genetics and Information Transfer)及互作(Interactions)主题。各主题包含的知识点如下:

BIG IDEA	GENERAL OUTLINE FOR THE EXAM CURRIUMLUM	PERCENTAGE OF COURSE

Ⅰ	1. Evolutionary Biology
	  a) Early evolution of life
	  b) Evidence for evolution
	  c) Mechanisms of evolution
	2. Classification
	  a) Evolutionary patterns
	  b) Phylogenetic classification
	  c) Evolutionary relationships
	  d) Survey of the diversity of life
		20%

Ⅱ	3. Chemistry of Life
	  a) Water
	  b) Organic molecules in organisms
	  c) Free energy changes
	  d) Enzymes
		30%

(Continued)

BIG IDEA	GENERAL OUTLINE FOR THE EXAM CURRIUMLUM	PERCENTAGE OF COURSE

II	4. Cells
	    a) Prokaryotic and eukaryotic cells
	    b) Membranes
	    c) Subcellular organization
	5. Cellular Energetics
	    a) Coupled reactions
	    b) Fermentation and cellular respiration
	    c) Photosynthesis
	6. Immune response
	    a) Humoral immune response
	    b) Cell-mediated immune response
	7. Homeostasis
	    a) Animal responding to environment
	    b) Plant responding to environment	

III	8. Heredity
	    a) Cell cycle and its regulation
	    b) Meiosis and gametogenesis
	    c) Eukaryotic chromosomes
	    d) Inheritance patterns
	9. Molecular Genetics
	    a) RNA and DNA structure and function
	    b) Gene regulation
	    c) Mutation
	    d) Viral structure and replication
	10. Nervous system
	    a) Structure of neuron
	    b) Impulse transmission in and between a neuron
	    c) Movement under nervous system control
	11. Endocrine system
	    a) Hormone
	    b) Coordination between hormone and nervous system
		30%

IV	12. Ecology
	    a) Population dynamics
	    b) Communities and ecosystems
	    c) Global issues
		20%

二、考试说明及注意事项

新 AP 生物学考试的题型及所占比例如下表所示:

Chapter 1 Things you should know about the AP Biology exams

	题型	考试时间	
客观题 （50%）	单选(Multiple Choice)[1]：共63题，从4个备选答案中选择正确的一项	90分钟	
	计算题(Grid-In Questions)[2]：共6题，新题型，要求将计算得出的结果填到答题卡上		
主观题[3] （50%）	论述题(Multi-Part Questions)：共2题，其中1题涉及实验	20～25分钟/题	90分钟
	简答题(Single-Part Questions)：共6题，用2～3句英语作答	3～10分钟/题	

  1. 考题中涉及某些生物过程会用简图表示，在使用本书时仔细理解书中出现的图表。

  2. 计算题的答题卡及填涂方式如下：

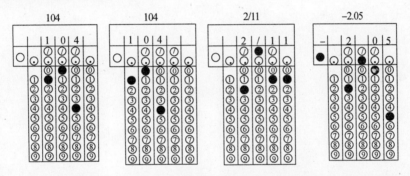

考试可使用简单计算器（可进行四则运算），全部客观题使用2B铅笔涂卡。

  3. 主观题部分用黑色不可更改的水笔作答，要求语言准确具有逻辑，必要时须提供恰当的例子以支持观点，因此在使用本书时留意相关知识点的英文表达。

CHAPTER 2

Chemistry of Life

Ⅰ. Water and Its Properties

Most cells are surrounded by water, and cells themselves are about 70%~95% water.

1. Because water is a **polar molecule(极性分子)**, water molecules are hydrogen bonded to each other.

    1) The **polarity (极性)**[1] of water molecule results from the **electronegativity(电负性)** of oxygen atom in water. Electronegativity is the tendency of an atom in a bond to attract shared bonding electrons. The bonds between hydrogen and oxygen are polar because oxygen is more electronegative than hydrogen.

    2) The polar structure of water has important consequences for the interactions that occur between water molecules. The most important interaction between water molecules is **hydrogen bond(氢键)**[2]. A hydrogen bond is the attractive interaction of a hydrogen atom with an electronegative atom, such as nitrogen, oxygen or fluorine that comes from another molecule or chemical group.

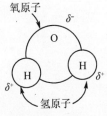

由于氢氧原子不同的电负性形成水分子内的极性

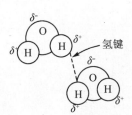

> 1. 水分子的极性:一个水分子由两个氢原子和一个氧原子组成,并具有极性。这源于氧原子是强电负性原子,即对电子的吸引力较强。在和氢原子形成共价键时,共用电子对会因氧原子的强电负性而更容易偏向氧原子,使得分子内部的共用电子对呈不平均分配,最终结果使得氧原子一端呈负极性,氢原子一端呈正极性。

> 2. 氢键:由于水分子有极性,当多个水分子存在时,一个水分子氧一端的负极性会吸引另一个水分子氢一端的正极性,由此形成水分子之间微弱的吸引力,这个吸引力就是氢键。氢键是分子间的吸引力,存在的条件是两个分子里一个有氢原子另一个分子含有强电负性的原子,如氮原子、氧原子和氟原子。

2. Water has many unique properties that make it essential to all life. Most of water's unique properties are a result of the hydrogen bonding between water molecules.

1) Water has high **cohesion(内聚力)** and **adhesion(黏附力)**[3]. Cohesion is the attractive force between similar molecules in the same phase. Individual water molecules tend to "stick" with other water molecules due to hydrogen bonding. Cohesion helps hold a column of water together against the force of gravity. Adhesion is the attractive force between molecules in one phase. Adhesion between water molecules and the molecules in tube-like structures in the tree trunk is also important in transporting water from a tree's roots to its leaves. Both cohesion and adhesion let the water from a tree's roots be transported all the way to its leaves.

> 3. 由于水分子之间存在氢键,使得水分子可以相互吸引,这种水分子内部微弱的吸引力便是内聚力。
>
> 黏附力是水分子与其他分子相互间的吸引力,也是由氢键产生的。产生的结果使水分子可以黏附在其他物体的表面。

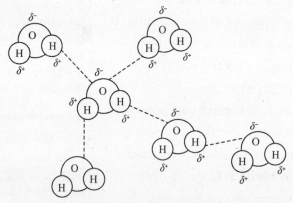

内聚力是水分子内部相互吸引的力

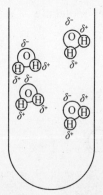

黏附力是水分子与其他物质表面相互吸引的力

2) Water has a high **specific heat capacity**(比热容)[4]. It takes a lot of energy to change the temperature of water. This characteristic makes water a good insulator and a good coolant. When you sweat, your body is using water as a coolant. The evaporating water removes heat with it. At night, oceans are a good insulator. The energy that the sun spent in heating the water all day is slowly released into the night.

3) Density of water decreases when water freezes[5]. Hydrogen bonding arranges water molecules into hollow "cells" when water freezes, making it less dense than liquid water. This characteristic of water is what allows fish in lakes and ponds to survive in the winter. When the water freezes, it becomes less dense and floats to the surface — leaving the bottom of the lake or pond unfrozen.

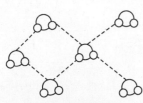 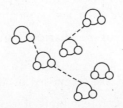

结冰状态下的氢键很稳定　　液态水状态下氢键被打断或再形成

4) Water is universal solvent, because it dissolves a great number of solutes[6]. Polar covalent compounds, because they too have charged poles, also dissolve in water. Nonpolar covalent compounds, however, do not dissolve in water. Thus polar covalent compounds are **hydrophilic**(亲水的) while nonpolar covalent compounds are **hydrophobic**(疏水的). This property facilitates chemical reactions both outside of and within living systems.

> 4. 比热容的定义为单位质量的某物质吸收（或放出）一定量能量时温度升高（或降低）的多少。水分子的高比热容也是由水分子之间的氢键导致的。当一个水体吸收能量时，部分能量先用于打破氢键，之后才用于增加水分子的运动速度升高水温。因此与其他物质相比，当吸收等量能量时，水温增加量小于其他物质的温度增加量。

> 5. 密度是描述物体致密程度的物理量。当水结冰时水分子之间会形成大量的氢键，氢键制约着水分子之间的距离，使其与液态相比致密程度下降，即密度下降。

> 6. 水的溶解性是由水的极性产生的。当水溶液存在极性分子或离子化合物的溶质时，水分子的负极和正极分别会与溶质的正极和负极吸引，从而溶解溶质。

Properties of water	Significance	Cause
Cohesion	Enable plant transport water from root to other organelle	Hydrogen bond
Adhesion		
High specific heat	Moderation of temperature	
Expansion as it solidifies	Insulation of organism of water by floating ice	
Universal solvent	Important mediate for metabolism in lives	Polarity of water

II. Life Substances

Life substances fall into four major groups: carbohydrates, lipids, proteins and nucleic acids.

1. Carbohydrates (碳水化合物)[7]

Carbohydrates provide fast energy (4 kcal/gram) for the human body. Some forms of complex carbohydrates serve as roughage and as the structural backbone of plant cell walls. Carbohydrates are typically classified according to the number of saccharide (sugar) units they have.

1) **Monosaccharides(单糖)**[8] are composed of a single sugar unit. They are the simplest kind of carbohydrate. **Fructose(果糖)** and **glucose(葡萄糖)** are two common monosaccharides. Glucose and fructose are **isomer(同分异构体)**, because they share the same formula ($C_6H_{12}O_6$) but the placement of the carbon atoms is different. Additionally, the placement of a H and OH group in a molecule of glucose determines whether it is α-glucose or β-glucose.

> 7. 碳水化合物的功能主要是储存能量及保护。所有碳水化合物满足 $C_nH_{2n}O_n$ 的结构通式。

> 8. 单糖是结构最简单的碳水化合物，因此也是碳水化合物的结构单位。果糖和葡萄糖是最常见的单糖，二者的化学式相同，但结构不同，因此称之为同分异构体。

Chapter 2　Chemistry of Life　9

Glucose

Fructose

2) **Disaccharides**(二糖)[9] are composed of two sugar units. They are formed through **dehydration reaction**(脱水缩合反应). The covalent bond connected 2 monosaccharides is called a **glycosidic linkage**(糖苷键). An example of a disaccharide is **sucrose**(蔗糖) (formed from fructose and glucose).

> 9. 两个单糖通过脱水缩合反应后形成一个二糖，如蔗糖。连接两个单糖的键称为糖苷键。

葡萄糖　果糖　糖苷键 蔗糖

葡萄糖和果糖经脱水缩合作用后形成蔗糖

3) **Polysaccharides**(多糖)[10] are composed of three plus sugar units. There are four main kinds of polysaccharides: **starch**(淀粉), **glycogen**(糖原), **cellulose**(纤维素), and **chitin**(几丁质). Starch is the storage form of sugar in plants. It is made of **amylose**(直链淀粉) and **amylopectin**(支链淀粉)—each thousands of glucose units in length. Glycogen is the storage form of sugar in animals. It looks like starch, but with more glucose branches attached. Cellulose is a structural carbohydrate that forms cell walls in plants. It is not digestible by either man or other animals. Chitin is a polysaccharide that contains nitrogen. It is found in the exoskeleton of arthropods and the cell walls of fungi.

> 10. 三个及三个以上的单糖脱水缩合后形成多糖。

2. Proteins(蛋白质)[11]

Almost every structure in an organism and all enzymes are composed of proteins.

1) Protein is made of **amino acids(氨基酸)**. Every amino acid has an **amine group(氨基)**, a **carboxyl group(羧基)**, and an **R (variable) group(R基)**. Amino acids are connected to form proteins by **peptide bonds(肽键)**, which are formed through dehydration synthesis. Thus, proteins are also called **polypeptides(多肽)**[12]. The function of protein is closely related to the order and number of amino acid groups.

Alanine(Ala,丙氨酸)
R基为疏水基团的非极性氨基酸

Threonine(Thr,苏氨酸)
R基为亲水基团的极性氨基酸

> 11. 蛋白质的结构单位是氨基酸。氨基酸由一个中心碳连接一个氨基、一个羧基、一个R基及一个氢组成。R基的性质决定该氨基酸是否具有极性或带电。

> 12. 多个氨基酸经脱水缩合后形成多肽,多肽经加工后形成具有功能的蛋白质。氨基酸的数目及顺序与蛋白质的性质密切相关。

Chapter 2 Chemistry of Life   11

[Chemical structure diagram showing peptide bond formation with dehydration, resulting in a tripeptide with 支链 (side chains) and 骨架 (backbone) labeled; 肽键 (peptide bond) arrows indicate the peptide bonds]

2) Protein has four types of structure[13].
- The **primary structure**(初级结构) of protein is a long polypeptide chain of amino acids.
- The **secondary structure**(次级结构) of protein is an alpha helix or a beta sheet. The twisting of the polypeptide chain occurs because of hydrogen bond between the amino groups and the acid groups.
- The **tertiary structure**(三级结构) of protein is globular or fibrous 3-D shape. **Hydrophilic interactions** (疏水作用)— interactions between R-groups with water — and disulfide bridges, van der Waals interactions and hydrogen bonds alter the shape of protein.
- The **quaternary structure**(四级结构) of protein involves more than one polypeptide chain. It refers to associating two or more polypeptide chains into a large protein.

13. 蛋白质的四级结构
  初级结构即氨基酸脱水缩合后形成的多肽,此时的分子尚未具有功能性,需进一步折叠、旋转后才是具有功能性的蛋白质。
  二级结构称为 α-helix 或 β-sheet。多肽内每个四个肽键间会形成一根氢键,由此使得多肽呈螺旋形或在空间上形成180°折叠。
  三级结构又称疏水作用,由各氨基酸的 R 基决定。亲水的 R 基使某一段多肽在水溶液中外翻迎向水,疏水的 R 基则使多肽向内卷,由此使得多肽具有一定三维结构。除此以外,肽键间的双硫键、范德华力及氢键可固定疏水作用。具有三级结构的多肽此时已具有功能性,若蛋白质只由一条多肽构成,三级结构即是该蛋白质的终极结构。
  对于某些由多条肽链组成的蛋白质,每条拥有三级结构的肽被叠加后形成蛋白质的四级结构。

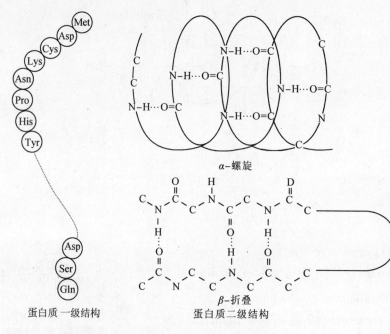

蛋白质一级结构

α-螺旋

β-折叠

蛋白质二级结构

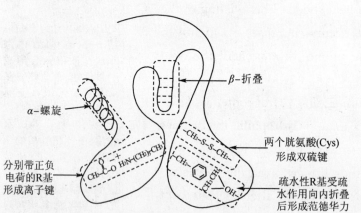

蛋白质三级结构

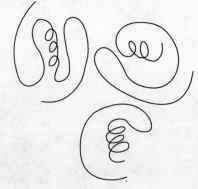

蛋白质四级结构

3) Protein shape is crucial to its function. Environmental factors such as heat, pH and formaldehyde cause it to lose its shape and its functionality, which is called **denaturation**(变性)[14].

| 14. 高温、强酸碱及某些化学物质会破坏蛋白质的二级和三级结构，使蛋白质失去空间构型，从而使蛋白质失去功能，这种现象叫做变性。|

3. Nucleic Acid (核酸)[15]

Nucleic acids are biological molecules essential for life, and include DNA (deoxyribonucleic acid, 脱氧核糖核酸) and RNA (ribonucleic acid 核糖核酸). Both DNA and RNA function in encoding, transmitting and expressing genetic information.

| 15. DNA 和 RNA 是两种核酸，它们是生物体遗传物质的载体。|

1) **Nucleotides** (核苷酸)[16] are subunits of nucleic acid, which have three components: a **nitrogenous base** (含氮碱基), a **pentose sugar** (五碳糖)—**ribose** (核糖) in RNA and **deoxyribose** (脱氧核糖) in DNA—and a **phosphate group** (磷酸基团). When the structure consists of only the pentose sugar and the nitrogenous base, it's called a **nucleoside** (核苷). Nucleotides are connected by dehydration reaction forming **phosphodiester bond** (磷酸二酯键).

| 16. 核酸的结构单位是核苷酸，其包含三部分：含氮碱基，五碳糖和磷酸基团。磷酸和含氮碱基构成核苷。核苷酸通过脱水缩合形成核酸，连接核苷酸的键为磷酸二酯键。|

2) DNA is double helix strand. Its nitrogenous bases are **adenine** (腺嘌呤), **thymine** (胸腺嘧啶), **cytosine** (胞嘧啶) and **guanine** (鸟嘌呤). RNA is single strand. It doesn't have thymine but has **uracil** (尿嘧啶) instead.

DNA 的结构

3) **Polymer**（多聚体）and **monomer**（单体）[17]

Carbohydrates, protein and nucleic acid are polymers, and sometimes they are also called macromolecules. Polymers are made of several repeated units called monomer. Two monomers join to form polymer through removing a H_2O molecule. This reaction is called dehydration reaction or **condensation reaction**（缩合反应）[18]. The reverse of this reaction called **hydrolysis**（水解）—H_2O is added to split polymer to form several monomers.

	17. 碳水化合物、蛋白质、核酸均是由多个相似的结构单位组成，因此被称为多聚体，各结构单位称为单体。
	18. 单体形成多聚体的反应称为缩合反应，由于反应过程中会失去水分子，因此又称为脱水反应。多聚体在水分子参与下被分解成为若干个单体的过程称为水解。

4. **Lipids**（脂类）[19]

Lipids include three major groups: **fats**（脂肪），**phospholipids**（磷脂）and **steroid**（类固醇）. All lipids are hydrophobic that means being insoluble in water. Lipids have many functions such as providing long-term storage of energy (9 kcal/gram) in humans, padding and insulation, storing fat-soluble vitamins (A, D, E, etc.), and forming the backbone of hormones and cell membranes.

1) Fats[20] are made of 1 **glycerol**（甘油）molecule and 3 **fatty acids**（脂肪酸）molecules. Fatty acids connect to glycerol also by dehydration reaction. They can be **saturated**（饱和的）or **unsaturated**（不饱和的）. The carbon chain of saturated fat is linked with as many single bonds as possible. Fats are considered unsaturated when there is a double bond in the carbon chain.

19. 脂类包括脂肪、磷脂和类固醇三大类，所有脂类均是疏水分子。脂类的功能主要有储存能量、提供缓冲、某些激素以及构成细胞膜的主要成分。

20. 脂肪由一分子甘油与三分子脂肪酸经脱水缩合而成。脂肪酸分为饱和脂肪酸和不饱和脂肪酸。脂肪酸上若全是C—C单键，为饱和脂肪酸。脂肪酸上若含有C=C双键，为不饱和脂肪酸。

$$
\begin{array}{l}
H-\overset{\overset{H}{|}}{\underset{|}{C}}-O-\overset{O}{\overset{\|}{C}}-(CH_2)_{13}-CH_3 \\
H-\overset{|}{\underset{|}{C}}-O-\overset{O}{\overset{\|}{C}}-(CH_2)_{13}-CH_3 \\
H-\overset{|}{\underset{|}{C}}-OH \;+\; HO-\overset{O}{\overset{\|}{C}}-(CH_2)_{13}-CH_3 \\
\overset{|}{H} \\
\downarrow \\
\rightarrow H_2O
\end{array}
$$

$$
\begin{array}{l}
H-\overset{\overset{H}{|}}{\underset{|}{C}}-O-\overset{O}{\overset{\|}{C}}-(CH_2)_{13}-CH_3 \\
H-\overset{|}{\underset{|}{C}}-O-\overset{O}{\overset{\|}{C}}-(CH_2)_{13}-CH_3 \\
H-\overset{|}{\underset{|}{C}}-O-\overset{O}{\overset{\|}{C}}-(CH_2)_{13}-CH_3 \\
\overset{|}{H}
\end{array}
$$

酯键

$$CH_3-(CH_2)_7-CH=CH-(CH_2)_7-COOH$$
单不饱和脂肪酸

$$CH_3-(CH_2)_7-CH=CH-CH_2CH=CH-(CH_2)_4-COOH$$
多不饱和脂肪酸

2) Phospholipids[21] are important structural component of the cell membrane. Phospholipids are similar to fats but a phosphate group and **choline group**（胆碱基） replace one of the fatty acid groups. This structure makes phospholipids **amphipathic**（双性的） molecule.

21. 磷脂是组成细胞膜的主要成分。它与脂肪不同之处在于磷酸基和胆碱基取代了一分子脂肪酸。这种变化使磷脂分子成为双性分子。

亲水
疏水
双性分子

脂肪，疏水分子

3) Steroids[22] consist of 4 fused carbon rings and include **cholesterol**（胆固醇） and **sex hormones**（性激素）.

22. 类固醇包括胆固醇与性激素。所有的类固醇都具有四个C环结构。

睾酮(Testosterone)   雌二醇(Estradiol)   胆固醇(Cholesterol)

III. Introduction of Metabolism and Enzyme

1. Metabolism and Energy

1) **Metabolism(新陈代谢)**[23] is a set of chemical reactions that happen in the cells of living organisms. Metabolism is usually divided into two categories.
   - **Catabolism(异化反应)** breaks down organic matters and produces energy in the process, for example to harvest energy in cellular respiration.
   - **Anabolism(同化反应)** uses energy to construct components of cells such as proteins and nucleic acids, which store energy.

2) Both catabolism and anabolism need energy in order to function. **Free energy(自由能)**[24], also known as Gibbs free energy (G), is the capacity of a system to do non-mechanical work and ΔG measures the non-mechanical work done on it. A key feature in the way cells manage their energy resources to do cell work is **energy coupling(能量耦合)**, the use of an **exergonic reaction(放热反应)** to drive an **endergonic reaction(吸热反应)**.
   - Endergonic reaction (also called a nonspontaneous reaction) is a chemical reaction in which the standard change in free energy is positive, or requires free energy.
   - Exergonic reaction is a chemical reaction where the change in the Gibbs free energy is negative, indicating a spontaneous reaction.

3) **ATP** or **adenosine triphosphate(三磷酸腺苷)** is the most important molecule in cellular energy.
   - ATP contains an adenosine and three phosphate groups. When the end phosphate bond is broken, ATP turning into **ADP (adenosine diphosphate, 二磷酸腺苷)**, energy is released.
   - Energy is also released when ADP loses a phosphate group and becomes AMP, adenosine mono-

> 23. 生物体内的所有化学反应称为新陈代谢。
> 把大分子分解为小分子同时释放能量的化学反应称为异化反应。
> 吸收能量利用小分子合成大分子的反应称为同化反应。

> 24. 在热力学当中,自由能指的是在某一个热力学过程中,系统减少的内能中可以转化为对外做功的部分。

phosphate. When a phosphate group is added to AMP and ADP, energy is stored for later use.
- ADP and ATP are universally present in all living organisms. ATP is so widespread and heavily used that it is sometimes referred to as the "energy currency" of life.

2. **Enzymes (酶)** are biological **catalysts (催化剂)**[25].
   1) Enzymes are protein. They speed up reactions by lowering the **activation energy (活化能)** (the energy required for a reaction to begin) but without changing the free energy change of the reaction.
   - Substrates are reactants in the enzymatic reaction. Substrates usually attach to the active site of enzyme to form an **enzyme-substrate complex (酶-底物复合物)**.
   - The **induced fit model (诱导契合模型)** describes how enzymes work. Each enzyme has **active sites (活性位点)** that are specific in shape, size, or polarity to the particular reactant. When the **substrate (底物)** binds to the active site, the enzyme changes shape to move the substrate into a new position for the reaction to occur.[26]

> 25. 酶是生物催化剂，在生物体内主要起到加速反应速率的作用。大部分的酶是蛋白质，加速反应速率的原理在于降低活化能。

> 26. 酶的关键区域是活性位点，此处为酶与底物即反应物结合的区域。活性位点能适当调整空间结构从而使其能与底物的结构吻合。这一系列变化称为诱导契合模型。

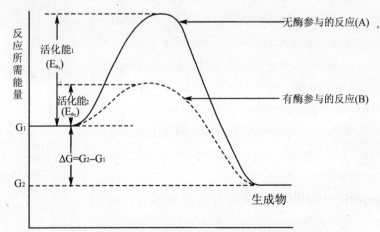

反应 A、B 前后自由能变化（ΔG）相同，但 $E_{a_1} > E_{a_2}$，即在酶的参与下，可降低反应所需的活化能（E_a），使反应易于进行。

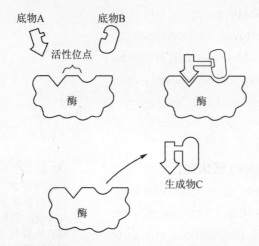

2) The activity of an enzyme can be regulated by several factors.
   - Substrate concentration. In a certain range, more substrates provide higher probability to attach to active site, which increases activity of enzyme.
   - Enzyme concentration. More enzymes provide higher probability to attach to substrates, which increases activity of enzyme.
   - Temperature and pH value. Since enzymes are protein, high temperature and pH will denature enzyme, which decreases activity of enzyme.
   - **Competitive inhibitors**(竞争性抑制剂)[27]. The inhibitor competes with the substrate for the same binding site on the enzyme. The addition of more substrates into the system would slightly speed up the reaction since there would be larger chance of substrate binding to the active site than inhibitor. The addition of more enzymes would also speed up the reaction since there would be more binding sites available. The removal of the inhibitor would also speed up the reaction.
   - **Noncompetitive inhibitors**(非竞争性抑制剂)[28]. Inhibitor temporarily binds to a site other than the binding site. The addition of more substrates into this system would have no effect on reaction rate. The addition of more enzymes into this system

27. 某些抑制剂会与酶的活性位点结合，使酶无法催化底物的反应，这类抑制剂称为竞争性抑制剂。竞争性抑制剂的影响因素可通过增加底物浓度来降低。

28. 某些抑制剂会结合到酶的非活性位点上，这类抑制剂称为非竞争性抑制剂。结合后改变了酶的空间结构，尤其是活性位点的结构，使底物无法与酶结合，从而降低酶的催化效率。非竞争性抑制剂的影响很难消除。

would speed up the reaction slightly. The addition of more inhibitors would slow down the reaction.
- **Cofactors**(辅基) and **coenzymes**(辅酶). Cofactors are minerals that are usually found near the active site and assist in binding substrates to the enzyme. Coenzymes are vitamins. They function as intermediate carriers of electrons, atoms, or functional groups.

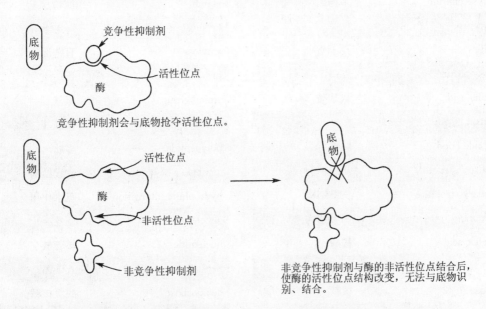

3) **Negative feedback inhibition**(负反馈抑制) is the end products of enzyme-driven reactions. Feedback inhibitors function by binding to an enzyme and distorting its shape so that the binding sites of other substrates on the same enzyme don't fit any more. This mechanism maintains a balance between the concentration of reactants and products in a cell.

本章词汇

polar molecule	极性分子
electronegativity	电负性
cohesion	内聚力

polarity	极性
hydrogen bond	氢键
adhesion	黏附力

specific heat capacity	比热容	hydrophilic	亲水的
hydrophobic	疏水的	carbohydrate	碳水化合物
monosaccharide	单糖	fructose	果糖
glucose	葡萄糖	isomer	同分异构体
disaccharide	二糖	dehydration reaction	脱水缩合反应
glycosidic linkage	糖苷键	sucrose	蔗糖
polysaccharide	多糖	starch	淀粉
glycogen	糖原	cellulose	纤维素
chitin	几丁质	amylose	直链淀粉
amylopectin	支链淀粉	protein	蛋白质
amino acid	氨基酸	amine group	氨基
carboxyl group	羧基	R group	R 基，可变基团
peptide bond	肽键	polypeptide	多肽
primary structure	初级结构	secondary structure	次级结构
tertiary structure	三级结构	hydrophilic interaction	疏水作用
quaternary structure	四级结构	denaturation	变性
nucleic acid	核酸	nucleotide	核苷酸
nitrogenous base	含氮碱基	pentose sugar	五碳糖
ribose	核糖	deoxyribose	脱氧核糖
phosphate group	磷酸基团	nucleoside	核苷
phosphodiester bond	磷酸二酯键	adenine	腺嘌呤
thymine	胸腺嘧啶	cytosine	胞嘧啶
guanine	鸟嘌呤	uracil	尿嘧啶
polymer	多聚体	monomer	单体
condensation reaction	缩合反应	hydrolysis	水解
lipid	脂类	fat	脂肪
phospholipid	磷脂	steroid	类固醇
glycerol	甘油	fatty acid	脂肪酸
saturated	饱和的	unsaturated	不饱和的
choline group	胆碱基	amphipathic	双性的
cholesterol	胆固醇	sex hormone	性激素
metabolism	新陈代谢	catabolism	异化反应

anabolism	同化反应	free energy	自由能
energy coupling	能量耦合	endergonic reaction	吸热反应
exergonic reaction	放热反应	ATP(adenosine triphosphate)	三磷酸腺苷
ADP(adenosine diphosphate)	二磷酸腺苷	enzyme	酶
catalyst	催化剂	activation energy	活化能
enzyme-substrate complex	酶-底物复合物	induced fit model	诱导契合模型
active site	活性位点	substrate	底物
competitive inhibitor	竞争性抑制剂	noncompetitive inhibitor	非竞争性抑制剂
cofactor	辅基/辅因子	coenzyme	辅酶
negative feedback inhibition	负反馈抑制		

本章重点

1. 水的特性及产生原理以及对生物体的意义。
2. 明确多聚体及对应单体,解释单体的序列与多聚体特性的联系。
3. 蛋白质的四级结构,每级结构的形成原理及最终对蛋白质功能的影响。
4. 判断及预测单体的改变对多聚体性质的影响。
5. 从酶活性位点与底物识别的角度,理解分子间作用对分子结构及功能的影响。
6. 列举影响酶活性的因素。

本章习题

1. What would be an expected consequence of changing one amino acid in a particular protein?
   a. The primary structure would be changed.
   b. The tertiary structure would be changed.
   c. The biological activity of this protein might be altered.
   d. All of the above are expected.

2. Which statement about amino acids is CORRECT?
   a. They always have at least one amino group and at least one carboxyl group.

b. In the formation of proteins, it is a condensation reaction that links the amino group of one amino acid to the variable side chain of the adjacent amino acid.
c. The variable side chains of all of the amino acids are highly reactive and carry a charge at neutral pH.
d. The peptide bond that links amino acids together in a protein is a type of ionic bond, which explains why proteins are unstable at high temperatures.

3. Which statement about nucleotides is CORRECT?
   a. Nucleotides contain phosphate groups, whatever they are components of RNA or DNA.
   b. Nucleotides are composed of only a pentose sugar and a nitrogenous purine or pyrimidine base.
   c. Nucleotides are subunits of fatty acids.
   d. Nucleotides contain a deoxyribose sugar if they are components of RNA, and a ribose sugar if they are components of DNA.

4. Which statement about proteins is CORRECT?
   a. Protein's quaternary structure is determined solely by the primary amino acid sequence.
   b. Protein sequences that span a lipid bilayer membrane usually contain a number of charged amino acids.
   c. Examples of protein's secondary structure include an α-helix or a β-sheet.
   d. Protein's tertiary structure is the result of the interaction of two or more independent polypeptide chains.

5. Which statement about macromolecules is FALSE?
   a. Monomers are the building blocks of polymers.
   b. Both DNA and RNA are linear polymers of nucleotides.
   c. A monosaccharide is a long-chain polymer formed of simple sugars.
   d. Both cellulose and starch are polymers of glucose.

6. Which statement about proteins is CORRECT?
   a. The primary structure of a protein is composed of many branched chains.
   b. Proteins always contain an amino group at one end and the amino acid methionine at the other end.
   c. The formation of disulfide bridges between cysteine amino acids can modify a

protein's primary structure.
d. The quaternary structure of proteins is the result of the interactions of two or more independent polypeptide chains.

7. Macromolecules are giant molecules formed by the joining of smaller molecules. The bonds that form between the units of macromolecules are:
   a. hydrogen bonds
   b. peptide bonds
   c. disulfide bonds
   d. covalent bonds

8. Which statement about enzymes is FALSE?
   a. They function best at a particular pH.
   b. All enzymes are catalysts.
   c. They function best at specific temperatures but break down at high temperatures.
   d. They undergo a major chemical change after reacting with their specific substrate.

9. Which statement about the properties of water and its role in biological systems is FALSE?
   a. In a water molecule, hydrogen atoms are linked to the oxygen atom by polar covalent bonds.
   b. The combination of hydrophobic and hydrophilic interactions of a protein with water can influence the shape of the protein.
   c. The solubility of NaCl in water is a product of the interactions between the water molecules and the ions in the salt.
   d. Water boils at 100℃ as a result of the breakage of the bonds between the hydrogen and oxygen atoms.

10. You are invited to a dinner party and decide to make salad dressing. You mix olive oil and balsamic vinegar (which is mostly water) together and notice they don't mix. Which of the following, when added to this mixture, would allow these two substances to mix?
    a. ATP.
    b. Phospholipid.
    c. Starch.
    d. Salt.

CHAPTER 3

Cell

Ⅰ. Comparing Two Types of Different Cells

1. Cells are the smallest units of life. It follows that they are separated from each other.
   1) The **plasma membrane(细胞膜)**[1] is the barrier between cells. All cells have a plasma membrane, but not all cells have the same internal structure. The main components in membranes are lipids and proteins, but some carbohydrates are also important.
      - The most abundant lipids are **phospholipids(磷脂)**. Phospholipids and most other membrane constituents are **amphipathic molecules(双亲分子)**. Amphipathic molecules have both hydrophobic regions and hydrophilic regions. The arrangement of phospholipids and proteins in biological membranes is described as **fluid mosaic model(流动镶嵌模型)**[2]. Besides phospholipid, **cholesterol(胆固醇)** is also an important lipid protecting cell membrane.
      - Proteins determine most of the membrane's specific functions. **Peripheral proteins(外周蛋白)** are not embedded in the lipid bilayer at all. **Integral proteins(整合蛋白)**[3] penetrate the hydrophobic core of the lipid bilayer, often completely spanning the membrane (as transmembrane proteins). The proteins of the plasma membrane have several functions such as transporting specific solutes into or out of cells, catalyzing one of a number of steps of a metabolic pathway, signal transduction and cell to cell recognition.

> 1. 所有的细胞都有细胞膜。细胞膜的基本结构为磷脂双分子层。磷脂为双亲分子,包括极性的亲水头部和非极性的疏水尾部。胆固醇也是细胞膜的组成成分之一,对于保持细胞膜的流动性和稳定性起到重要的作用。

> 2. 流动镶嵌模型的定义:细胞膜由结构和功能上不对称的磷脂双分子层所组成,蛋白质以镶嵌样模式分布在膜的表面与内部,并能在膜内运动。

> 3. 整合蛋白插入磷脂双分子层的疏水核心中,多为跨膜蛋白。

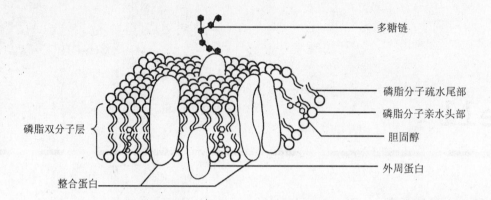

2) **Prokaryotic cells(原核细胞)**[4] don't have membrane-enclosed internal compartments. Organisms with this type of cell are called **prokaryotes(原核生物)**. Prokaryotes are single-celled organisms, roughly one micrometer in diameter. The cell's internal fluid is called **cytosol(细胞质基质)**. Its genetic material consists of a large DNA molecule compacted in an area called **nucleoid region(核区)**. The plasma membrane encases the cytosol and its contents. Large members of prokaryotes have a cell wall surrounding the plasma membrane. A flagellum gives the organism mobility.

3) **Eukaryotic cells(真核细胞)**[5] do contain membrane-enclosed compartments. Their DNA is enclosed in a membrane-covered compartment called **nucleus(细胞核)**. Eukaryotic cells also contain other membrane-enclosed compartments that isolate certain molecules and chemical reactions from the rest of the cell. Organisms containing eukaryotic cells are called **eukaryotes(真核生物)**.

> 4. 原核细胞没有膜包裹的内部结构。由原核细胞构成的生物体称为原核生物。细胞质基质是指细胞膜内部的液体成分。原核细胞没有细胞核,其遗传物质——大型环状DNA分子存在的区域叫做核区。

> 5. 真核细胞具有膜包裹的内部结构。其DNA分子存在于核膜包裹的细胞核中。由真核细胞构成的生物称做真核生物。

Ⅱ. Subcomponents of Eukaryotic Cells

Only eukaryotic cells have intracellular sub-divisions. A eukaryotic cell has extensive and elaborate internal membranes, which partition the cell into compartments.

1. Nucleus and Ribosome

The eukaryotic cells' genetic instructions are housed in the nucleus and carried out by the ribosomes.

Cell nucleus is one of the largest organelles found in cells and also plays an important biological role. It composes about 10% of the total volume of the cell and is found near the center of eukaryotic cells. Its importance lies in its function as a storage site for DNA, our genetic material. The cell nucleus is composed of two membranes that form a porous **nuclear envelope(核膜)**[6], which allows only selected molecules in and out of the cell.

Ribosomes(核糖体)[7], containing rRNA and protein, are the organelles that carry out protein synthesis. Cell types that synthesize large quantities of proteins (e.g. pancreas cells) have large numbers of ribosomes and prominent nucleoli. Some ribosomes, **free ribosomes(游离核糖体)**, are suspended in the cytosol and synthesize proteins that function within the cytosol. Other ribosomes, **bound ribosomes(附着核糖体)**, are attached to the outside of the endoplasmic reticulum or nuclear envelope. Both eukaryotic cells and prokaryotic cells contain ribosomes.

2. **Endomembrane System(内膜系统)**[8]
   1) The **endoplasmic reticulum (ER,内质网)**[9] accounts for half the membranes in a eukaryotic cell. **Rough endoplasmic reticulum(粗面内质网)** is a kind of endoplasmic reticulum that is coated with ribosomes and involved in protein synthesis. **Smooth endoplasmic reticulum(滑面内质网)** is naked endoplasmic reticulum that lacks ribosomes and is more involved in lipid synthesis.
   2) **Golgi apparatus(高尔基体)**[10], a membrane-bound organelle found near the cell nucleus in eukaryotic cells, is responsible for sorting and packaging proteins for secretion to various destinations in the cell.
   3) **Lysosomes(溶酶体)** are digestive compartments. A lysosome is a membrane-bound sac of hydrolytic enzymes that an animal cell uses to digest macromolecules.

> 6. 细胞核由核膜包裹。核膜为双层膜,每层膜均由磷脂双分子层构成。核膜上具有核孔,允许特定的分子进出细胞。

> 7. 核糖体是由rRNA与蛋白质构成的、与蛋白质合成相关的、非膜包裹的细胞器。细胞质基质中的核糖体成为游离核糖体;附着在内质网或者核膜上的核糖体为附着核糖体。

> 8. 内膜系统是指内质网、高尔基体、溶酶体和液泡等四类膜结合细胞器,因为它们的膜是相互流动的,处于动态平衡,在功能上也是相互协同的。

> 9. 内质网属于细胞的内膜系统。粗面内质网上附着有核糖体,因此与蛋白质合成相关;滑面内质网参与脂质的合成。

> 10. 高尔基体与蛋白质的分选、加工和分泌相关。溶酶体中含有水解酶,帮助动物细胞消化大分子物质。

4) Vesicles and vacuoles (larger versions) are membrane-bound sacs with varied functions. **Food vacuoles(食物液泡)**[11] are formed by **phagocytosis(胞吞；吞噬作用)** and fuse with lysosomes. **Contractile vacuoles(收缩液泡)**, found in freshwater protists, pump excess water out of the cell to maintain the appropriate concentration of salts. A large **central vacuole(中央液泡)** is found in many mature plant cells.

3. Organelles performing various metabolic functions
   1) Much of cell respiration is carried out within **mitochondria(线粒体)**[12]. Mitochondria have a smooth **outer membrane(外膜)** and a convoluted **inner membrane(内膜)** with infoldings called **cristae(嵴)**. The inner membrane encloses the **mitochondrial matrix(线粒体基质)**, a fluid-filled space with DNA, ribosomes, and enzymes.
   2) **Chloroplast(叶绿体)**[13] is one of several members of a generalized class of plant structures called **plastids(质体)**. The contents of the chloroplast are separated from the cytosol by an envelope consisting of two membranes separated by a narrow intermembrane space. Inside the innermost membrane is a fluid-filled space, the **stroma(基质)**, in which float membranous sacs, the **thylakoids(类囊体)**.
   3) **Peroxisomes(过氧化物酶体)**[14] contain enzymes that transfer hydrogen from various substrates to oxygen.

4. **Cytoskeleton(细胞骨架)**[15]
   Cytoskeleton is a network of fibers extending throughout cytoplasm. It organizes cell structures and activities, provides mechanical support, maintains cell shape and provides anchorage for organelles. Cytoskeleton is made of **microtubules(微管)**, **microfilaments(微丝)** and **intermediate filament(中间纤维)**. Microtubules are the central structural supports in **cilia(纤毛)** and **flagella(鞭毛)**. In animal cells, the **centrosome(中心体)** has a pair of

---

11. 生物体细胞内的液泡主要有3种形式。
    食物液泡通过细胞吞作用形成。在细胞内可与溶酶体融合后，经溶酶体内水解酶分解液泡中物质。
    收缩液泡是某些单细胞原生生物进行渗透调节的结构。
    中央液泡存在于成熟的植物细胞中，可储存某些有机分子和离子，并进行渗透调节。

12. 线粒体是细胞呼吸的主要场所，是具有双层膜的细胞器。线粒体的内膜向内折叠形成嵴。包裹在线粒体内膜中的液体成分称为线粒体基质。

13. 叶绿体是细胞进行光合作用的重要场所，属于质体的一种。叶绿体也具有双层膜结构。基质填充在类囊体垛叠成的基粒与内膜之间。类囊体上有与光合作用相关的色素。

14. 过氧化物酶体是一种由膜包起来的胞质细胞器，含有各种利用或产生过氧化氢的酶。其主要功能是使有毒物质失活、氧化脂肪酸和含氮物质代谢。

15. 细胞骨架是细胞质中的网状纤维结构，其主要功能是提供机械支持、维持细胞结构并帮助细胞器定位。细胞骨架分为微管、微丝和中间纤维。微管是纤毛和鞭毛的核心结构。微管构成中心粒，相互垂直的中心粒构成中心体。中间纤维构成核纤层——位于细胞核内膜与染色质之间的纤维网状结构。

centrioles(中心粒), each with nine triplets of microtubules arranged in a ring. Before a cell divides, the centrioles replicate.

The nucleus gains support from intermediate filaments that both form the surrounding **nuclear lamina**(核纤层) and makes direct contact with the endoplasmic reticulum.

	Diameter (nm)	Function
Microtubules	25	1. Formation of cilia and flagella for cell motility 2. Formation of spindle fibers for chromosome movement during cell division
Microfilaments	7	1. Formation of actin for muscle contraction 2. Formation of cleavage furrow for cell division
Intermediate filaments	8~12	Formation of nuclear lamina for cell shape maintaining

5. **Cell Walls**(细胞壁)[16]

Cell walls are found in prokaryotes, fungi, and some protists. In plants, the cell wall consists of cellulose and protects the cell, maintains its shape, and prevents excessive uptake of water. Plant cells are perforated with **plasmodesmata**(胞间连丝), channels allowing cytosol to pass between cells.

[16]. 植物细胞细胞壁的主要成分是纤维素。植物细胞利用胞间连丝将两个细胞的细胞质联系起来。动物细胞没有细胞壁,而通过细胞外基质提供支持和附着功能。

6. **Extra Cellular Matrix (ECM,细胞外基质)**

Lacking cell walls, animal cells do have an elaborate extra cellular matrix functioning in support, adhesion, movement and regulation. The ECM is connected to the cytoskeleton. The interconnections from the ECM to the cytoskeleton permit the interaction of changes inside and outside the cell.

Neighboring cells in tissues, organs, or organ systems often adhere, interact, and communicate through direct physical contact. The most common connection between animal cells is **gap junctions**(缝隙连接).

III. Cellular Transportation

1. **Passive Transport**(被动运输)[17]

    1) **Diffusion**(扩散) is the tendency of molecules of any substance to spread out in the available space. Each substance diffuses down its own concentration gradient, independent of the concentration gradients of other substances. Because membranes are selectively permeable, the interactions of the molecules with the membrane play a role in the diffusion rate. The diffusion of a substance across a biological membrane is passive transport because it requires no energy from the cell to make it happen. The concentration gradient itself represents potential energy and drives diffusion.

    2) Many polar molecules and ions that are normally impeded by the lipid bilayer of the membrane diffuse passively with the help of transport proteins that span the membrane. The passive movement of molecules down their concentration gradient via transport proteins is called **facilitated diffusion**(协助扩散)[18]. Two types of transport proteins facilitate the movement of molecules or ions across membranes: **channel proteins**(通道蛋白) and **carrier proteins**(载体蛋白). Water channel proteins, **aquaporins**(水通道蛋白), greatly facilitate the diffusion of water. Many ion channels function as **gated channels**(门控通道). These channels open or close depending on the presence or absence of a chemical or physical stimulus.

    3) The diffusion of water across a selectively permeable membrane is called **osmosis**(渗透)[19]. The direction of osmosis is determined only by a difference in total solute concentration.
        - The solution with the higher concentration of solutes is **hypertonic**(高渗的) relative to the other solution. The solution with the lower concentration of solutes is **hypotonic**(低渗的) relative to the other

17. 物质进入细胞膜可以通过被动运输和主动运输两种方式进行。被动运输不需要消耗能量。根据是否有蛋白质参与,又分为扩散和协助扩散。扩散又称为简单扩散或单纯扩散,是指物质从高浓度向低浓度运动。

18. 协助扩散不需要能量,但是需要通道蛋白或者载体蛋白的协助。水通道蛋白也称为水孔蛋白,就是一种能够协助水分子进入细胞的通道蛋白。许多离子通道为门控通道,其打开和关闭需要特定的因素刺激,如离子浓度的高低。

19. 水分子通过扩散进出选择透过性膜的过程称为渗透。高渗溶液是指溶质在细胞膜外的浓度高于其在细胞膜内的浓度;此时进入细胞的水分子少于渗出细胞的水分子。在等渗溶液中,水分子进出细胞的速率相等。

solution. Solutions with equal solute concentrations are **isotonic**(等渗的).

- The hypertonic solution has a lower water concentration than the hypotonic solution. When two solutions are isotonic, water molecules move at equal rates from one to the other, with no net osmosis. The movement of water by osmosis is crucial to living organisms.
- An animal cell (or other cell without a cell wall) immersed in an isotonic environment experiences no net movement of water across its plasma membrane. The same cell in a hypertonic environment will lose water, shrivel, and probably die. A cell in a hypotonic solution will gain water, swell, and burst. The cells of most land animals are bathed in extracellular fluid that is isotonic to the cells. A plant cell in a hypotonic solution will swell until the elastic cell wall opposes further uptake. At this point the cell is turgid (very firm), a healthy state for most plant cells.

	Hypertonic solution	Hypotonic solution	Isotonic solution
Plant cell	Cells lose water and become plasmolyzed.	Cells uptake water and become turgid (normal for plant cell).	No net movement of water, cells are flaccid.
Animal cell	Cells lose water and become shriveled.	Cells uptake water and will be lysed.	No net movement of water, cells stay normal.

2. **Active Transport**(主动运输)[20]

1) Some carrier proteins can move solutes across membranes against their concentration gradient, from the side where they are less concentrated to the side where they are more concentrated. This active transport requires the cell to expend metabolic energy. ATP supplies the energy for most active transport.

> 20. 主动运输是逆浓度梯度的跨膜运输方式，既需要蛋白质载体也需要 ATP 提供能量。

All cells maintain a voltage across their plasma membranes.

- Voltage is electrical potential energy due to the separation of opposite charges. The voltage across a membrane is called a **membrane potential（膜电位）**[21].
- The cytoplasm of a cell is negative in charge compared to the extracellular fluid because of an unequal distribution of cations and anions on opposite sides of the membrane. The membrane potential favors the passive transport of cations into the cell and anions out of the cell. Two combined forces, collectively called the **electrochemical gradient（电化学梯度）**, drive the diffusion of ions across a membrane. One is a chemical force based on an ion's concentration gradient. The other is an electrical force based on the effect of the membrane potential on the ion's movement. An ion does not simply diffuse down its concentration gradient but diffuses down its electrochemical gradient.
- Special transport proteins, **electrogenic pumps（生电泵）**, generate the voltage gradient across a membrane. The **sodium-potassium pump（钠-钾泵）** in animals restores the electrochemical gradient not only by the active transport of Na^+ and K^+, setting up a concentration gradient, but because it pumps two K^+ inside for every three Na^+ that it moves out, setting up a voltage across the membrane. It is the major electrogenic pump of animal cells. In plants, bacteria, and fungi, a **proton pump（质子泵）** is the major electrogenic pump, actively transporting H^+ out of the cell.

> 21. 细胞膜两侧电荷总量的差异称为膜电位。细胞膜两侧某一物质浓度的差异称为浓度梯度。质子跨膜运输是一个电压生成的过程。因为质子带电，所以其跨膜转运使得膜两侧的电荷和质子浓度均发生了变化；膜两侧即形成电位差，也形成浓度梯度，两种梯度合称为电化学梯度。
>
> 生电泵是进行主动运输的载体蛋白，能够通过主动运输使膜两侧产生电位差，细胞内常见的生电泵如钠-钾泵和质子泵。

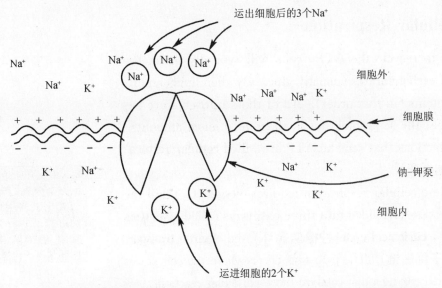

由于自身代谢的需要,某些细胞内外电荷呈内负外正分布。细胞内外钠离子分布为内低外高,钾离子为外低内高(由上图所示)。当细胞继续向外运输钠离子时,要逆钠离子浓度梯度运输(即"electrochemical gradient"的"chemical"部分);细胞向外运输 3 个钠离子,向内运输 2 个钾离子后,净向外运输一个阳离子,运输结果增加了膜电势(此为"electro"部分),因此需要额外的能量(ATP)投入来完成运输工作。

凡运输离子时,需同时考虑浓度梯度和膜电势,运输小分子时,则只需考虑浓度梯度。

2) In **cotransport(协同运输)**[22], a membrane protein couples the transport of two solutes. A single ATP-powered pump that transports one solute can indirectly drive the active transport of several other solutes. As the solute that has been actively transported diffuses back passively through a transport protein, its movement can be coupled with the active transport of another substance against its concentration gradient.

3) Large molecules, such as polysaccharides and proteins, cross the membrane **exocytosis(胞吐;外排)**[23] and **endocytosis(胞吞;内吞)**. During exocytosis, a transport vesicle budded from the Golgi apparatus is moved by the cytoskeleton to the plasma membrane. During endocytosis, a cell brings in macromolecules and particulate matter by forming new vesicles from the plasma membrane. There are three types of endocytosis: phagocytosis(吞噬)("cellular eating"), **pinocytosis(胞饮)**("cellular drinking"), and **receptor-mediated endocytosis(受体介导的内吞作用)**.

22. 协同运输是一类靠间接提供能量完成的主动运输方式。物质跨膜运动所需要的能量来自膜两侧离子的电化学浓度梯度,而维持这种电化学势的是钠-钾泵或质子泵。动物细胞中常常利用膜两侧 Na^+ 浓度梯度来驱动,植物细胞和细菌常利用 H^+ 浓度梯度来驱动。

23. 除主动运输和被动运输这类跨膜运动外,物质,特别是大分子物质,进出细胞的方式还包括细胞的内吞和外排。内吞又分为吞噬作用、胞饮和受体介导的内吞作用。

IV. Cellular Respiration

In order to recycle the ATP, cells will typically break the bonds of carbohydrates (usually glucose), then lipids and finally proteins (in that order). All of those nutrients are being used at the same time but in those mentioned amounts. These reactions that remake ATP are called **cellular respiration(细胞呼吸)**[24].

Complete cellular respiration requires oxygen(O_2) and the entire process is divided into three pathways called **glycolysis(糖酵解)**, **citric acid cycle(柠檬酸循环)** and **electron transport chain(电子传递链)**. The pathways occur where the cell stores the required enzymes that catalyze those particular reactions.

> 24. 细胞呼吸是将葡萄糖完全分解，产生水和二氧化碳并生成能量的过程。共分为三个阶段：糖酵解、柠檬酸循环和电子传递链。

1. Glycolysis
   - In glycolysis (which occurs in the cytosol), the degradation of glycose begins as it is broken into two molecules of pyruvate.
   - There is an ATP-consuming phase and an ATP-producing phase, which results in a net gain of 2 ATP.
   - 2 NADH are also produced, which will be utilized in the electron transport system to produce ATP.
2. The Junction between Glycolysis
   - Pyruvate, in the cytosol, uses a transport protein to move into the matrix of the mitochondria.
   - The matrix, an enzyme complex removes a CO_2, strips away electrons to convert NAD^+ to NADH, and adds coenzyme A to form acetyl CoA.
   - 2 acetyl CoA molecules are produced per glucose. Acetyl CoA now enters the enzymatic pathway termed the citric acid cycle.
3. Citric Acid Cycle
   - Citric acid cycle (also called Kreb's cycle), which occurs in the mitochondrial matrix, the job of breaking down glucose is completed with CO_2 released as a waste product.
   - The total products of the citric acid cycle are usually

listed as the result of two cycles: $4CO_2$, 6 NADH, $2FADH_2$, and 2ATP.
- ATP is generated in glycolysis and Kreb's cycle results from transferring a phosphate group from an organic molecule (the substrate) to ADP forming ATP. This pathway called **substrate-level phosphorylation(底物水平磷酸化)**[25].

4. Electron Transport Chain (ETC) and Chemiosmosis in Oxidative Phosphorylation
   1) Electron transport chain
      - The ETC is embedded in the cristae. The electrons from NADH or $FADH_2$ continue along the chain that includes several **cytochrome proteins(细胞色素蛋白)**, and ultimately pass to oxygen—the terminal electron acceptor.
      - The movement of electrons along the ETC produces the proton gradient. The potential energy the electrons lose pushes H^+ across the membrane into the inter membrane space. This concentration of H^+ is also called **proton-motive force(质子动力势)**[26].
   2) Chemiosmosis
      - A protein complex, ATP synthetase, in the cristae, actually makes ATP from ADP and Pi. The ATP synthetase is the only place that allows H^+ to diffuse back to the matrix. The enzyme to generate ATP, a process called **chemiosmosis(化学渗透)**, uses the flow of H^+ stored during electron transport chain.
      - ATP uses the energy of an existing proton gradient to power ATP synthesis, and the energy is originally stored in the electrons carried by NADH and $FADH_2$ before transport.
   3) ATP produced in this whole pathway called **oxidative phosphorylation(氧化磷酸化)**[27], a metabolic pathway that uses energy released by the oxidation of nutrients to produce ATP.

> 25. 将底物上的磷酸转移至ADP从而形成ATP的过程称为底物水平磷酸化,这是细胞内合成ATP的一种方式。

> 26. 高能电子在电子传递链上传递的过程中使质子由基质泵至内外膜间隙,在内膜的两侧形成质子浓度差异,称为质子动力势。质子浓度梯度推动质子由膜间隙经ATP合成酶进入基质,这一过程称为化学渗透。

> 27. 氧化还原反应与磷酸化相耦联形成ATP的过程称为氧化磷酸化,这是细胞呼吸合成ATP的主要方式。

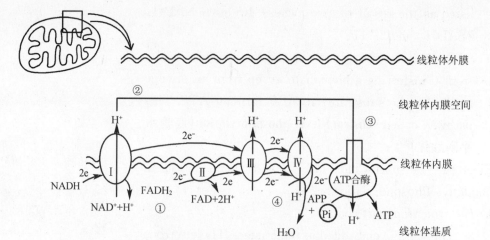

① 线粒体内膜上分布着大量的细胞色素蛋白(图中Ⅰ,Ⅱ,Ⅲ,Ⅳ),经过糖酵解和柠檬酸循环产生的 NADH 和 $FADH_2$ 将在此处进行电子传递。NADH 的电子按Ⅰ→Ⅲ→Ⅳ的顺序传递,而 $FADH_2$ 则按Ⅱ→Ⅲ→Ⅳ的顺序传递。电子每传递一次,能量便释放一部分,释放的能量用于主动运输 H^+,将 H^+ 从线粒体基质逆浓度运往内膜空间。

② 细胞色素蛋白不仅是传递电子的媒介,也是一种质子泵,它将氢离子从线粒体基质向内膜空间逆化学梯度运输,主动运输所需的能量来自于电子从 NADH 或 $FADH_2$ 在细胞色素蛋白间传递释放。运输的结果增加了内膜的膜电势,即电子传递释放出的能量(传递前储存于 NADH 和 $FADH_2$ 内)转化为膜电势。

③ 当内膜空间内的 H^+(即膜电势)积累到一定程度,H^+ 便通过内膜上的 ATP 合成酶从内膜空间通过协助扩散的方式转移到基质中,此时膜电势下降,即暂时储存的能量便释放出来,在 ADP 和 Pi 的参与下,通过 ATP 合成酶的催化合成 ATP。这一过程即是化学渗透,可形象解释为"先蓄水,再开闸放水发电"。"蓄水"即主动运输 H^+ 后储存在内膜空间内,"放水"即 H^+ 通过 ATP 合成酶回到基质,释放膜电势,"发电"即 ATP 合成。NADH 内的电子在传递过程中经历 3 次 H^+ 主动运输,可简单理解为 NADH 内的能量完全释放合成 3 分子 ATP,而 $FADH_2$ 则可合成 2 分子 ATP。

④ 传递至Ⅳ处的电子需要一个最终电子载体,否则Ⅰ,Ⅱ,Ⅲ,Ⅳ无法接收从新的 NADH 和 $FADH_2$ 处传递的电子,NADH 和 $FADH_2$ 也就无法被还原成 NAD^+ 和 FAD 参与新的糖酵解和柠檬酸循环。在有 O_2 的情况下,O_2 便可接受来自Ⅳ的电子,与基质中的 H^+ 生成 H_2O,同时也使 NAD^+ 与 FAD 参与新的反应。

5. Fermentation

Under anaerobic conditions, NADH and $FADH_2$ can't pass their electron to oxygen because of the absence of oxygen, then **fermentation (发酵)**[28] occurs, which consists of glycolysis plus reduction of pyruvate to either lactate or to alcohol and CO_2 (depending on the organism).

1) **Alcoholic fermentation (乙醇发酵)**[29], carried out by yeasts, converting glucose to pyruvic acid via the glycolysis pathways, then go one step farther, converting pyruvic acid into ethanol.

2) **Lactic acid fermentation(乳酸发酵)**, carried out by human and certain bacteria, produces lactic acid (lactate).

> 28. 当处于无氧条件时,NADH 和 $FADH_2$ 无法将电子传递给氧气,这时发酵将会发生,糖酵解产生的丙酮酸将会进一步反应生成乳酸或乙醇和二氧化碳。

> 29. 乙醇发酵:如酵母,糖酵解产生的丙酮酸经反应形成乙醇。
> 乳酸发酵:如人类,丙酮酸最终生成乳酸。

Complete glucose breakdown to CO_2 and H_2O during cellular respiration represents a potential yield of 686 kcal of energy, while two ATP produced per glucose molecule during fermentation in glycolysis is equivalent to 14.6 kcal, far less efficient than complete breakdown of glucose. Despite a low yield of two ATP molecules, fermentation provides a quick burst of ATP energy for muscular activity.

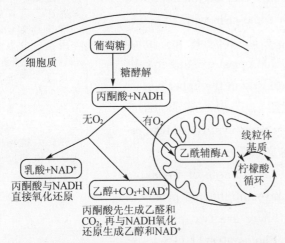

Normal cells	From	To	$NADH+H^+$	$FADH_2$	CO_2	ATP
Glycolysis	Glucose	2 Pyruvic acid	2	0	0	2
2 Acetyl-CoA formation	2 Pyruvic acid	2 Acetyl-CoA	2	0	2	0
Citric acid	2 Acetyl-CoA		6	2	4	2
Electron transport chain	$NADH+H^+$ $FADH_2$	NAD^+ FAD	-10	-2	0	34
Total			0	0	6	38

Nerve cells, muscle cells	From	To	$NADH+H^+$	$FADH_2$	CO_2	ATP
Glycolysis	Glucose	2 Pyruvic acid	2	0	0	2
2 Acetyl-CoA formation	2 Pyruvic acid	2 Acetyl-CoA	2	0	2	0
Citric acid	2 Acetyl-CoA		6	2	4	2
2 NADH pass through the mitochondria membrane	$2NADH+2H^+$	$2FADH_2$	-2	2	0	0
Electron transport chain	$NADH+H^+$ $FADH_2$	NAD^+ FAD	-8	-4	0	32

	From	To	NADH+H$^+$	CO$_2$	ATP
Glycolysis	Glucose	2 Pyruvic acid	2	0	2
Lactic acid fermentation	2 Pyruvic acid	2 Lactic acid	−2	0	0
Alcoholic fermentation	2 Pyruvic acid	2 Ethanol	−2	2	0

Ⅴ. Photosynthesis[30]

Photosynthesis occurs in the plant cell organelle called chloroplast. All plants have at least some cells with these organelles. Those plant cells that have chloroplasts are found mainly in leaves. Within the leaves, chloroplast existing in cells called **mesophyll cells(叶肉细胞)** are mostly in the upper surface in an area named **palisade layer(栅栏层)**. The entire photosynthesis requires two sets of reactions, or pathways, called **light reaction(光反应)** and **Calvin cycle(卡尔文循环)**.

1. Light reaction, occurring on the membrane of thylakoid in chloroplast, requires water and sunlight and produces some ATP, NADPH and O$_2$. There are two photosystems involved in light reaction, **Photosystem Ⅰ(PSⅠ,光系统Ⅰ)** and **Photosystem Ⅱ(PSⅡ,光系统Ⅱ)**.

   1) Both two photosystems consist of two parts, **light-harvesting complex(光捕获复合体)** and **reaction center (反应中心)**. Each part of them is constructed by protein and chlorophyll.

      - Each light-harvesting complex consists of pigment molecules (which may include chlorophyll a, chlorophyll b, and carotenoid molecules) bound to particular proteins. Together, these light-harvesting complexes enhance the absorption of light and transfer the energy to the reaction centers.
      - Two families of reaction centers, Photosystem Ⅰ and Photosystem Ⅱ exist in Photosystems. Each photosystem can be identified by the wavelength of light to which it is most reactive. PSⅠ has a reaction center chlorophyll a, named as **P700**[31] **(色素 700)** that has an absorption peak at 700 nm, and PSⅡ has **P680(色素 680)** that has an absorption peak at 680 nm.

> 30. 光合作用在植物细胞的细胞器——叶绿体中进行。叶绿体主要存在于叶片栅栏层的叶肉细胞中。光合作用主要分为光反应和卡尔文循环两部分。
> 　光反应的场所在类囊体的膜上。光系统Ⅰ和光系统Ⅱ参与光反应的电子传递过程。两种光系统均由光捕获复合体和反应中心两部分构成。

> 31. P700 和 P680 均为叶绿素 a,根据最大吸收峰的不同进行分类。
> 　P700 为最大吸收峰值在 700 nm 的叶绿素 a,P680 为最大吸收峰值在 680 nm 的叶绿素 a。

Chapter 3　Cell

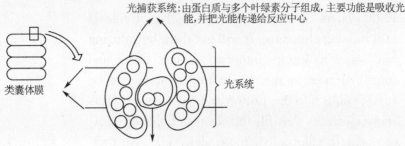

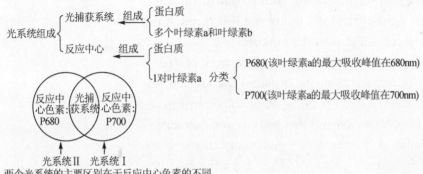

两个光系统的主要区别在于反应中心色素的不同

2) Two types of electron flow are found in plants. **Linear (Noncyclic) electron flow(非循环电子传递)**[32] starts from PhotosystemⅡ when light energy (photons), especially blue and red photons of visible light strike a reaction center's chlorophyll pigments. This leads a pair of outer electrons from chlorophyll to become so energized that are ejected. It is at this exact moment that solar energy has been transformed into chemical energy. The electron pumped from chlorophyll flow along thylakoid membrane assisting by some organic molecules and protein.

- In Photosystem Ⅱ these energized electrons do chemical work. Their energy is used to pump protons (H^+) from stroma into thylakoid disc, which creates a high concentration gradient of H^+ inside the thylakoid disc. The protons then diffuse back out, through an enzyme called ATP synthetase, which combines ADP and Pi forming ATP, an ATP production pathway similar to oxidative phosphorylation called **photophosphorylation(光合磷酸化)**[33].

32. 非循环电子传递经过两个光合系统,生成ATP 和 NADPH。电子传递是一个开放的通道。

33. 由光照所引起的电子传递与磷酸化作用相耦联而生成 ATP 的过程,称为光合磷酸化,是光合作用合成ATP 的方式。

- Photosystem II center's chlorophyll molecule is still missing electrons. It will get them by splitting two water molecules into two oxygen atoms and four hydrogen atoms. A hydrogen atom can be further split into one proton and one electron. It is these electrons that fill the electron holes of Photosystem II chlorophyll molecules. The two oxygen atoms combine forming O_2, which can either be used by the plant during cellular respiration or if there is a surplus it will diffuse out of the chloroplast, out of the cell, out of the leaf through the open stomata and into the atmosphere.
- The ejected electrons, after doing the work of "pumping" the protons inside the thylakoid disc are now less energy poor and attach to the other chlorophyll molecules from Photosystem I that had electron "vacancies" as a result of its own earlier electron ejections. Some of the hydrogen's protons (H^+), from the split water, will be used along with Photosystem I chlorophyll's electrons to remake complete hydrogen atoms. Hydrogen will then be picked up by an empty hydrogen carrier molecule called $NADP^+$, which is reduced to NADPH. Together with ATP, NADPH is used in Calvin cycle.

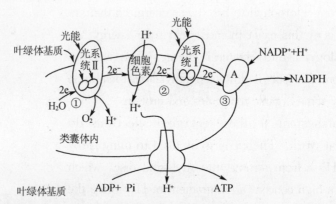

① P680 的电子被光能激发出后,需要从 H_2O 内"抢夺"电子以便进行下一轮反应。H_2O 于是被分解成 O_2 和 H^+,这个过程称为光解。
② 从光系统 II 处激发的电子延类囊体膜进行传递,细胞色素蛋白接受电子后传递给光系统 I,同时将 H^+ 从叶绿体基质主动运输进类囊体内,并耦联 ATP 合成酶生成 ATP,该过程与细胞呼吸电子传递链相似。
③ 光系统 I 接受电子后,在 $NADP^+$ 还原酶(图中 A 处)的参与下,将电子传递给 $NADP^+$,生成 NADPH,NADPH 与 ATP 共同进入下一个反应。

3) **Cyclic electron flow(循环电子传递)**[34] will be stimulated when NADPH accumulates because ATP in plant cells is consumed faster than NADPH. Unlike linear electron flow, this alternative flow only uses Photosystem I producing ATP by chemiosmosis but no NADPH.

> 34. 循环电子传递的电子传递是一个闭合的回路,只经过光系统 I,不需要 NADP⁺ 作为最终电子受体。

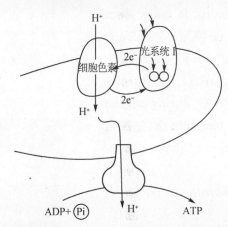

光系统 I 也可单独进行光反应。P700 的电子波激发后传递给细胞色素分子,细胞色素又将电子返还给光系统 I 以填补 P700 电子的空缺,同时耦联 ATP 合成酶生成 ATP。此循环传递电子的过程不发生光解,也不生成 NADPH。

	Photosystem usage	Outcome
Cyclic electron flow	Photosystem I	Produces ATP
Linear (Noncyclic) electron flow	Photosystem I & Photosystem II	Photolysis occurs and produces ATP and NADPH

2. The Calvin cycle occurs in the stroma of chloroplast[35]. Stroma is the goo inside of the chloroplast but outside of the thylakoid. The Calvin cycle uses the ATP and NADPH from light reaction as well as atmospheric carbon dioxide that diffuses from the atmosphere into the leaf cells and into their chloroplasts.

> 35. 卡尔文循环在叶绿体的基质中进行。
> 　二氧化碳与二磷酸核酮糖在二磷酸核酮糖羧化酶的作用下结合形成两分子三碳化合物—磷酸甘油酸。

1) Carbon dioxide is carried into Calvin cycle by an enzyme called **rubisco(二磷酸核酮糖羧化酶)**. This enzyme only works when activated by light. Rubisco combines carbon dioxide with a five carbon molecule called **ribulose bisphosphate (RuBP,二磷酸核酮糖)**, which results in a very unstable six carbon molecule that breaks into two three carbon molecules called

PGA. After ATP and NADPH adding on hydrogens and raising the energy level of these molecules, two PGAL (or G_3P, Glyceraldehyde-3-phosphate) are the result; one remains in the cycle and the other is combined with more PGAL until another RuBP is formed and the Calvin cycle can occur again. It takes three "turns" of the Calvin cycle and three CO_2 molecules to make one surplus PGAL, and six "turns" of the Calvin cycle and six CO_2 molecules to make two surplus PGAL. The plant can either use PGAL during cellular respiration to remake ATP or for **biosynthesis(生物合成)**[36]. Biosynthesis is the production of other organic compounds.

- Carbohydrate product of photosynthesis is, somewhat incorrectly, represented as glucose ($C_6H_{12}O_6$) but it is more accurately PGAL. The balanced formula, meaning the total number and types of atoms on the left/reactant side equals the total number and kinds of atoms on the right/product side, for photosynthesis is:

$$6CO_2 + 12H_2O \longrightarrow C_6H_{12}O_6 + 6O_2 + 6H_2O$$

- Plants fix CO_2 in this pathway are called **C_3 plants (C_3 植物)**[37], because the carbon dioxide is first "fixed" or added to a five carbon molecule to make two PGA(3-phosphoglycerate) molecules. If there is too much O_2, it will compete with CO_2 and instead some of rubisco will combine with O_2. Since some of rubisco isn't carrying carbon dioxide to Calvin cycle, this will result in less photosynthesis. When this happens, it is called **photorespiration(光呼吸)**.

2) Other plants are called **C_4 plants(C_4 植物)**[38] for avoiding the problems associated with rubisco and photorespiration. C_4 plants carry out the light reactions of photosynthesis in the mesophyll cells like other plants, but they carry out the light-independent reac-

---

36. 生物合成是生物体内合成有机分子的统称。

37. C_3 植物固定二氧化碳的途径的第一步为：二氧化碳与二磷酸核酮糖在羧化酶的作用下结合形成两分子三碳化合物——磷酸甘油酸。
当植物因外界气温升高关闭气孔，CO_2 吸收量下降时，卡尔文循环会因 CO_2 不足而受到抑制。此时植物细胞内进行光呼吸，即利用光反应产生的 O_2 与 RuBP 反应，分解 RuBP。

38. C_4 植物光合作用的光反应发生在叶肉细胞中，暗反应发生在维管束鞘细胞中。在叶肉细胞中，磷酸烯醇式丙酮酸在羧化酶的作用下与二氧化碳结合形成苹果酸，转移到维管束鞘细胞中，再在脱羧酶的作用下释放二氧化碳参与卡尔文循环。

tions in the bundle sheath cells. The enzyme in the C_4 plants' mesophyll cells, PEP carboxylase, has a higher affinity for grabbing carbon dioxide than rubisco. This gives C_4 plants a better chance of survival in tightly packed areas where carbon dioxide may be limited. They usually can make more PGAL, grow faster. Examples of such fast growing C_4 plants are corn and sugarcane.

3) The **CAM pathway (Crassulacean Acid Metabolism pathway,景天酸代谢途径)**[39] is utilized by cacti, other succulents, and members of crassulaceae. CAM plants open their stomates at night to take in CO_2 and close them (reducing water loss) in the day. They also carry out Calvin cycle in daytime but use CO_2 accumulated in earlier night.

39. 景天酸代谢途径的特点是：在夜间细胞中磷酸烯醇式丙酮酸作为二氧化碳接受体，在磷酸烯醇式丙酮酸羧化酶催化下，形成草酰乙酸，再还原成苹果酸，并贮于液泡中；白天苹果酸则由液泡转入叶绿体中进行脱羧释放二氧化碳，再通过卡尔文循环转变成糖。

Reaction	Location
Light-dependent reaction	Thylakoid membrane
Light-independent reaction	Stroma
Glycolysis	Cytoplasm
Citric acid	Matrix of mitochondria
Electron transport chain of cellular respiration	Inner membrane of mitochondria
Fermentation	Cytoplasm

VI. Cell Signal Pathway

Unicellular organisms are completely immersed in their environment, and need only move materials across their cell membrane to regulate internal conditions and functions. Multicellular organisms are encased in multiple protective layers, and most of their cells are far removed from the outside world, having them surrounded by an aqueous internal environment. They maintain homeostasis through the close coordination of organs and organ systems. Whatever the organisms consist of, in order to maintain homeostasis, they must detect and communicate with other cells and external environment. Cell-to-cell communication or called cell signaling is ubiquitous in biological systems, from unicellular to multicellular organisms.

1. Cell Signaling Pathway[40]

   To survive, organisms must be able to sense changes in their external and internal environments, and respond accordingly.

   Cell-to-cell contact, like gap junctions of animal cell and plasmodesma of plant cell, is most often done through cell signaling, where an exogenous molecule is received by a cell and converted into a response by the receiving cell. The pattern is remarkably similar in all cells, probably evolved early, before first multicellular system (maybe in single cell prokaryotes) has been highly conserved in today's ancestral cells. Stages of cell signaling mechanism include **reception(感应)**, **transduction(转导)** and **response(反应)**.

   1) Reception
      - Certain cells that help trigger organisms respond can detect important cues that mean signals from environment, such as day length, temperature, and chemicals. These cells are called **target cells(靶细胞)**[41]. Target cells receive information from environment through a class of proteins known as **receptors(受体)**. Receptors that are plasma-membrane proteins usually affect the cell through multistep signal transduction pathways. These pathways allow for amplification of signals and signal coordination and regulation.
      - Chemical signals that activate (or, in some cases, inhibit) receptors can be classified as hormones, neurotransmitters, cytokines, and growth factors, but all of these are called receptor ligands. The ligand fits like a key in a lock and triggers a change in the receptor molecule.
      - The details of ligand-receptor interactions are fundamental to cell signaling. All cells can potentially come in contact with a signal, but only those that

> 40. 细胞信号传递分为三个阶段：感应阶段主要是信号分子与受体的结合；转导阶段是信号分子与受体结合后，将胞外信号转化为胞内信号的过程；效应阶段将产生一系列的生物学效应。

> 41. 靶细胞是受到特定环境信号影响的细胞。靶细胞上有一类特别的膜蛋白称为受体，受体能够识别和选择性结合信号分子。

have a specific receptor for that signal will respond. Although different types of cells may have specific receptors for the same signal, they will respond to that signal in different ways. In other words, the receptor decodes the signal message, but the specificity of the response is determined by the nature of the cell that responds, not by the signal.

2) Signal transduction[42]

Signal transduction converts the change in the receptor to a form that can bring about a cellular response. Shape change results in that receptor interacts with other intracellular molecules, and result in multiple, structural changes in other cellular proteins. All these steps can alter and amplify the effect of signal. **Second messengers**(第二信使) and **protein kinases**(蛋白激酶) are often involved in signal transduction.

Second messengers are small non-protein molecules that act as intermediaries in signal transmission. Two important second messengers are **cyclic AMP**(环化腺核苷一磷酸)[43] and **calcium ions**(钙离子).

- Cyclic AMP acts as a second messenger in pathways initiated by both G-protein-linked receptors and receptor tyrosine kinases.
- Calcium ions also act as second messengers in signal transduction pathways that are responsible for many important physiological functions, such as in muscle contraction.

A protein kinase catalyzes the transfer of phosphate groups from ATP to another protein. This modification is known as phosphorylation, which can turn an inactive protein into active form. More often than not, the activated protein is also a protein kinase, which may act on still another protein kinase. One kinase may activate many molecules of the next type of kinase in the chain, thus amplifying the signal, until the last kinase activates many

---

42. 细胞内信号转导主要依靠第二信使和大量蛋白激酶。

细胞外的信号与受体作用后,细胞内最早产生的信号分子称为第二信使。

蛋白激酶,也称为蛋白质磷酸化酶,催化蛋白质磷酸化反应。

43. cAMP 和 Ca^{2+} 是两个重要的第二信使。G 蛋白耦联受体和酪氨酸蛋白激酶受体均影响细胞内 cAMP 的水平。Ca^{2+} 主要参与肌肉收缩相关的信号转导通路。

molecules of the protein that carries out the final cellular response.

3) Response[44]

In the third stage of cell signaling, the transduction process brings about a cellular response. This can be any of many different cellular activities, such as activation of a certain enzyme, rearrangement of the cytoskeleton, or activation of specific genes.

> 44. 细胞信号传递的最终反应阶段可能是激活某些酶或是激活基因表达合成蛋白质。

2. Important Signal Pathways in Organisms

1) G-protein-coupled receptors

G-protein-coupled receptors(G 蛋白耦联受体)[45] are transmembrane proteins that pass through the plasma membrane. Their ligand-binding sites are exposed outside the surface of the cell and effector sites extend into the cytosol.

Binding of the ligand to the receptor activates a G protein associated with the cytoplasmic terminal. This initiates the production of cyclic AMP. The second messenger, in turn, initiates a series of intracellular events such as phosphorylation and activation of enzymes release of Ca^{2+} into the cytosol from stores within the endoplasmic reticulum. In the case of cAMP, these enzymatic changes activate the transcription factor. The cell begins to produce the appropriate gene products in response to the signal it had received at its surface.

Once activated, one subunit of G protein swaps GDP for GTP. However, this subunit is a GTPase and quickly converts GTP back to GDP restoring the inactive state of the receptor.

> 45. G蛋白耦联受体参与的信号传递是信号分子与受体结合后，复合物需要首先活化G蛋白，然后活化的G蛋白再进一步活化靶蛋白，在细胞内产生第二信使，将细胞外的信号传递到细胞内。G蛋白的全称是GTP结合调节蛋白，位于细胞膜胞浆一侧，它的活化能够起始cAMP的合成。

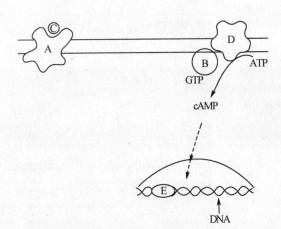

① 当信号分子(C)未与G蛋白耦联受体(A)相结合时,G蛋白(B)处于非活性状态

② 信号分子与受体识别并结合后,GDP被GTP取代,从而激活G蛋白

③ 激活的G蛋白进一步激活腺苷酸活化酶(D),该酶可将ATP转化为cAMP,cAMP介导各级传递过程后,可激活细胞核内调控因子(E),从而调控DNA合成蛋白质

2) Receptor tyrosine kinases

The receptors tyrosine kinases are also transmembrane proteins that span the plasma membrane.

Binding of the ligand to two adjacent receptors forms an active homodimer. This activated dimer is a tyrosine kinase; an enzyme that attaches phosphate groups to certain tyrosine residues — first on itself, then on other proteins converting them into an active state. Many of these other proteins are also tyrosine kinases and in this way a cascade of expanding phosphorylation occurs within the cytosol. Some of these cytosolic tyrosine kinases act directly on gene transcription by entering the nucleus and transferring their phosphate to transcription factors thus activating them. Others act indirectly through the production of second messengers.

For the receptors tyrosine kinases, this is done through quickly engulfing and destroying the ligand-receptor complex by receptor-mediated endocytosis.

本章词汇

plasma membrane	细胞膜	phospholipid	磷脂
amphipathic molecule	双亲分子	fluid mosaic model	流动镶嵌模型
cholesterol	胆固醇	peripheral protein	外周蛋白
integral protein	内在蛋白；整合蛋白	prokaryotic cell	原核细胞
prokaryote	原核生物	cytosol	细胞质基质
nucleoid region	核区，拟核	eukaryotic cell	真核细胞
nucleus	细胞核	eukaryote	真核生物
nuclear envelope	核膜	ribosome	核糖体
free ribosome	游离核糖体	bound ribosome	附着核糖体
endomembrane system	内膜系统	endoplasmic reticulum (ER)	内质网
rough endoplasmic reticulum	粗面内质网	smooth endoplasmic reticulum	滑面内质网
Golgi apparatus	高尔基体	lysosome	溶酶体
food vacuole	食物液泡	phagocytosis	胞吞；吞噬作用
contractile vacuole	伸缩液泡；收缩液泡	central vacuole	中央液泡
mitochondria	线粒体	outer membrane	外膜
inner membrane	内膜	cristae	嵴
mitochondrial matrix	线粒体基质	chloroplast	叶绿体
plastid	质体	stroma	基质
thylakoid	类囊体	peroxisome	过氧化物酶体

cytoskeleton	细胞骨架	microtubule	微管
microfilament	微丝	intermediate filament	中间纤维
cilia	纤毛	flagella	鞭毛
centrosome	中心体	centriole	中心粒
nuclear lamina	核纤层	cell wall	细胞壁
plasmodesmata	胞间连丝	extra cellular matrix (ECM)	细胞外基质
gap junction	缝隙连接	passive transport	被动运输
diffusion	扩散	facilitated diffusion	协助扩散
channel protein	通道蛋白	carrier protein	载体蛋白
aquaporin	水通道蛋白	gated channel	门控通道
osmosis	渗透	hypertonic	高渗的
hypotonic	低渗的	isotonic	等渗的
active transport	主动运输	membrane potential	膜电位
electrochemical gradient	电化学梯度	electrogenic pump	生电泵
sodium-potassium pump	钠-钾泵	proton pump	质子泵
cotransport	协同运输	exocytosis	胞吐;外排
endocytosis	胞吞;内吞	pinocytosis	胞饮
receptor-mediated endocytosis	受体介导的内吞作用	cellular respiration	细胞呼吸
glycolysis	糖酵解	citric acid cycle	柠檬酸循环
electron transport chain	电子传递链	substrate-level phosphorylation	底物水平磷酸化
cytochrome protein	细胞色素蛋白	proton-motive force	质子动力势
chemiosmosis	化学渗透	oxidative phosphorylation	氧化磷酸化
fermentation	发酵	alcoholic fermentation	乙醇发酵
lactic acid fermentation	乳酸发酵	mesophyll cell	叶肉细胞
palisade layer	栅栏层	light reaction	光反应
Calvin cycle	卡尔文循环	Photosystem Ⅰ (PSⅠ)	光系统Ⅰ

Photosystem Ⅱ (PSⅡ)	光系统Ⅱ	light-harvesting complex	光捕获复合体
reaction center	反应中心	P700	色素700
P680	色素680	noncyclic electron flow	非循环电子传递
photophosphorylation	光合磷酸化	cyclic electron flow	循环电子传递
rubisco	二磷酸核酮糖羧化酶	ribulose bisphosphate (RuBP)	二磷酸核酮糖
biosynthesis	生物合成	C_3 plant	C_3 植物
photorespiration	光呼吸	C_4 plant	C_4 植物
CAM pathway	景天酸代谢途径	reception	感应
transduction	转导	response	反应,效应
target cell	靶细胞	receptor	受体
second messenger	第二信使	protein kinase	蛋白激酶
cyclic AMP	环化腺核苷—磷酸	calcium ion	钙离子
G-protein-coupled receptor	G蛋白耦联受体		

本章重点

1. 细胞膜的特性以及细胞膜对细胞及相关细胞器的意义。
2. 细胞跨膜运输的方式及所需条件。
3. 动植物细胞在不同渗透环境下的表现及产生原理。
4. 通过计算细胞比表面积,比较不同细胞扩散的快慢,理解细胞体积和形状对细胞功能的影响。
5. 真核细胞与原核细胞的区别。
6. 内膜系统中各细胞器间的相互作用。
7. 线粒体和叶绿体结构与功能的相似性与区别。
8. 理解细胞光合作用和呼吸作用转化能量的过程以及影响因素,了解细胞信号传递的过程。
9. 区分底物磷酸化、氧化磷酸化及光合磷酸化。
10. 比较呼吸作用和光合作用中化学渗透的异同。

本章习题

1. Which of the following would NOT be found in the cell of bacterium?
   a. DNA.
   b. Ribosomes.
   c. Plasma membrane.
   d. Mitochondria.

2. Which statement is FALSE?
   a. The Golgi complex forms vesicles that fuse to form the endoplasmic reticulum.
   b. Cell walls generally contain high levels of carbohydrate.
   c. If a lysosome bursts, its contents can seriously damage the cytoplasm of a cell.
   d. Secreted proteins are initially formed by ribosomes attached to the endoplasmic reticulum.

3. If a plant cell has its cell wall removed and is placed in a hypotonic solution, what will happen to the cell?
   a. The cell will already be dead because plant cells cannot survive without a cell wall.
   b. The cell will expand and eventually burst.
   c. The cell will shrink because the vacuole gets smaller.
   d. Nothing obvious would happen.

4. If you could suddenly remove all the protein molecules from the plasma membrane of a cell (without destroying the cell), which of the following would you expect to happen?
   a. Transport of all molecules across the plasma membrane would stop.
   b. Transport of most ions across the plasma membrane would stop.
   c. The amount of cholesterol in the plasma membrane would decrease.
   d. Amino acids would rapidly aggregate on the plasma membrane and replace the missing proteins.

5. A scientist cultured some single-celled amoebae which he fed with cells of smaller single-celled organisms. If he genetically modified these amoebae so that the hydrogen ion pumps found in the membrane of lysosomes only worked at temperatures below 16℃, what would happen if the temperature was raised to 20℃?
   a. The lysosomes would burst open.

b. The amoebae would die instantly because of the high level of hydrogen ions in the cytoplasm.

c. The amoebae would swell and burst.

d. The amoebae would starve to death.

6. In cellular respiration, an excess of positive charge from hydrogen ions builds up _____.
   a. in the cytoplasm
   b. in the matrix of the mitochondrion
   c. in the endoplasmic reticulum
   d. in the space between the two mitochondrial membranes

7. During the light-dependent reactions of photosynthesis (photophosphorylation), light energy is converted to chemical potential energy through the process of chemiosmosis in the chloroplasts. Which of the following statements about this process is FALSE?
   a. The electron carriers of photophosphorylation are located in the thylakoid membranes of the chloroplasts.
   b. During photophosphorylation, the chloroplast stroma becomes more acidic than the interior of the thylakoid membranes.
   c. Protons diffuse through protein channels which are ATP synthetase molecules.
   d. ATP is synthesized from ADP and Pi on the stroma side of the thylakoid membranes in the chloroplast.

8. A scientist added a chemical (cyanide) to an animal cell to stop aerobic respiration. Which of the following is most likely to have been affected by this treatment?
   a. Active transport of substances across the plasma membrane.
   b. Passive transport of substances across the plasma membrane.
   c. Diffusion of substances across the plasma membrane.
   d. The size of the ribosomes in the cytoplasm.

9. Which statement comparing the biochemical processes of photosynthesis and cellular respiration is FALSE?
   a. Both biochemical processes take place in specialized organelles that have complex systems of internal membranes.
   b. ATP synthesis in both processes relies on the chemiosmotic mechanism, involving the pumping of protons through a membrane.
   c. Both processes involve the passing of electrons from carrier to carrier in a series of

oxidation-reduction reactions which liberate energy.
d. The initial source of electrons which pass from carrier to carrier is from high-energy food molecules in both processes.

10. Which statement about the two pathways of photosynthesis is FALSE?
    a. The first pathway (the light reactions) captures light energy and produces ATP and NADPH+H$^+$.
    b. The second pathway (the Calvin-Benson cycle) uses the products of the first pathway and CO_2 to produce sugars.
    c. The second pathway is also known as the dark reactions because none of its reactions uses light directly.
    d. The light reactions occur within chloroplasts; the Calvin-Benson cycle takes place in the cytosol.

11. Which statement about cellular respiration is FALSE?
    a. All organisms perform cellular respiration.
    b. Carbon dioxide is a product of the Krebs (citric acid) cycle.
    c. Glycolysis and fermentation are carried out in mitochondria under anaerobic conditions.
    d. Glycolysis results in the breakdown of glucose to pyruvate molecules.

12. Which event occurs during the light reactions of photosynthesis?
    a. Fixation of carbon dioxide, reduction of NADP$^+$, formation of ATP.
    b. Oxidation of water, reduction of NADP$^+$, formation of ATP.
    c. Oxidation of water, reduction of NADP$^+$, hydrolysis of ATP.
    d. Fixation of carbon dioxide, release of oxygen, synthesis of glucose.

13. Which metabolic pathway occurs in both fermentation and cellular respiration?
    a. Calvin (Calvin-Benson) cycle.
    b. Citric acid (Krebs) cycle.
    c. Glycolysis.
    d. Electron transport chain.

14. Match the component or process in the left column with the proper compartment or membrane in the right column (e. g. : The citric acid cycle occurs within the...).
    i. Citric aid cycle   p. Stroma of chloroplast
    ii. RuBP carboxylase/oxygenase (Rubisco)   q. Matrix of mitochondrion

iii. Glycolysis
iv. Photosystem II

r. Thylakoid membrane
s. Cytoplasm

a. i-q, ii-p, iii-s, iv-r
b. i-q, ii-s, iii-r, iv-p
c. i-r, ii-s, iii-p, iv-q
d. i-q, ii-p, iii-r, iv-s

15. Why is photosynthetic CO_2 fixation dependent on light?
    a. ATP and NADPH are required for the regeneration of ribulose bisphosphate (RuBP).
    b. The conversion of RuBP and CO_2 to 3-phosphoglycerate (3PG) requires ATP.
    c. Phosphoenolpyruvate (PEP) regeneration requires NADPH.
    d. The movement of CO_2 from the air into the leaf requires ATP.

CHAPTER 4

Genetics

Ⅰ. Cellular Reproduction

Cellular reproduction, also known as cell division, is a process by which cells duplicate their contents and then divide to yield new cells.

There are two different types of cell reproduction—**mitosis(有丝分裂)** and **meiosis(减数分裂)**[1]. These processes are responsible for creating two different types of cells. Mitosis is a process that creates a nearly exact copy of the original cell. **Somatic cells(体细胞)**, such as skin cells, are created by this process. Meiosis is a different form of reproduction that leads to the production of **gamete(配子)**, or sex cells mainly referring **sperm(精子)** and **egg(卵子)**. It is a type of cellular reproduction that results in the formation of four haploid cells from one diploid cell.

The difference between mitosis and meiosis can also be thought of the difference between sexual and **asexual reproduction(无性生殖)**[2]. Mitosis makes it possible for organisms to reproduce asexually. In asexual reproduction, a single individual is the sole parent and passes copies of all its genes on to its offspring. Many single-celled organisms and some multicellular ones reproduce asexually. Humans and other organisms that reproduce sexually in which meiosis is needed to take into account the genetic contribution of the two parent organisms.

The most important cellular components during cell reproduction are the chromosomes, which contain all the genetic information for a cell and lead to the specific features, traits,

1. 细胞通过有丝分裂和减数分裂两种方式进行繁殖。体细胞只能进行有丝分裂，而生殖细胞可以进行减数分裂形成配子，雄配子为精子，雌配子为卵子。

2. 无性生殖是以单一个体为亲代产生后代的生殖方式。

and capabilities of a cell. DNA is packaged into chromosomes in eukaryotic cells. In higher organisms each cell usually contains two similar copies of each chromosome. One of these copies is a maternal contribution and the other is a paternal contribution. Together, these are called a pair of **homologous chromosome(同源染色体)**[3] and each alone is called a homologue.

- The **haploid(单倍体)**[4] number of a cell refers to the total number of homologous pairs in a cell (or the number of unique chromosomes). This number varies from species to species; in humans it is 23. The **diploid(二倍体)** number of a cell refers to the total number of chromosomes in a cell and is equal to two times the haploid number.
- If the haploid number is thought of as N, the diploid number would be 2N. In humans the diploid number is 46.

1. Mitosis and Cell Cycle

   Mitosis in cell division is usually a small segment of a larger **cell cycle(细胞周期)**[5], an ordered sequence of events in the life of a eukaryotic cell from its origin in the division of a parent cell until its own division into two daughter cells. It can be divided into two periods: **interphase(间期)** and **mitosis (M) phase(有丝分裂期)**.

   1) During interphase, cell is not dividing but cellular metabolic activity is high, chromosomes and organelles are duplicated, and cell size may increase. It accounts for 90% of the cell cycle and is subdivided into G_1 **phase(合成前期)**, **S phase(合成期)** and G_2 **phase(合成后期)**[6].

      - The G_1 and G_2 phases are periods of protein synthesis and organelle production.
      - The S phase is when DNA replication occurs. Cells that undergo mitosis duplicate their chromosomes, resulting in cells with two times their normal haploid or diploid numbers. Newly synthesized chromosomes remain closely associated with their like-

> 3. 在体细胞中,有一对形态结构相似的染色体,一条来自父方,一条来自母方。这样的染色体叫做一对同源染色体。

> 4. 单倍体数目是指细胞内不同的染色体的个数;二倍体数目是指细胞内所有染色体的数目,且为单倍体的数目的二倍。

> 5. 细胞周期分为间期和有丝分裂期两部分。间期又分为合成前期、合成期和合成后期。

> 6. 合成前期和合成后期主要是合成蛋白质和细胞器的时期。合成期的主要事件是DNA的复制和姐妹染色单体的形成。

chromosome. These two identical chromosomes are called **sister chromatids(姐妹染色单体)**.
- The cytoplasm of a cell in late interphase contains two centrosomes, each of which may contain a pair of centrioles. One or more nucleoli are present.

2) Mitosis, division of the nucleus and its chromosomes, is divided into four phases: **prophase(前期)**, **metaphase(中期)**, **anaphase(后期)**, and **telophase(末期)**. Mitosis is followed by **cytokinesis(胞质分裂)**[7], when the cytoplasm splits to form two separate daughter cells.

- During prophase, the nucleoli disappear and chromatin fibers coil up to become discrete chromosomes. The two identical sister chromatids making up one chromosome, join at the centromere. Microtubules grow out from the two centrosomes, initiating formation of the mitotic spindle. The nuclear envelope breaks into fragments. Some of the spindle fibers reach the chromosomes and attach to **kinetochores(着丝点)**[8], structures made of proteins and specific sections of DNA at the centromeres. Nonkinetochore microtubules overlap with those coming from the opposite pole.
- At metaphase, the mitotic spindle is fully formed, and the microtubules find and attach to kinetochores moving the chromosomes to the **metaphase plate(赤道板)**, an imaginary plane equidistant from the poles.
- Anaphase begins when centromeres divide, the proteins that bind sister chromatids together are cleaved freeing the two sister chromatids from each other. Sister chromatids then are pulled to opposite poles as the attached microtubules shorten.
- In telophase, the spindle apparatus disassembles. The nuclear membrane begins to reform around the identical sets of chromosomes at the two poles of the cell and the chromosomes become less tightly

7. 有丝分裂期分为前期、中期、后期和末期四个阶段。有丝分裂后细胞还需要进行胞质分裂才能最终形成两个子细胞。

8. 着丝粒由蛋白质和着丝粒附近的 DNA 序列构成,是纺锤丝附着的位置。纺锤丝将牵引着染色体排列在赤道板上。
着丝点是纺锤丝与染色体接触的位置。

coiled.

- Cytokinesis is technically not even a phase of mitosis, but rather a separate process, necessary for completing cell division. In animal cells, cytokinesis begins with the formation of a **cleavage furrow** (卵裂沟)[9]. At the site of the furrow, a ring of microfilaments contracts, pinching the cell in two and separating the two identical daughter cells. Plant cells are separated by several vesicles that containing cellulose collect in the middle of the cell. The vesicles fuse, forming a large sac called the **cell plate**(细胞板). The cell plate grows outward until its membrane fuses with the plasma membrane, separating the two daughter cells.

3) The cell cycle is carefully controlled.

The cell cycle is controlled by both internal and external signals. A signal, we have discussed in last chapter, is a molecule that either stimulates or inhibits a metabolic event.

A cell uses three main **checkpoints**(检验点)[10] to both assess the internal state of the cell and integrate external signals. The G1/S checkpoint is the primary point at which the cell decides to divide; the G2/M checkpoint represents a commitment to mitosis; and the spindle checkpoint ensures that all chromosomes are attached to the spindle in preparation for anaphase. Proteins in the cytoplasm control the passage of a cell through the cell cycle. Two groups of proteins, **cyclins**(细胞周期蛋白) and **Cdks**(周期蛋白依赖性激酶)[11], interact and regulate the cell cycle.

- Cyclin must be present for the cell to move from the G1 stage to the S stage, and from the G2 stage to the M stage. Their levels in the cell rise and fall with the stages of the cell cycle.
- Cdks must bind the appropriate cyclin (whose levels fluctuate) in order to be activated. They add

9. 在动物细胞中，由微丝形成的卵裂沟的出现，标志着胞质分裂的开始。在植物细胞中，高尔基体产生的囊泡融合成细胞板，帮助细胞进行胞质分裂。

10. 细胞周期的调控点，在这一时间，细胞会对细胞周期内应当发生的重要事件和出现的错误进行检测，以决定细胞活动是否向下进行。

11. 细胞周期蛋白和周期蛋白依赖性激酶相互作用，对细胞周期进行调控。
  细胞周期蛋白是细胞从G1期进入S期和从G2期进入M期所必需的。周期蛋白依赖性激酶必须与细胞周期蛋白结合才能够活化，将其他控制细胞周期的蛋白磷酸化。

phosphate groups to a variety of protein substrates that control processes in the cell cycle. Their levels in the cell remain fairly stable. They turn active form to inactive when cyclin is gradated.

Cells also receive other protein signals (growth factors) that affect cell division. Growth factors are external signals received at the plasma membrane, which will stimulate cell division. For example, the growth factor PDGF (platelet-derived growth factor) binds to its receptor, an integral membrane protein embedded in the plasma membrane. Binding of a growth factor to its receptor triggers a cascade of signaling events within the cytosol. In most cases, phosphorylation activates the protein and eventually transfers the signal into the nucleus. Then phosphorylation activates transcription factors that bind to promoters and enhancers in DNA, turning on their associated genes. In this case, cell division won't happen without growth factors.

Once cell escapes cell cycle control, it will become **cancer cell**(癌细胞)[12]. A cancer is an uncontrolled proliferation of cells. Many reasons involve cancel cell formation, and we will talk about in later section.

12. 一旦细胞不再受到细胞周期的控制,其将会变成癌细胞,即不受控制无限增殖的细胞。

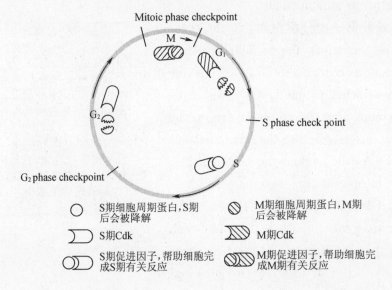

2. Meiosis

Like mitosis, meiosis is preceded by an interphase, during which the chromosomes replicate. The centrosome also duplicates in preparation for cell division. However, meiosis in diploid organisms consists of two rounds of division, **meiosis Ⅰ(减数第一次分裂)** and **meiosis Ⅱ(减数第二次分裂)**[13], but replication only occurs at the beginning of meiosis Ⅰ.

1) Meiosis Ⅰ

Prophase Ⅰ(减数第一次分裂前期)[14] begins with condensation of the chromosomes. Homologous chromosomes, each made up of two sister chromatids, come together in pairs. This pairing is called **synapsis(联会)**. Each homologous chromosome pair is called a **tetrad(四分体)**, a complex of four chromatids. Chromatids of homologous chromosomes **cross over(交换)** each other and exchange parts at **chiasmata(交叉)** (singular, chiasma). Meanwhile, other cellular components prepare for the division of the nucleus. The centrosomes move away from each other, and spindle microtubules form between them. The nuclear envelope and nucleoli disperse. Finally, spindle microtubules capture the kinetochores that form on the chromosomes, and the chromosomes begin moving to the metaphase plate.

At **metaphase Ⅰ(减数第一次分裂中期)**[15], the chromosome tetrads are aligned on the metaphase plate. For each tetrad, kinetochore microtubules from one pole of the cell are attached to one homologous chromosome, while kinetochore microtubules from the other pole of the cell are attached to the other chromosome of the pair. Thus, the homologous chromosomes are poised to move to opposite poles of the cell.

During **anaphase Ⅰ(减数第一次分裂后期)**, each pair of homologous chromosomes is pulled apart, and each one moves toward the opposite pole. Note that sister chromatids remain attached at their centromeres and

13. 减数分裂分为减数第一次分裂和减数第二次分裂两个时期。减数第一次分裂又分为减数第一次分裂前期、减数第一次分裂中期、减数第一次分裂后期和减数第一次分裂末期。

14. 发生在减数第一次分裂前期的主要事件是同源染色体的联会。发生联会的同源染色体称为四分体,含有四个姐妹染色单体。同源染色体非姐妹染色单体间会发生交换。交叉结构标志着交换的产生。

15. 减数第一次分裂中期同源染色体成对排列在赤道板上。
　　减数第一次分裂后期同源染色体相互分离,非同源染色体自由组合。
　　减数第一次分裂末期和胞质分裂完成后,形成两个单倍体子细胞,但是此时姐妹染色单体未分离。

move as a unit toward the same pole.

The chromosomes finish their journey during **telophase Ⅰ(减数第一次分裂末期)**, and cytokinesis occurs, producing two haploid daughter cells. Note that each chromosome still consists of two sister chromatids. Meiosis isn't over yet; remember that it consists of two consecutive divisions. During meiosis Ⅱ, the sister chromatids will be separated.

2) Meiosis Ⅱ

The second division of meiosis—meiosis Ⅱ—is essentially the same as mitosis. The important thing to remember is that meiosis Ⅱ begins with a haploid cell.

- During **prophase Ⅱ(减数第二次分裂前期)**, a spindle forms in each cell and the chromosomes move toward the middle of each cell.
- During **metaphase Ⅱ(减数第二次分裂中期)**, the chromosomes align on the metaphase plate.
- Sister chromatids are pulled apart in **anaphase Ⅱ (减数第二次分裂后期)**[16].
- In **telophase Ⅱ(减数第二次分裂末期)**, nuclei form at opposite poles of each dividing cell, and cytokinesis splits the cells apart. Meiosis has produced four haploid cells, each with one set of chromosomes.

3) Unique features of meiosis contribute genetic variation[17].
- In prophase Ⅰ of meiosis, homologues pair in synapsis and crossing over occurs, allowing nonsister chromatids to exchange chromosomal material.
- In metaphase Ⅰ, the tetrads, not chromosome, line up at the metaphase plate randomly. At the end of meiosis I each pair of chromosomes within a tetrad separates and sorts into daughter cell independently.
- The result of meiosis is the production of gamete. Both female and male gametes will combine to restore the diploid cell, **zygote(合子/受精卵)**[18], during **fertilization(受精作用)**. The random nature of fertilization doubles the genetic variation arising from meiosis.

16. 减数第二次分裂后期,姐妹染色单体相互分离。

17. 减数第一次分裂前期发生的同源染色体非姐妹染色单体间发生的交换和减数第一次分裂后期发生的非同源染色体自由组合增加了配子的基因多样性。

18. 单倍体的配子通过受精作用,精子和卵子结合,形成受精卵或称为合子。

3. Variety of Sexual Life Cycles among Organisms

Alternation of fertilization and meiosis occurs in all sexual life cycles. However, the timing of meiosis and fertilization does vary among species.

1) In most animals, including humans, gametes are the only haploid cells. Gametes do not divide further but fuse to form zygote that divides by mitosis to produce a multicellular organism[19].

2) Most fungi and some protists have an opposite type of life cycle. Their gametes fuse to form a zygote that undergoes meiosis to produce haploid cells called **spores(孢子)**. Spores grow by mitosis to form the haploid multicellular adult organism. The haploid adult produces gametes by mitosis[20].

3) Plants and some algae have a third type of life cycle called alternation of generations that includes two multicellular stages, one haploid and one diploid. Once a zygote is formed, the zygote develops into a multicellular organism by mitosis. This diploid multicellular stage called **sporophyte(孢子体)** produces spores through meiosis. Each spore has the ability to grow into a multicellular **gametophyte(配子体)** plant. This stage of plant is called a gametophyte because it produces gametes. Gametes then fuse to form a new zygote after maturing[21].

19. 对于动物,包括人类来说,配子是单倍体且不再进行分裂。两个配子融合形成合子后(二倍体)再进行有丝分裂以产生多细胞个体。个体可通过减数分裂产生配子。

20. 对于真菌和原生动物来说其单倍体配子细胞融合形成合子后会经减数分裂产生单倍体孢子。孢子经有丝分裂形成单倍体的多细胞个体。单倍体个体经有丝分裂产生单倍体配子。

21. 植物的生命周期会出现世代更替的现象。植物的合子经有丝分裂产生多细胞个体,二倍体多细胞个体处于孢子体时期;单倍体多细胞个体处于配子体时期,可产生配子;配子融合形成合子。

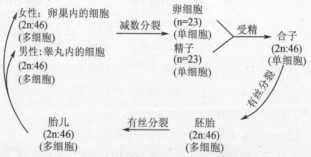

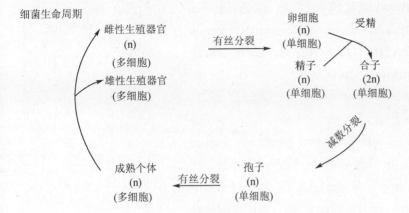

II. Mender's Law of Genetics

Mendel studied peas. In nature, pea plants typically self-fertilize. Mendel hybridized two contrasting, true-breeding pea varieties. The true-breeding parents are the **P generation (亲代)** and their hybrid offspring are the **F₁ generation (子一代)**[22]. Mendel would then allow the F₁ hybrids to self-pollinate to produce the **F₂ generation (子二代)**. Mendel developed two principles of heredity: **the law of segregation (分离定律)** and **the law of independent assortment (自由组合定律)**[23].

1. Mendel's monohybrid crosses and law of segregation

    Mendel's experiments that tested a single character are called **monohybrid crosses (单因子杂交)**. In each case Mendel found one parental dominating in the F₁ hybrid,

> 22. 亲代杂交形成子一代,子一代杂交形成子二代。

> 23. 分离定律:配子形成时,等位基因随着同源染色体的分开而分离,随配子独立遗传给后代。
> 自由组合定律:减数分裂形成配子时,等位基因随着同源染色体的分开而分离,非同源染色体上的非等位基因自由组合。

and after **self-fertilization**(自花传粉)[24] in F_2 generation both parental characters appeared in the proportion of three-fourths to one-fourth. He performed each experiment on several thousand plants and counted all the plants in F_2 progeny which gave an average ratio of 3∶1.
Segregation of Genes: From his experiments Mendel concluded that each parent contributes one factor for a character to the F_1 hybrid. In this way the F_1 hybrid has two factors for each character. When the F_1 hybrid forms gametes the two factors separate from each other. There is no mixing up of factors thus emphasizing the purity of gametes. The separation of two factors into separate gametes is summarized as Mendel's law of segregation.

> 24. 只选择一对相对性状为研究对象的杂交方式称为单因子杂交。
> 子一代自花传粉（自交）产生子二代。表型比例为3∶1。

```
P        高(纯种)×矮(纯种)        ……杂交
遗传因子   TT       tt
配子      T        t
F₁             高(杂交种)⊗高(杂交种)  ……自交
               Tt         Tt
配子          T,t        T,t
F₂代          高          矮
            (TT, Tt, tT)  (tt)
```

Terms used in Mendel's Crosses:
Dominant(显性) versus ***Recessive***(隐性)[25]: When two pure breeding varieties are crossed, the parental character that expresses itself unchanged in the F_1 generation hybrids is dominant; the other one that does not appear in F_1 but appears in F_2 is called recessive. In the above cross three-fourths of the F_2 progeny show the dominant character and one-fourth the recessive character.

> 25. 具有一对相对性状的两个纯合亲本杂交，子一代中表现出来的性状为显性性状，另一性状为隐性形状。

Alleles(等位基因): Factors which control contrasting expressions of a character are said to be alleles of each other. In the above cross the character in consideration is height, and factors T and t which control tallness are alleles of each other. So, Mendel's law of segregation also can be summarized as the separation of alleles into separate gametes.

Homozygous(纯合子) and ***Heterozygous***(杂合子)[26]: Mendel had concluded that each character is controlled by

> 26. 控制相对性状的基因叫做等位基因。等位基因相同的个体叫做纯合子，等位基因不相同的个体叫做杂合子。

a pair of factors. When both factors are identical such as TT and tt, the individual is said to be homozygous for that character. When the factors are different (for example *Tt*), the term heterozygous is used.

***Phenotype*(表型)** and ***genotype*(基因型)**[27]: A description of an organism's traits is its phenotype. A description of its genetic makeup is its genotype.

***Test Cross*(测交)**[28]: In the cross between tall and dwarf pea plants, the F_1 hybrids were all phenotypically tall but their genotypes were not only *TT* but also *Tt*. Test cross then was used to determine the genotype of an individual with a dominant phenotype and can be explained diagrammatically below:

> 27. 对于个体性状的描述为个体的表型；个体的等位基因组成为个体的基因型。

> 28. 未知基因型的个体与隐性纯合个体杂交，可通过子代的表型预测未知个体的基因型。

```
P       高      ×    矮           高      ×    矮
        Tt           tt           TT           tt
配子  T(50%)  t(50%)  t(100%)  或  T(100%)  (100%)
F₁      高           矮                高
        Tt            t                Tt
        50%          50%              100%
```

2. Mendel's dihybrid cross and law of independent assortment

   Mendel made crosses between pea plants differing in two characters such as texture of seed and color of cotyledons. Such a cross in which inheritance of two characters is considered is called a **dihybrid cross(双因子杂交)**[29].

   Mendel crossed true-breeding plants that had yellow, round seeds (*YYRR*) with true-breeding plants that had green, wrinkled seeds (*yyrr*). From the results of his dihybrid crosses, Mendel realized the following facts. At the time of gamete formation, the segregation of alleles into separate gametes occurs independently. In this way Mendel proved that when two characters are considered in a cross, there is independent assortment of genes for each character, and this became the law of independent assortment.

> 29. 双因子杂交以两对相对性状为研究对象。子二代的表型比例为 9:3:3:1。

P		黄圆(纯种)	×	绿皱(纯种)	
		RRYY		rryy	
配子		RY		ry	
F_1		黄,圆	⊗	黄,圆	
		RrYy		RrYy	
配子		RY,Ry,rY,ry		RY,Ry,rY,ry	
F_2	表现型	黄,圆	绿圆	黄皱	绿皱
	表现型比例	9	3	3	1
	基因型	YYRR,YYRr,YyRR,YyRr	yyRR,yyRr	YYrr,Yyrr	yyrr
	基因型比例	1 2 2 4	1 2	1 2	1

3. Many human diseases are inherited by Mendelian genetics.[30]
   ***Cystic fibrosis*(囊性纤维化)**: The abnormal, recessive allele doesn't allow for Cl^- transport and the mucus becomes thicker and stickier than normal and favors bacterial infections.
   ***Tay-Sachs disease*(泰-萨氏症)**: Another lethal recessive disorder caused by a dysfunctional enzyme that fails to break down specific brain lipids.
   ***Sickle-cell disease*(镰刀型细胞贫血症)**: It's caused by the substitution of a single amino acid in hemoglobin. Red cells are sickled and don't carry oxygen well.
   ***Huntington's disease*(亨廷顿舞蹈症)**: A degenerative disease of the nervous system. The dominant lethal allele has no obvious phenotypic effect until an individual is about 35 to 45 years old.
   ***Phenylketonuria*(PKU, 苯丙酮尿症)**: Individuals with PKU accumulate the amino acid phenylalanine to toxic levels, which leads to mental retardation.

4. Extension of Two Laws of Inheritance
   The heterozygous F_1 offspring of Mendel's crosses always looked like one of the parental varieties because one allele was dominant to the other. This kind of inheritance demonstrates that one gene controls one character; of the two alleles of a gene, one allele is **completely dominant(完全显性)**[31] over the other.
   1) Some alleles show **incomplete dominance(不完全显性)** where heterozygotes show a distinct intermediate phenotype, not seen in homozygotes. Incomplete domi-

---

30. 囊性纤维化:患者呼吸道上皮细胞缺乏运输 Cl^- 的能力,导致呼吸道因渗透压异常而易受细菌感染。
泰-萨氏症:患者因正常基因缺失而无法分解脑中的脂类。
镰刀型细胞贫血症:患者因血红蛋白异常使得红细胞呈镰刀形。
亨廷顿舞蹈症:一种神经系统紊乱的遗传病。患者通常要到35~45岁才表现出症状。
苯丙酮尿症:患者因苯丙氨酸代谢异常,尿液中会有大量苯丙酮积累。
以上5种遗传疾病均为伴常染色体遗传。除亨廷顿舞蹈症由显性致病基因决定,其余4种由隐性致病基因决定。

31. 完全显性:子代杂合体完全表达双亲之一的性状。
不完全显性:子代杂合体不表达纯合双亲的任意一性状,表达介于双亲性状之间的中间性状。
共显性:子代杂合体同时表达两个纯合双亲的性状。
复等位基因:三个以上的等位基因控制统一形状。

nance is the blending of two characteristics to form an intermediate characteristic, such as red and white carnations produce pink offspring.

2) In **codominance**(共显性) the heterozygote expresses both the parental phenotypes equally or both traits will show, such as in roan cattle, with patches of red and white hair.

3) **Multiple alleles**(复等位基因) occur when there are more than two allelic forms of a gene, such as in ABO blood type.

III. Chromosomal Basis of Inheritance

1. Sex Determination and Sex-linked Inheritance

    In humans and other mammals, there are two varieties of sex **chromosomes**(性染色体), X and Y. The rest chromosomes are called **autosomes**(常染色体). In both testes (XY) and ovaries (XX), the two sex chromosomes segregate during meiosis and each gamete receives one.

    Each egg receives an X chromosome. Half the sperm receive an X chromosome and half receive a Y chromosome. Because of this, each conception has about a fifty-fifty chance of producing a particular sex.

    In addition to their role in determining sex, the sex chromosomes, especially the X chromosome, have genes for many characters unrelated to sex. If a sex-linked trait is due to a recessive allele, a female has this phenotype only if homozygous.[32] Any male receiving the recessive allele on the X (from his mother) will express the trait. Therefore, males are far more likely to inherit sex-linked recessive disorders than females.

    - ***Duchenne muscular dystrophy***(杜氏肌营养不良症): Absence of an X-linked gene for a key muscle protein. Patients are progressive weakening on the muscles and losing coordination and usually fatal.
    - ***Hemophilia***(血友病): A sex-linked recessive trait defined by the absence of one or more clotting factors.

> 32. 因为 Y 染色体上没有与 X 染色体对应的等位基因。所以对于男性个体来说,X 染色体上如果有隐性等位基因,那么个体将表达隐性性状。杜氏肌营养不良和血友病是两种伴 X 隐性遗传病。

Individuals with hemophilia have prolonged bleeding because a firm clot forms slowly.

Disease	Pattern	Mutation
Cystic fibrosis	Autosomal recessive	Deletion of three nucleotide
Tay-Sachs disease	Autosomal recessive	Single base insertions and deletions, splice phase mutations, missense mutations
Sickle-cell disease	Autosomal recessive	Point mutation
Phenylketonuria	Autosomal recessive	
Huntington's disease	Autosomal dominate	Too much trinucleotide repeat
Duchenne muscular dystrophy	X-linked recessive	Deletions of one or more exons
Hemophilia	X-linked recessive	

2. Barr Bodies

Although female mammals inherit two X chromosomes, only one X chromosome is active. During female development, one X chromosome per cell condenses into a compact object, a **Barr body(巴氏小体)**[33].

Formation of Barr body inactivates most of its genes. The condensed Barr body chromosome is reactivated in ovarian cells that produce ova. In humans, this mosaic pattern is evident in women who are heterozygous for a X-linked mutation that prevents the development of sweat glands. A heterozygous woman will have patches of normal skin and skin patches lacking sweat glands. Similarly, the orange and black pattern on tortoiseshell cats is due to patches of cells expressing an orange allele while others have a non-orange allele.[34]

3. Gene Linkage Inheritance

1) **Linked genes(连锁基因)**[35] tend to be inherited together because they are located on the same chromosome. These linked genes tend to be inherited together because the chromosome is passed along as a unit. Genes located on the same chromosome tend to move together through meiosis and fertilization.

> 33. 在女性个体发育过程中,每个细胞中的一条X染色体上的基因会被关闭。这条染色体会高度压缩,称为巴氏小体。

> 34. 对于其中一条X染色体上控制汗腺发育的基因发生突变的杂合体女性来说,就可能因为其中一条染色体的关闭而导致其部分皮肤正常,部分皮肤缺少汗腺的情况发生。

> 35. 连锁基因位于同一染色体上,所以在减数第一次分裂后期时不能进行自由组合,总是连锁在一起遗传。但是由于减数第一次分裂前期同源染色体的非姐妹染色单体会发生交换,所以后代中也有少量个体表现出连锁基因控制的性状发生交换的现象。可通过交换率进行基因作图,寻找基因的相互位置。

When genes are linked, they do not assort independently. That is, from a testcross involving an individual heterozygous for each of two genes, the offspring will not exhibit a 1∶1∶1∶1 phenotypic ratio expected for independently assorting genes. Instead, there will be an excess of the parental phenotypes. Results of such testcrosses can be used to calculate the map distance between the two genes involved.

2) Crossing over and genetic mapping[36]

Crossing over occurs during prophase I, which results in the production of more types of gametes than one. It would be predicted by Mendelian rules alone. Crossing over of linked genes is used to develop a method for constructing a chromosome map. The farther apart a gene is to the centromere, the more likely the number of crossing-overs.

36. 相对交换率的测定：如果只发生一次交换，相对交换率可用重组率表示。重组率＝[重组型/(重组型＋亲本型)]×100%。假设 a^+b^+ 连锁，$a^+a^+b^+b^+$ 个体与 aabb 个体杂交得到 a^+ab^+b 个体。

a^+ab^+b 个体与 aabb 个体测交，那么后代中 a^+ab^+b 个体和 aabb 个体为亲本组合且数目较多，a^+abb 个体和 aab^+b 个体为重组合且数目较少

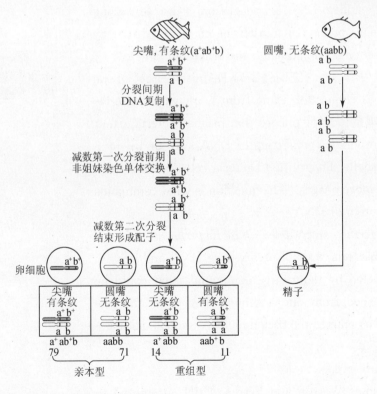

$$\text{重组率}\% = \frac{\text{重组型后代}}{\text{后代总数}} \times 100\%$$

$$= \frac{14+11}{79+71+14+11} \times 100\%$$

$$= 14\%$$

a与b在染色体上的相对距离为

```
  a b
 ─────
  14%
或
  b a
 ─────
  14%
```

IV. Molecular Genetics

1. DNA is the genetic material.
   1) *Bacterial Transformation*[37]. Griffith and Avery in 1928 found that they could transfer an inherited characteristic (e.g. the ability to cause pneumonia), from one strain of bacteria to another, by exposing a harmless bacteria strain to DNA extracted from a disease causing strain. This process of transferring an inherited trait by an extract of DNA is called **transformation(转化)**.

   2) *Bacterial Invaders*(细菌侵染). Definitive proof of the gene-DNA connection came from work with **bacteriophages(噬菌体)** (or phages that means bacteria eater) which are viruses consisting of DNA surrounded by a protein shell. They infect bacteria cells causing them to make more phages. The question is what commands this? Protein or DNA?

   3) *Alfred Hershey and Martha Chase Experiment*. Exposed E. coli bacteria with phages whose DNA and protein were labeled by radioactive compounds that could be distinguished from one another, they found that the phage DNA entered the bacteria but the protein did not.

37. 肺炎双球菌转化试验和噬菌体侵染试验证明了DNA是遗传物质。

2. The Structure of DNA
   In 1951, James Watson and Francis Crick attempted to build a model that would show the molecular structure of DNA that until that time was largely unknown.

1) What was known about DNA at that time:
   a) DNA is a polymer of nucleotides, each one having a phosphate group, the sugar deoxyribose, and a nitrogenous base.
   b) Erwin Chargaff, formulated ***Chargaff's Rules***[38]:
      - *The number of purines in DNA always equals the number of pyrimidines.*
      - *The amount of adenine equals the amount of thymine; the amount of cytosine equals the amount of guanine.*
   c) Rosalind Franklin and Maurice Wilkins had prepared an X-ray detraction photograph of DNA indicating that DNA was long and skinny, helical and consisted of 2 parallel strands.

> 38. 查加夫法则：双链 DNA 中，嘌呤数目＝嘧啶数目；A＝T,C＝G。

2) The model proposed by Watson and Crick suggested the following features of DNA:
   - The DNA molecule is composed of 2 nucleotide chains oriented in opposite directions. In each strand each phosphate group is attached to one sugar at the 5' position and to the other at the 3' position. They suggested that the two DNA strands are twisted together to form intertwined helices or **double helix(双螺旋)**[39].
   - The DNA molecule is analogous to the structure of a ladder. The bases on the 2 strands are directed inward and form the rung of the ladder, while the sugar-phosphate face outside and act as the sides of the ladder.
   - **Complimentary base pairing(碱基互补配对)**[40]. Bases A and T are always paired and G and C always paired.

> 39. DNA 的两条链反向平行，构成双螺旋结构。

> 40. A 与 T 配对，C 与 G 配对。

3. Experiments determine the method of DNA replication. Matthew Meselson and Franklin W. Stahl designed an experiment to determine the method of DNA replication. Three models of replication were considered likely:
   1) ***Conservative replication*(全保留复制)**[41] would somehow produce an entirely new DNA strand during replication when the entire DNA molecule acted as a template.

> 41. 全保留复制是以整条 DNA 双链为模板，复制一条新链。

2) **Semiconservative replication**（半保留复制）[42] would produce two DNA molecules, each of which was composed of one-half of the parental DNA along with an entirely new complementary strand. During replication, the double stranded DNA molecule lent itself to replicate because each strand could serve as a template for the formation of a complimentary strand.

3) **Dispersive replication**（分散复制）[43] involved the breaking of the parental strands during replication. This would synthesize the DNA in short pieces alternating from one strand to the other and somehow, a reassembly of molecules that were a mix of old and new fragments on each strand of DNA.

> 42. 半保留复制是指DNA复制时两条链均作为模板通过碱基互补配对原则合成另一条互补链，所以子代DNA中有一条链（一半）来自于母链。

> 43. 分散复制是将母链打断进行分段复制，然后将复制的片段进行组装，这样产生的DNA分子既包含旧链也包含新链。

The Meselson-Stahl experiment involved the growth of *E. coli* bacteria on a growth medium containing heavy nitrogen (Nitrogen^{15} as opposed to the more common, but lighter molecular weight isotope, Nitrogen^{14}). The first generation of bacteria was grown on a medium where the sole source of N was Nitrogen^{15}. The bacteria were then transferred to a medium with light (Nitrogen^{14}) medium. Watson and Crick had predicted that DNA replication was semi-conservative. If it was, then the DNA produced by bacteria grown on light medium would be intermediate between heavy and light. It was.

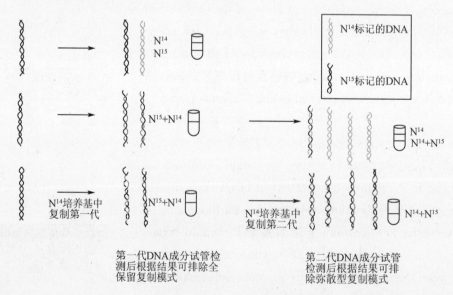

4. Details of DNA Replication
   1) Origination

      The replication of a DNA molecule begins at special sites, **origins of replication**(复制起始位点)[44], where the double helix unwinds and unzips. At the origin sites, the DNA strands are separated by **helicase**(解旋酶) enzyme forming a replication "bubble" with replication forks, the y-shaped junction at the spot where the 2 strands are unwinding.

      In eukaryotes, there may be thousands of origin sites per chromosome. The replication bubbles elongate in both directions and eventually fuse until the entire molecule is copied.

   2) DNA polymerase can only add nucleotides to the growing DNA strand from 5' to 3' direction. At the replication fork, DNA replication is continuous on this side of the template and is discontinuous on the other template. Only one parental strand (3' to 5' into the fork) can be used as a template for a continuous complimentary **leading strand**(前导链)[45]. The other parental strand (5' to 3' into the fork) is copied away from the fork for the **lagging strand**(滞后链) in short segments (Okazaki fragments). **Okazaki fragments**(岗崎片段) are joined by **DNA ligase**(连接酶). To summarize, at the replication fork, the leading stand is copied continuously. The lagging strand is copied in short segments, each requiring a new primer.

   3) DNA polymerase proofreads during replication. DNA polymerase proofreads each new nucleotide against the template nucleotide as soon as it is added. If there is an incorrect pairing, the enzyme removes the wrong nucleotide and then resumes synthesis.

   4) The ends of eukaryotic chromosomal DNA molecules, the **telomeres**(端粒)[46], have special nucleotide sequences. Telomeres protect genes from being eroded through multiple rounds of DNA replication.

> 44. 复制起始位点即 DNA 复制开始的位点，DNA 首先在这里解旋和解链。解旋酶打开 DNA 双链形成复制叉。

> 45. 在 DNA 复制中，以 3'→5'方向的 DNA 模板链合成的新链为前导链；以 5'→3'方向的模板链合成的新链为滞后链。前导链合成是连续的；滞后链则呈片段化合成，这些片段称为岗崎片段。岗崎片段经 DNA 连接酶连接后形成完整的新链。

> 46. 真核细胞染色体末端的 DNA 分子呈特殊结构，称为端粒。端粒保护 DNA 序列不在复制过程中受到损伤。

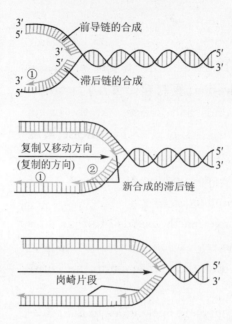

5. Gene Expression and Protein Synthesis

   Genes, functional subunits of DNA, are located on chromosomes directing synthesis of protein. The genetic material contained in DNA is stored and used in cells after it has been synthesized during replication, which involves 2 processes—transcription and translation.

   1) **Transcription(转录)**[47]

      During transcription, a DNA strand, **template strand (模板链)**, provides a template for the synthesis of a complementary RNA strand, called **messenger RNA (mRNA,信使RNA)**. Uracil is used instead of thymine.

      a) **RNA polymerase(RNA 聚合酶)** separates the DNA strands and bonds the RNA nucleotides as they base-pair along the DNA template, making mRNA. Like DNA polymerases, RNA polymerases can add nucleotides only to the 3' end of the growing polymer. As RNA polymerase moves along the DNA, it untwists the double helix. The enzyme adds nucleotides to the 3' end of the growing strand. A single gene can be transcribed simultaneously by several RNA polymerases at a time. This helps the cell make the encoded protein in large amounts.

> 47. 在转录过程中，DNA双链中的一条链作为模板链提供mRNA合成所需要的信息。RNA聚合酶打开DNA双链并连接核糖核苷酸形成RNA链。

b) Specific sequences of nucleotides along the DNA mark where gene transcription begins and ends. RNA polymerase attaches and initiates transcription at the **promoter(启动子)**[48]. The **terminator(终止子)** signals the end of transcription. When a terminator code is reached, transcription stops.

2) RNA processing in eukaryotic cells

In eukaryotes, transcription occurs at nucleus. After the mRNA strand called transcript unit is formed, it passes from the nucleus to the cytoplasm where it becomes associated with ribosomes. But, before it leaves the nucleus, the mRNA is modified or processed.

- The addition of extra nucleotides 5'-cap and poly A-tail to the ends of the RNA transcript.
- **RNA splicing(RNA 剪接)**[49]. DNA is comprised of long stretches of noncoding regions, **introns(内含子)** that interrupt nucleotide sequences coding for amino acids. The coding regions, the parts of the gene that are expressed, are called **exons(外显子)**. Both exons and introns are transcribed from DNA into RNA. Before the RNA leaves the nucleus, the introns are removed and the exons are joined to produce the mRNA with a continuous coding sequence.

> 48. RNA 聚合酶识别启动子并与之结合，起始 RNA 的合成；当 RNA 聚合酶沿 DNA 模板移动至终止子位置时,转录终止。

> 49. 真核细胞的 DNA 分为非编码区的内含子和可表达蛋白的外显子。因此,真核细胞的 mRNA 并不能全部用于编码蛋白质。RNA剪接就是切除内含子,连接外显子。

3) **Translation**(翻译)[50]

During translation the sequence of bases of the mRNA is translated into a sequence of amino acids. The information contained in mRNA is used to determine the amino acid sequence of a polypeptide.

- *Origination*. 3 nucleotide units of the mRNA that code for an amino acid is called a **codon**(密码子)[51], e. g. CGU codes for Arginine. Also, there are 3 codons called **stop codons**(终止密码子), which serve as a signal of polypeptide chain termination, e. g. UAA, UAG, UGA. One codon is a **start codon**(起始密码子) that signals to begin polypeptide synthesis, e. g. AUG. Codon is redundant: there is more than one code for the twenty amino acids.

- *Initiation*[52]. The mRNA molecule binds (5' end) to **rRNA**(核糖体 RNA) of small ribosomal subunit initiating translation at the start codon.

- *Elongation*. **Transfer RNA**(**tRNA**,转录 RNA) transfers amino acids to a ribosome. The ribosome adds each amino acid carried by tRNA to the growing end of the polypeptide chain. Each tRNA carries a specific amino acid at one end and has a specific nucleotide triplet, an anticodon, at the other. The ribosome moves down the length of the mRNA in 5' to 3' direction.

- *Termination*. The process continues until the ribosome encounters one of three possible stop codons. There is no tRNA to recognize these codons; instead a release factor will bind to the stop codon. The last tRNA is released and the polypeptide chain is freed. The polypeptides may then go to the ER where further synthesis occurs (e. g. secondary, tertiary structure). Some go to the cellular organelles e. g. mitochondria and chloroplasts.

50. 翻译：以 mRNA 为模板，根据 mRNA 的信息，合成氨基酸序列的过程。

51. 在 mRNA 上，三个连续的核苷酸为一个氨基酸编码。这三个连续的核苷酸称为一个密码子。UAA，UAG，UGA 为终止密码子，标志着氨基酸链合成的终止。AUG 为起始密码子，标志着氨基酸合成的开始。存在多个密码子为同一个氨基酸编码的情况。

52. 起始：mRNA 与核糖体小亚基中的 rRNA 结合，在起始密码子处起始翻译。

延伸：tRNA 携带氨基酸至正在延伸的多肽链末端，tRNA 上的反密码子与 mRNA 上的密码子配对。

终止：当核糖体移动至终止密码子处，由于没有相应的 tRNA 携带氨基酸并识别终止密码子，翻译终止。

6. Genetic Regulation in Prokaryotic Cells

The bacterial genes are organized into units, called

operon(操纵子)[53], so that functionally related genes are together. Operons are stretches of DNA that contain both **regulatory sequences**(调控序列) and structural genes that code for polypeptides. This organization of the genome into operons is important because it allows functionally related genes to be regulated together. An operon consists of the components as follows:

- The **promoter site**(启动位点)[54] is the attachment site for RNA polymerases.
- The structural genes code for the proteins.
- The **operator site**(操纵位点) is the attachment site for the **repressor protein**(阻遏蛋白/阻遏物).
- The regulatory gene codes for the repressor protein. Regulatory sequences control the level of transcription of structural genes by blocking RNA polymerase, or by allowing it to bind to the DNA sequence.
- The repressor protein is different for each operon and is custom fit to the regulatory metabolite. The type of operon determines whether or not the repressor protein can bind to the operator site.

> 53. 操纵子是原核细胞转录的功能单位。很多功能上相关的基因前后相连成串，由一个共同的控制区进行转录的控制，包括结构基因以及调节基因的整个DNA序列。主要见于原核生物的转录调控。

> 54. RNA聚合酶与启动位点结合起始转录。
> 阻遏蛋白与操纵位点结合可阻止RNA聚合酶进行转录。
> 操纵基因编码阻遏蛋白。

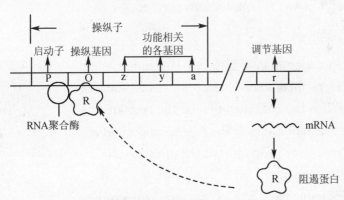

1) In the **repressible operon**(阻遏型操纵子)[55], the product is the regulatory metabolite. When the concentration of the product increases, the product binds to the repressor protein allowing the repressor protein to bind to the operator site — shutting the operon down. Trp operon[56] is repressible. Structural genes of Trp operon coding for the proteins are responsible for tryp-

> 55. 阻遏型操纵子：新陈代谢产物与阻遏蛋白结合，使阻遏蛋白与操纵位点结合，关闭操纵子。

tophan synthesis. Tryptophan acts as **corepressor(辅阻遏物)** that will bind to repressor protein and activate it. Corepressor-repressor complex binds to promoter blocking RNA polymerase binding to promoter, thus turning off transcription.

> 56. 色氨酸操纵子即是一种阻遏型操纵子。色氨酸为辅阻遏物,可与阻遏蛋白构成复合体,与启动子结合后阻挡抑制 RNA 聚合酶与启动子结合从而关闭转录。

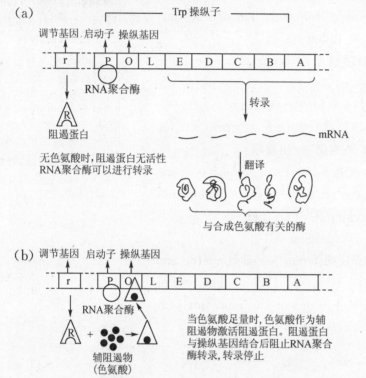

2) In the **inducible operon(诱导型操纵子)**[57], the reactant is the regulatory metabolite, which serves as **inducer(诱导物)**. When the concentration of the reactant increases, the reactant binds to the repressor protein removing the repressor protein from the operator site — turning on the system.

Lac operon is inducible. E. Coli bacteria can synthesize lactase, which is an enzyme that breaks down lactose. Lactase is only synthesized in the presence of lactose. If there is no lactose in the environment, the gene is repressed. With lactose, the repressor is inactivated which enables RNA polymerase to bind to the promoter. Without lactose, the lac repressor binds to the operator site. Then RNA is transcribed, which is

> 57. 在诱导型操纵子中,底物作为诱导物,与阻遏蛋白结合,使阻遏蛋白从操纵位点脱离,起始转录,如乳糖操纵子。

then translated, and becomes the lactase enzyme. The logic of the lac operon is that the proteins required to use lactose are only made when their substrate (lactose) is available. This prevents wasteful expression of enzymes when their substrates are not available.

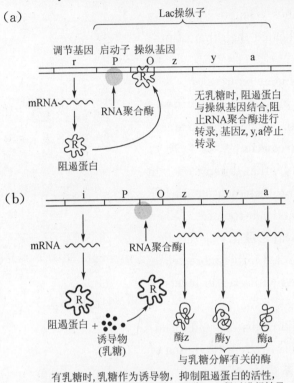

3) Both inducible and repressible operons are referred to as a **negative control system(负调控)**[58] because the repressor, the product of the regulatory gene, acts to turn off transcription of structural genes. **Positive control(正调控)** of transcription has been demonstrated in E. Coli through studies on the effect of glucose on the expression of genes encoding enzymes that lead to breakdown (catabolism) of other sugars, such as lactose. Activated by low levels of glucose, adenylyl cyclase converts ATP to cyclic AMP (CAMP). CAMP then binds to a transcriptional regulatory protein called **catabolic activator protein (CAP, 降解物激活蛋白)**, which interacts with the RNA polymerase to ini-

58. 负调控：调控方式主要通阻遏物实现。阻遏型负调控关闭结构基因表达,诱导型负调控起始基因表达。
正调控：复合物与DNA结合,促进DNA的表达。如葡萄糖水平降低时,cAMP浓度增加,与CAP结合形成复合物,促进乳糖操纵子中相关结构基因的表达。

tiate transcription.

7. Genetic Regulation in Eukaryotic Cells
Eukaryotic cells express only a small fraction of the total genes present in their DNA. The typical human cell expresses only around 5% of its genes. Genetic regulation of eukaryotes is much more complicated than that of prokaryotes.
   1) Package of DNA also regulates gene expression.
      - DNA sequences pack with proteins called **histones** (组蛋白)[59] into chromatin. Genes that are expressed are found in **euchromatin**(常染色质), which is less condensed. DNA that doesn't contain genes is highly condensed into **heterochromatin**(异染色质) such as telomeres and centromeres. When the histone tails are **acetylated**(乙酰化)[60], the condensed chromatin is transformed into a more relaxed structure that is associated with greater levels of gene transcription.
      - **Methyl group**(甲基) can modify histone tails leading to an opposite result. Meanwhile **methylation of DNA sequence**(DNA 序列甲基化)[61] at cytosine also can reduce transcription in eukaryotic cells.
      - The formation of Barr bodies in female mammals also results from heavy methylation, another example of using chromatin condensation to regulate gene expression. The second X chromosome in females is kept highly condensed, so its genes aren't expressed.
   2) Regulation during transcription by enhancers
      a) In general, proteins that bind to specific regulatory sequences are called **enhancers**(增强子)[62] and modulate the activity of RNA polymerase controlling transcription in eukaryotic cells. An enhancer is a sequence of DNA that increases the rate of transcription of nearby genes. Enhancers do not act on

59. 真核细胞的 DNA 与组蛋白构成染色质。常染色质表示转录活跃区域，DNA 较为松散；异染色质处的 DNA 高度密集，较少表达。

60. 组蛋白乙酰化使染色质较为松散易于 DNA 表达，而组蛋白的甲基化则会压缩 DNA 抑制其表达。

61. 真核细胞 DNA 序列中，胞嘧啶的甲基化同样能够抑制转录。

62. 增强子是 DNA 序列中通过调节 RNA 聚合酶，增加附近基因转录的序列。

the promoter region itself. They function by binding transcription factors that act by regulating RNA polymerase. These activator proteins interact with the mediator complex, which recruits. Enhancers can also be found within introns. The binding of specific transcriptional regulatory proteins to enhancers is responsible for the control of gene expression during development, differentiation and in response of cells to hormones and growth factors.

b) Chromosomal rearrangement can also increase the expression of a gene. This rearrangement places a gene, next to an enhancer that originally increased the expression of a different gene. The expression of the new gene increases, because the enhancer affects it. It's the one major reason that gives rise to cancer cell mutation.

3) Alternative splicing

In eukaryotic cells, pre-mRNA synthesized in nucleus needs modification after transcription, in which introns are removed and exons are joined. In many cases, the splicing process can create a range of unique proteins by varying the exon composition of the same messenger RNA. This phenomenon is then called **alternative splicing(可变剪接)**[63].

63. 在真核细胞当中，细胞核中合成的同一前体 mRNA，可以通过不同的内含子剪切和外显子连接方式，形成不同的 mRNA，以合成不同的蛋白质。

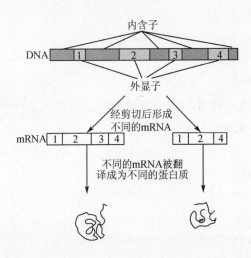

8. Changes of DNA Leading to Mutation

In the living cell, DNA undergoes frequent chemical changes, especially when it is being replicated (in S phase of the eukaryotic cell cycle). Most of these changes are quickly repaired. Those that are not result in a mutation. Thus, mutation is a failure of DNA repair.

1) **Single base substitutions(单碱基替换)**[64] are also called point mutations that one single base is replaced by another. Substitution may lead to three results:

- With a **missense mutation(错义突变)**, the new nucleotide alters the codon so as to produce an altered amino acid in the protein product.
- With a **nonsense mutation(无义突变)**, the new nucleotide changes a codon that specifies an amino acid to one of the stop codons (TAA, TAG, or TGA). Therefore, translation of the messenger RNA transcribed from this mutant gene will stop prematurely. The earlier in the gene this occurs, the more truncated the protein product and the more likely that it will be unable to function.
- Most amino acids are encoded by several different codons. For example, if the third base in the TCT codon for serine is changed to any one of the other three bases, serine will still be encoded. Such mutations are said to be **silent(沉默)** because they cause no change in their product and cannot be detected without sequencing the gene (or its mRNA).

2) **Frameshift mutation(移码突变)**[65]

Extra base pairs may be added (insertions) or removed (deletions) from the DNA of a gene. The number can range from one to thousands. Collectively, these mutations are called frameshift mutation.

Frameshift mutation involving one or two base pairs (or multiples of two) can have devastating consequences to the gene because translation of the gene is "frameshifted". Shifting the reading frame one nucleo-

> 64. 单碱基替换也叫做点突变,是指一个碱基被另一个碱基取代。
> 　错义突变:碱基替换造成密码子的改变,从而造成蛋白质产物中单个氨基酸的改变。
> 　无义突变:碱基替换使终止密码子提前出现,使得氨基酸链的合成提前终止。
> 　由于一个氨基酸可以由多个密码子编码,因此有时碱基的替换并不会改变氨基酸序列,这样的情况叫做沉默。

> 65. 碱基对的插入和删除可导致读码框的改变而造成移码突变,造成突变位点后的氨基酸顺序的改变。

tide to the right, the same sequence of nucleotides encodes a different sequence of amino acids.

3) Mutations can involve large sections of DNA becoming duplicated, deleted and inverted, sometimes through genetic recombination[66].
- **Duplications(重复/插入)** are a doubling of a section of the genome.
- **Deletions(缺失/删除)** of large chromosomal regions lead to losing the genes within those regions.
- **Inversion(倒位/转位)** is a chromosome rearrangement in which a segment of a chromosome is reversed end to end.
- **Translocations(易位)** are the transfer of a piece of one chromosome to a nonhomologous chromosome. Translocations are often reciprocal; that is, the two nonhomologues swap segments.

4) During meiosis, **nondisjunction(不分离现象)**[67] causing wrong distribution of chromosomes is also a source of mutation.
- **Aneuploidy(异倍体)**[68], the gain or loss of whole chromosomes, is the most common chromosome abnormality. It is caused by the failure of chromosomes to correctly separate homologues during meiosis Ⅰ or sister chromatids during meiosis Ⅱ.
- **Monosomy(单体)**, zygotes missing one chromosome, cannot develop to birth.
- **Trisomy(三体)**, three of the same chromosome is also lethal like trisomy 21, the cause of Down's syndrome.

9. Cancer and Mutation

Cancer cells are cells that lack control of cell division. They often result from mutation in genes that are involved in mitosis. Two types mutated genes are considered as most related to cancer cells.
1) **Oncogenes(致癌基因)**[69] are genes that contribute to converting a normal cell into a cancer cell when muta-

---

66. 有时突变是大段DNA序列的变化,包括重复、缺失、倒位和易位。
重复:染色体中有重复片段。
缺失:染色体中缺少部分片段。
倒位:某一片段的顺序与原顺序相反。
易位:片段出现在其他染色体上。

67. 不分离现象是由减数第一次分裂同源染色体分离时或减数第二次分裂姐妹染色单体分离时产生的错误导致。

68. 异倍体:具有不成套染色体组的细胞或个体。
单体:一对同源染色体缺失某一条染色体。
三体:一对同源染色体多一条染色体,如唐氏综合症患者的第21号染色体。
单体和三体同属异倍体。

69. 致癌基因:基因突变或高表达时可能使正常细胞转化为癌细胞。

ted or expressed at abnormally-high levels. Their mutated or over-expressed products stimulate mitosis even though normal growth signals are absent.

For example, Ras gene expresses Ras protein[70], a G-protein associated with G-protein receptor to initiate cell division in the present of growth factors. Ras gene in normal cells growing in culture will not divide unless they are stimulated by one or more growth factors present in the culture medium (see cell cycle control). Ras protein then shifts inactive to turn off signal transduction pathway. A mutated Ras gene expresses hyperactive Ras protein that cannot be inactivated, which stimulates cell division even in absence of growth factor.

> 70. Ras 基因突变可导致过度活化且不易失活的 Ras 蛋白的产生,在没有生长因子存在的条件下也能刺激细胞分裂。

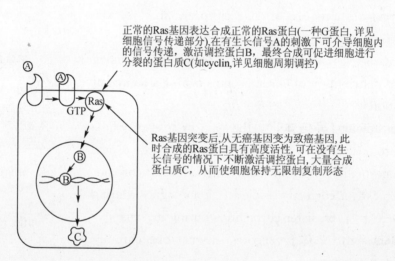

正常的Ras基因表达合成正常的Ras蛋白(一种G蛋白,详见细胞信号传递部分),在有生长信号A的刺激下可介导细胞内的信号传递,激活调控蛋白B,最终合成可促进细胞进行分裂的蛋白质C(如cyclin,详见细胞周期调控)

Ras基因突变后,从无癌基因变为致癌基因,此时合成的Ras蛋白具有高度活性,可在没有生长信号的情况下不断激活调控蛋白,大量合成蛋白质C,从而使细胞保持无限制复制形态

2) **Tumor repressor gene(肿瘤抑制基因)**[71]

Cancers begin as a primary tumor. Some genes that suppress tumor formation are tumor repressor genes. Their protein product inhibits mitosis.

The product of the tumor repressor gene $p53$[72] is a protein of 53 kilodaltons (hence the name). The $p53$ protein prevents a cell from completing the cell cycle if its DNA is damaged. When the damage occurs, $p53$ halts the cell cycle until the damage is repaired. A mutated $p53$ gene cannot stop cell division.

> 71. 肿瘤抑制基因是抑制肿瘤生长的基因,其蛋白质产物可抑制有丝分裂。

> 72. $p53$ 基因的蛋白产物可在细胞周期出现问题时,抑制细胞的继续分裂,直至细胞被修复。如果突变导致 $p53$ 蛋白失活,将无法阻止问题细胞的分裂。

Meanwhile, *p53* gene also can trigger the cell to commit suicide by apoptosis. Apoptosis is the pattern of events that cells undergo programmed suicide when they are damaged by injury, such as by mechanical damage or exposure to toxic chemicals.

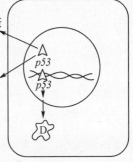

正常的*p53*基因是一种肿瘤抑制基因,其表达合成的*p53*蛋白是一种调控蛋白,该蛋白可激活抑制细胞分裂的蛋白质D的合成,使细胞停止分裂

变异的*p53*基因表达后的*p53*蛋白失去激活作用,可抑制细胞分裂的蛋白质D便无法合成,细胞仍可进行无限制的分裂活动

本章词汇

mitosis	有丝分裂	meiosis	减数分裂
somatic cell	体细胞	gamete	配子
sperm	精子	egg	卵子
asexual reproduction	无性生殖	homologous chromosome	同源染色体
haploid	单倍体	diploid	二倍体
cell cycle	细胞周期	interphase	间期
mitosis (M) phase	有丝分裂期	G_1 phase	合成前期
S phase	合成期	G_2 phase	合成后期
sister chromatid	姐妹染色单体	prophase	前期
metaphase	中期	anaphase	后期
telophase	末期	cytokinesis	胞质分裂
kinetochore	着丝点	centromere	着丝粒
metaphase plate	赤道板	cleavage furrow	卵裂沟/缢痕
cell plate	细胞板	checkpoint	检验点
cyclin	细胞周期蛋白	Cdks	周期蛋白依赖性激酶
cancer cell	癌细胞	meiosis I	减数第一次分裂
meiosis II	减数第二次分裂	prophase I	减数第一次分裂前期
synapsis	联会	tetrad	四分体

cross over	交换	chiasmata	交叉
metaphase I	减数第一次分裂中期	anaphase I	减数第一次分裂后期
telophase I	减数第一次分裂末期	prophase II	减数第二次分裂前期
metaphase II	减数第二次分裂中期	anaphase II	减数第二次分裂后期
telophase II	减数第二次分裂末期	zygote	合子/受精卵
fertilization	受精作用	spore	孢子
sporophyte	孢子体	gametophyte	配子体
P generation	亲代	F_1 generation	子一代
F_2 generation	子二代	the law of segregation	分离定律
the law of independent assortment	自由组合定律	monohybrid crosses	单因子杂交
self-fertilization	自花授粉	dominant	显性
recessive	隐性	allele	等位基因
homozygous	纯合子	heterozygous	杂合子
phenotype	表型	genotype	基因型
test Cross	测交	dihybrid cross	双因子杂交
cystic fibrosis	囊性纤维化	Tay-Sachs disease	泰-萨氏症
sickle-cell disease	镰刀型细胞贫血症	Huntington's disease	亨廷顿舞蹈症
phenylketonuria (PKU)	苯丙酮尿症	completely dominant	完全显性
incomplete dominance	不完全显性	codominance	共显性
multiple allele	复等位基因	sex chromosome	性染色体
autosome	常染色体	Duchenne muscular dystrophy	杜氏肌营养不良症
hemophilia	血友病	Barr body	巴氏小体
linked gene	连锁基因	transformation	转化
bacteriophage	噬菌体	double helix	双螺旋
complimentary base pairing	碱基互补配对	conservative replication	全保留复制
semiconservative replication	半保留复制	dispersive replication	分散复制
origin of replication	复制起始位点	helicase	解旋酶
leading strand	先导链/前导链	lagging strand	后随链/滞后链
Okazaki fragment	冈崎片断	DNA ligase	连接酶
telomere	端粒	transcription	转录
template strand	模板链	messenger RNA (mRNA)	信使RNA
RNA polymerase	RNA聚合酶	promoter	启动子
terminator	终止子	RNA splicing	RNA剪接

intron	内含子		exon	外显子
translation	翻译		codon	密码子
stop codon	终止密码子		start codon	起始密码子
rRNA	核糖体 RNA		transfer RNA(tRNA)	转录 RNA
operon	操纵子		regulatory sequence	调控序列
promoter site	启动位点		operator site	操纵位点
repressor protein	阻遏蛋白/阻遏物		repressible operon	阻遏型操纵子
corepressor	辅阻遏物		inducible operon	诱导型操纵子
inducer	诱导物		negative control system	负调控
positive control	正调控		catabolic activator protein (CAP)	降解物激活蛋白/分解代谢基因激活蛋白
histones	组蛋白		euchromatin	常染色质
heterochromatin	异染色质		acetylated	乙酰化
methyl group	甲基		methylation of DNA sequence	DNA 序列甲基化
enhancer	增强子		alternative splicing	可变剪接
single base substitution	单碱基替换		missense mutation	错义突变
nonsense mutation	无义突变		silent	沉默
frameshift mutation	移码突变		duplication	重复/插入
deletion	缺失/删除		inversion	倒位/转位
translocation	易位		nondisjunction	不分离现象
aneuploidy	异倍体		monosomy	单体
trisomy	三体		oncogene	致癌基因
tumor repressor gene	肿瘤抑制基因			

本章重点

1. 有丝分裂中染色体的变化及有丝分裂的意义。
2. 有丝分裂的调控原理及意义。
3. 减数分裂中能产生变异的重要阶段及减数分裂的意义。
4. 不同生物体在不同生命周期中细胞倍性的变化。
5. 孟德尔两大遗传定律及衍生的遗传现象。
6. 根据结果分析染色体基因连锁交换的情况,计算重组率。
7. 利用概率知识计算遗传概率。
8. 核酸是遗传物质的证明。
9. DNA 半保留复制的验证及 DNA 的复制过程。

10. DNA 指导蛋白质合成的过程。
11. 原核生物与真核生物基因表达调控的方式。
12. 基因突变的原因及结果。
13. 结合细胞信号传递机制,理解基因表达调控与癌症的关系。

本章习题

1. A cell cycle consists of _____.
   a. mitosis and meiosis
   b. G1, the S phase, and G2
   c. prophase, metaphase, anaphase, and telophase
   d. interphase and mitosis

2. How many times does cytokinesis occur during the entire process of meiosis?
   a. 1.
   b. 2.
   c. 3.
   d. 4.

3. Which statement is FALSE?
   a. Cells that do not divide are usually arrested in the G2 phase.
   b. Within the centrosome of an animal cell are a pair of centrioles.
   c. The kinetochore is the point of attachment of the spindle fibre to the chromatid.
   d. Anaphase begins the instant the sister chromatids begin to separate.

4. If the haploid number for a species is three, how many chromatids at anaphase will each dividing diploid cell during mitosis have?
   a. 3.
   b. 6.
   c. 9.
   d. 12.

5. How are cells at the completion of meiosis compared with the diploid cell from which they were derived?
   a. They have twice the amount of cytoplasm and half the amount of DNA.

b. They have half the number of chromosomes and half the amount of DNA.
c. They have the same number of chromosomes and half the amount of DNA.
d. They have the same number of chromosomes and the same amount of DNA.

6. In corn, the trait for tall plants (T) is dominant to the trait for dwarf plants (t) and the trait for coloured kernels (C) is dominant to the trait for white kernels (c). In a particular cross of corn plants, the probability of an offspring being tall is 0.5 and the probability of a kernel being coloured is 0.75. Which of the following most probably represents the parental genotypes?
    a. TtCc×TtCc
    b. TtCc×ttCc
    c. TtCc×ttcc
    d. TTCc×ttCc

7. In the pedigree shown below, individuals with the solid symbols suffer from a genetic disease caused by a recessive allele at an autosomal locus. You would counsel the couple marked A and B that the probability that each of their children will have the disease is _____.

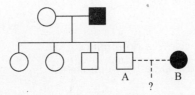

    a. 0
    b. 25%
    c. 50%
    d. 75%

8. A man who carries an X-linked allele will pass it on to _____.
    a. all of his daughters
    b. half of his daughters
    c. all of his sons
    d. half of his sons

9. Individuals afflicted with haemophilia suffer from excessive bleeding due to the failure of the normal clotting mechanism. The disease is associated with a sex-linked recessive gene.

Two brothers are haemophiliacs; their parents do not suffer from excessive bleeding. The probability that their sister inherited the gene for haemophilia is most likely:
a. 0
b. 1/4
c. 1/2
d. 3/4

10. Tay-Sachs disease is an autosomal recessive disorder. Children with this disease generally die before their fifth birthday. The carrier frequency in Ashkenazi Jewish individuals is approximately 3%. If two individuals of Ashkenazi descent have a child with Tay-Sachs, what is the probability that their second child will be a carrier of the disease?
a. 0.5
b. 0.25
c. 0.03
d. 1

11. The frequency of crossing over between any two linked genes is _____.
a. higher if they are recessive
b. difficult to predict
c. determined by their relative dominance
d. proportional to the distance between them

12. You have a summer job in a lab breeding fruit flies. You are given your first mating pair of flies, both of which have grey bodies and normal wings. You are asked to start a population of flies that share these characteristics with their parents. But upon mating the two flies, you end up with a large amount of variation, as described in the table below. Which statement best explains the outcome of your cross?

Traits	Number of fly offspring
Grey body, normal wings	45
Black body, shrivelled wings	5
Grey body, shrivelled wings	15
Black body, normal wings	10

a. The alleles for body colour and wing shape assort independently.
b. Crossing over failed to occur during meiosis, generating an unexpected ratio of

traits.

c. Grey body and normal wings are incompletely dominant traits.

d. The body colour and wing shape traits are polygenic.

13. The requirement for stable hydrogen bonding between base pairs requires that, if one strand of double-stranded DNA consists of the sequence 3'-ATTCGTAC-5', the complementary sequence must be _____.
    a. 5'-UAAGCAUG-3'
    b. 3'-ATTCGTAC-5' in the reverse direction
    c. 3'-TAAGCATG-5'
    d. 5'-TAAGCATG-3'

14. When a DNA molecule is replicated before mitosis the result is _____.
    a. two DNA molecules, one of which carries all of the original DNA molecule, while the other is newly synthesized
    b. two DNA molecules, each of which contains half of the original DNA molecule
    c. two DNA molecules, one of which carries all of the original DNA molecule, while the other is newly synthesized, plus the RNA template used as an intermediate
    d. two DNA molecules, each of which contains half of the original DNA molecule, plus the RNA template used as an intermediate

15. What aspect of DNA allows it to function as a hereditary molecule, faithfully carrying information from generation to generation?
    a. The simple composition of four nitrogenous bases.
    b. The complementary base pairing during semi-conservative replication.
    c. The incorporation of thymine instead of uracil.
    d. The capacity for methylation of cytosines and adenines.

16. As part of a science competition, a student is asked to identify an unknown molecule as either DNA or RNA. Which of the following characteristics would be the strongest evidence that the unknown molecule is DNA?
    a. The presence of phosphate and sugar.
    b. The absence of uracil.
    c. The presence of thymine.
    d. The presence of adenine, guanine, and cytosine.

17. Which statement about protein synthesis is CORRECT?
    a. A mutation that suppresses the formation of small nuclear RNA (snRNA) would increase the average size of mRNA.
    b. Transcription factors act at the level of the ribosome during protein synthesis.
    c. Introns contain tRNA sequences that fuse with rRNA to form spliceosomes.
    d. Redundancy of the genetic code means that a single codon can code for more than one amino acid.

18. How does a ribosome interact with the cell's genetic material during translation?
    a. It enters the cell's nucleus in order to directly translate the cell's DNA sequence into a sequence of amino acids.
    b. A molecule of mRNA brings amino acids to the ribosome, which the ribosome then assembles into tRNA.
    c. A ribosome translates the amino acid sequence of a tRNA molecule into mRNA, which then assembles the protein.
    d. A ribosome translates the sequence of an mRNA molecule into a sequence of amino acids, which are retrieved by tRNA molecules.

19. A frameshift mutation could result from _____.
    a. a base insertion only
    b. a base deletion only
    c. a base substitution only
    d. either an insertion or a deletion of a base

20. The lac operon of E. Coli is a segment of DNA that includes a promoter, an operator, and three structural genes that code for lactose-metabolizing enzymes. In the lac operon, RNA polymerase _____.
    a. binds to the operator when the repressor is activated by lactose
    b. binds to the promoter region when the repressor is inactivated by lactose
    c. is inactivated by binding to the repressor protein
    d. is coded for by the structural gene of the lac operon

21. The lac operon, found in E. Coli, codes for three enzymes that breakdown lactose. The three enzymes are coded by genes Z, Y, and A. The repressor of the lac operon is coded by gene I and is found at a separate locus. Lactose acts as an inducer by stopping the action of the repressor. In which of the following circumstances will

the Z, Y, and A genes be expressed?

i. If there is a mutation in gene I that prevents the repressor from binding to the operator.

ii. If there is a mutation in gene I that prevents the inducer from binding to the repressor.

iii. If there is a mutation in the promoter that prevents the RNA polymerase from binding.

iv. If lactose is present.

v. If lactose is absent.

a. i and iv
b. iii and v
c. ii and iii
d. iv only
e. i and ii

CHAPTER 5

Evolution

Ⅰ. Darwin and the Theory of Evolution

Charles Darwin is considered as the father of modern evolution. His theory consisted of two main points[1]:

- *Diverse groups of animals evolve from one or a few common ancestors, which explains the natural world is like and how and why it became that way.*
- *The mechanism by which this evolution takes place is natural selection, the forces that drive changes in species.*

1. Evolution and Natural Selection

One of the most important contributions made to the science of evolution by Charles Darwin is the concept of natural selection. The idea that members of a species compete with each other for resources and that individuals that are better adapted to their lifestyle have a better chance of surviving to reproduce revolutionized the field of evolution. He hypothesized that there must be some process that led to such diversity and adaptation, and he proposed these changes occurred through time according to a mechanism called **survival of the fittest(适者生存)** or **natural selection(自然选择)**. In *On the Origin of Species*, he eventually settled on four main points of the theory[2]:

- **Adaptation(适应)**: All organisms adapt to their environment.
- **Variation(变异)**: All organisms are variable in their traits.

> 1. 多个物种可能拥有共同的祖先,自然选择是物种进化的根本动力。

> 2. 所有的个体都适应其生存环境并在性状上存在一定的变异;个体产生超过环境容量的后代,通过自然选择,更适应环境的个体生存下来,并产生更多的后代。

- **Over-reproduction(过度繁殖)**: All organisms tend to reproduce beyond their environment's capacity to support them (this is based on the work of Thomas Malthus, who studied how populations of organisms tended to grow geometrically until they encountered a limit on their population size).
- Survival of the fittest: Since not all organisms are equally well adapted to their environment, some will survive and reproduce better than others — this is known as natural selection. In reality this merely deals with the **reproductive success(生殖成效)**[3] of the organisms, not solely their relative strength or speed.

> 3. 使基因能够遗传至下一代并保证继续向下遗传的能力,通常由个体所能产生后代的数目来衡量。

2. Types of Natural Selection

Natural selection is the ability of an organism to survive to reproduce in their environment based on their genetic makeup. It may act to change a trait in many different ways.

1) **Stabilizing selection(稳定选择)**[4]

- When selection pressures favor the average form of the traits, selection is said to be stabilizing. Stabilizing selection favors the intermediate form out of a range of phenotypes. The extreme and unusual phenotypes are eliminated.
- Infants weighing significantly less or more than 7.5 pounds have higher rates of infant mortality.

> 4. 稳定选择:选择中间性状,如高于或低于7.5磅的婴儿的死亡率均会升高。
> 定向选择:选择其中一个极端性状。
> 双歧选择:选择极端性状(两个)。

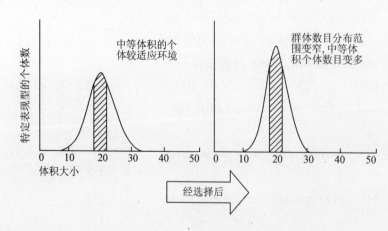

2) **Directional selection(定向选择)**
   - Directional selection occurs when selection pressures favor one extreme of the trait distribution. It tends to favor traits at one extreme of the range of variation.
   - A famous example is the peppered moth (Biston betularia). Before the Industrial Revolution in the 18th and early 19th centuries, only light-colored moths were collected in light-colored woodlands in England. There was a rare dark form. With the pollution caused by the burning of coal, the light-colored tree trunks became darker due to soot. The once rare dark-colored moths became more prevalent, while the once-common light-colored moths became increasingly rare. The color that had the greatest contrast with the background (tree trunk) was at a disadvantage. Cleanup of the forest during the 1950s caused the allele frequencies of light and dark moths to reverse to pre-Industrial Revolution levels: Dark moths are now rare; light moths are now common.

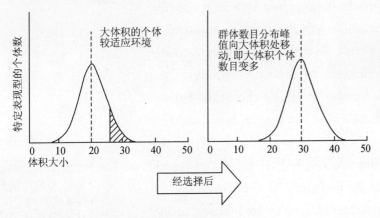

3) **Disruptive selection(双歧选择)**
   - Disruptive selection occurs when the environment favors extreme traits over common traits. Disruptive selection favors individuals at both extremes of variation: Selection is against the middle of the

curve. This causes a discontinuity of the variations, causing two or more morphs or distinct phenotypes.
- The African swallowtail butterfly (Papillo dardanus) produces two distinct morphs, both of which resemble brightly colored but distasteful butterflies of other species. Each morph gains protection from predation although it is in fact quite edible.

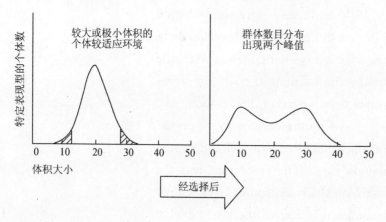

4) In addition to natural selection, there are two other types of selection leading to changes of species.
- **Sexual selection(性选择)**[5], which Darwin believed was distinct from natural selection, involves the selection of traits based on their role in courtship and mating. Sexual selection is the selection of a mate based on a trait. In male competition the male that wins the contests of strength, agility, etc. mates with the female. In female choice the female mates with the male that she prefers based on certain characteristics.

5. 性选择：对与吸引异性相关的第二性征的选择。

- **Artificial selection(人工选择)**[6] is a form of selection carried out by humans. Artificial selection is the selective breeding of species by humans to increase desirable traits, though the traits do not necessarily have to confer greater fitness.

6. 人工选择：人类根据自身喜好选择性培育具有特定性状的个体，无论这些性状是否适应环境。

3. Evidence of Evolution
   1) **Paleontology(古生物学)**[7]. Today, whereas molecular

biology might be used to study microevolution, or the development of individual species, paleontology is used to study macroevolution, or large evolutionary trends.

Fossils(化石) provide the only direct evidence of the history of evolution. The fossil record has revealed the extinction of certain species, the beginning of new species, and the evolution of other species. The discovery of fossils showing forms of animals that had never previously been seen began to cast serious doubt upon creationist theories. The fossil record also provides abundant evidence that the complex animals and plants of today were preceded by earlier simple ones. In addition, it shows that multicellular organisms evolved only after the first single-celled ones. This fits the predictions of evolutionary theory. New technological techniques such as radioactive carbon dating help determine the absolute ages of fossils.

> 7. 进化的古生物学证据：化石。化石是唯一的进化史的直接证据。化石揭示物种的灭绝和新物种的形成；复杂结构的物种由结构简单的物种进化而来；多细胞物种由单细胞物种进化而来。放射性定年法可测定化石产生的年代。

2) **Biogeography(生物地理学)**[8] has revealed that organisms in similar environments around the world tend to acquire the same adaptations for their survival, which is another clue to patterns of past evolution found in the natural geographic distribution of related species. It is clear that major isolated land areas and island groups often evolved their own distinct plant and animal communities. The most likely explanation for the existence of Australia's, New Zealand's, and Hawaii's mostly unique biotic environments is that the life forms in these areas have been evolving in isolation from the rest of the world for millions of years.

> 8. 进化的生物地理学证据：生存环境相似的物种其适应性特征也相似。

3) **Embryology(胚胎学)**[9] has revealed that there are similar stages in development among related species. Most notable is the fact that gill slits and tails are found in fish, chicken, pig, and human embryos.

> 9. 进化的胚胎学证据：脊椎动物胚胎早期都存在鳃裂和尾等结构。

4) **Biochemistry(生物化学)**[10]
- All living things on earth share the ability to create

> 10. 进化的生物化学证据：构成生命体的元素相似；DNA 为大多数生物体的遗传物质；蛋白质由 20 种氨基酸构成，使用相同的密码子系统。

complex molecules out of carbon and a few other elements. In fact, 99% of the proteins, carbohydrates, fats, and other molecules of living things are made from only 6 of the 92 most common elements.
- All plants and animals receive their specific characteristics from their parents by inheriting particular combinations of genes. Molecular biologists have discovered that genes are, in fact, segments of DNA molecules in our cells.
- All of the tens of thousands of types of proteins in living things are made of only 20 kinds of amino acids. Despite the great diversity of life on our planet, the simple language of the DNA code is the same for all living things. This is the evidence of the fundamental molecular unity of life.

5) **Comparative anatomy(比较解剖学)**[11] also supports the theory of evolution.

- **Homologous structures(同源结构)** in the forelimbs of various vertebrates support the concept of a common ancestor. The arms of humans, the forelegs of dogs and cats, the wings of birds, and the flippers of whales and seals all have the same types of bones (humerus, radius, and ulna), because they have retained these traits of their shared common ancient vertebrate ancestor.
- **Analogous structures(同功结构)** in organisms that live in similar environments (like fins whales and fish) support the concept that the environment affects the development of organisms. Bird wings and insect wings are an analogous trait, or a trait that has developed independently in two groups of organisms from unrelated ancestral traits.

Ⅱ. Modern Study of Evolution

Darwin proposed that evolution is the process by which

> 11. 进化的比较解剖学证据：同源结构，脊椎动物的前肢均包含相同类型的骨骼（肱骨/桡骨/尺骨），证明其来自共同的祖先；同功结构，生存在相似环境中的生物，为适应相似的环境而产生结构不同但功能相同的结构。

modern organisms have descended from ancient ancestors. Unfortunately, he could not explain how natural selection caused the changes in species he observed because the field of genetics had not yet been discovered, much less studied. In the early 1900s, however, genetics became widely studied, and Darwin's theory found support in the evidence uncovered in this and other fields. Since the late 19th century, there have been many important discoveries about the mechanisms of inheritance and evolution.

1. Evolution involves changes in the gene pool of a population.
   1) A population is a group of potentially interbreeding organisms living in the same geographical area and sharing a common **gene pool(基因库)**[12].
   The gene pool is the sum of all genetic information carried by the members of a population. The members of a population vary from one another. This variation results from genetic diversity. The proportion of all copies of a gene that is made up of a particular gene variant (allele) in a population is called **allele frequency(等位基因频率)** or **gene frequency(基因频率)**. It can be expressed for example as a percentage. In population genetics, allele frequencies are used to depict the amount of genetic diversity at the individual, population, and species levels.
   Consider a population of 100 individuals all typed for the simplest test at the AB blood group locus. At its most simplistic form this locus can be reduced to a codominant system with two alleles A and B. (In reality it is considerably more complex than this but this simple form will suffice for our examples.) Every individual in the population will be either A (having two A alleles), AB (heterozygous), or B (having two B alleles). Suppose the blood typing results are as follows: 30 type A individuals, 60 type AB individuals, and 10 type B individuals.

> 12. 同一种群中所有的基因构成该种群的基因库。
> 某一等位基因在控制该性状的所有等位基因中出现的频率称为等位基因频率或基因频率。

- The gene frequency of the A allele in the above population of 100 individuals[13]:
  100 individuals each have two alleles at the blood type locus＝200 genes
  Each A individual has 2 A alleles, 30×2＝60 A alleles
  Each AB individual has 1 A allele, 60×1＝60 A alleles
  There are a total of 120 A genes in a population of 200 genes. The gene frequency of the A allele is 120/200＝0.6
- The gene frequency of the B allele:
  Each AB individual has 1 B allele, 60×1＝60 B genes
  Each B individual has 2 B genes, 10×2＝20 B genes
  Again, there is a total of 200 genes in the population for the AB locus. The gene frequency of the B allele is 80/200＝0.4
- Notice that when there are only two alleles in the population, their gene frequencies must add up to 1.

Gene frequency＝(2×homozygote＋heterozygote)/(2×population)

Gene frequency for one allele＝1－gene frequency of the other allele

2) The biological sciences now generally define evolution as being the sum total of the genetically inherited changes in the individuals who are the members of a population's gene pool. It is clear that the effects of evolution are felt by individuals, but it is the population as a whole that actually evolves. Evolution is simply a change in frequencies of alleles in the gene pool of a population[14].

For instance, there is a trait that is determined by the inheritance of a gene with two alleles—B and b. If the parent generation has 92％ B and 8％ b and their offspring collectively have 90％ B and 10％ b, evolution

---

13. 等位基因 A 的基因频率:
每个个体决定血型的基因座有 2 个,100 个个体即共有 200 个基因座。
每个 A 型血(AA)个体有 2 个等位基因 A,30 名 A 型血个体即有 60 个等位基因 A。
每个 AB 型血(AB)个体有 1 个等位基因 A,60 名 AB 型血个体即有 60 个等位基因 A。
$A\% = \frac{2 \times 30 + 60}{2 \times 100} \times 100\% = 60\%$
同理:
$B\% = \frac{60 + 10 \times 2}{2 \times 100} \times 100\% = 40\%$

14. 种群是进化的最小单位。从遗传学角度理解,当一个种群的基因库内等位基因频率改变时,该种群就进化了。

has occurred between the generations. The entire population's gene pool has evolved in the direction of a higher frequency of the b allele—it was not just those individuals who inherited the b allele who evolved.

3) Hardy-Weinberg equation

The definition of evolution was developed largely as a result of independent work in the early 20th century by Godfrey Hardy, an English mathematician, and Wilhelm Weinberg, a German physician. They went to develop a simple equation that can be used to discover the probable genotype frequencies in a population and to track their changes from one generation to another. This has become known as the Hardy-Weinberg equilibrium equation. In this equation

$$p^2+2pq+q^2=1^{15}$$

p is defined as the frequency of the dominant allele and q as the frequency of the recessive allele for a trait controlled by a pair of alleles (A and a).

In other words, p equals all of the alleles in individuals who are homozygous dominant (AA) and half of the alleles in people who are heterozygous (Aa) for this trait in a population. In mathematical terms, this is

$$p=\frac{\text{number of homozygous dominant individuals}+\text{1/2 number of heterozygous individuals}}{\text{total numbers of individuals in population}}\times 100\%$$

15. p 为某种群中显性等位基因频率，q 为该种群中隐性等位基因频率。

$$p=\frac{\text{显性纯合体个数}+1/2\text{杂合体个数}}{\text{总个数}}\times 100\%$$

$$q=\frac{\text{隐性纯合体个数}+1/2\text{杂合体个数}}{\text{总个数}}\times 100\%$$

Likewise, q equals all of the alleles in individuals who are homozygous recessive (aa) and the other half of the alleles in people who are heterozygous (Aa).

$$q=\frac{\text{number of homozygous recessive individuals}+\text{1/2 number of heterozygous individuals}}{\text{total number of individuals in population}}\times 100\%$$

Because there are only two alleles in this case, the frequency of one plus the frequency of the other must equal 100%, which is to say

$$p+q=1$$

Since this is logically true, then the following must al-

so be correct:
$$p = 1 - q$$
There were only a few short steps from this knowledge for Hardy and Weinberg to realize that the chances of all possible combinations of alleles occurring randomly is
$$(p+q)^2 = 1$$
or
$$p^2 + 2pq + q^2 = 1$$
In this equation, p^2 is the predicted frequency of homozygous dominant (AA) people in a population, $2pq$ is the predicted frequency of heterozygous (Aa) ones, and q^2 is the predicted frequency of homozygous recessive (aa) ones. From observation of phenotypes, it is usually only possible to know the frequency of homozygous recessive people, or q^2 in the equation, since they will not have the dominant trait. Those who express the trait in their phenotype could be either homozygous dominant (p^2) or heterozygous ($2pq$)[16].

The Hardy-Weinberg equation allows us to predict which ones they are. Since $p = 1 - q$ and q is known, it is possible to calculate p as well. Knowing p and q, it is a simple matter to plug these values into the Hardy-Weinberg equation ($p^2 + 2pq + q^2 = 1$). This then provides the predicted frequencies of all three genotypes for the selected trait within the population.

Albinism: a sample Hardy-Weinberg problem

Albinism is a rare genetically inherited trait that is only expressed in the phenotype of homozygous recessive individuals (aa). The most characteristic symptom is a marked deficiency in the skin and hair pigment melanin. This condition can occur among any human group as well as among other animal species. The average human frequency of albinism in North America is only about 1 in 20,000.

16. p^2：显性纯合体个数
$2pq$：杂合体个体
q^2：隐性纯合体个数

Referring back to the Hardy-Weinberg equation, the frequency of homozygous recessive individuals (aa) in a population is q^2. Therefore, in North America the following must be true for albinism:

$$q^2 = 1/20\ 000 = 0.000\ 05$$

By taking the square root of both sides of this equation, we get:

$$q = 0.007$$

In other words, the frequency of the recessive albinism allele (a) is 0.007 or about 1 in 140. Knowing one of the two variables (q) in the Hardy-Weinberg equation, it is easy to solve for the other (p).

$$p = 1 - q$$
$$p = 1 - 0.007$$
$$p = 0.993$$

The frequency of the dominant, normal allele (A) is, therefore, 0.993 or about 99 in 100.

The next step is to plug the frequencies of p and q into the Hardy-Weinberg equation:

$$p^2 + 2pq + q^2 = 1$$
$$(0.993)^2 + 2 \times 0.993 \times 0.007 + (0.007)^2 = 1$$
$$0.986 + 0.014 + 0.000\ 05 = 1$$

This gives us the frequencies for each of the three genotypes for this trait in the population:

p^2 = *predicted frequency of homozygous dominant individuals*
      = 0.986 = 98.6%

$2pq$ = *predicted frequency of heterozygous individuals*
      = 0.014 = 1.4%

q^2 = *predicted frequency of homozygous recessive individuals (the albinos)*
      = 0.000 05 = 0.005%

The Hardy-Weinberg law stating an equilibrium of allele frequencies in a gene pool remains in effect in each succeeding generation of a sexually reproducing population if five conditions are met[17].

No mutation: No allelic changes occur.

> 17. 哈温公式的适用条件是种群基因频率未发生改变,即种群没有进化。因此,当某种群可用哈温公式进行基因频率或性状频率推算时,也说明该种群没有进化。

No gene flow: Migration of alleles into or out of the population does not occur.

Random mating: Individuals pair by chance and not according to their genotypes or phenotypes.

No genetic drift: The population is large so changes in allele frequencies due to chance are insignificant.

No selection: No selective force favors one genotype over another.

These conditions of the Hardy-Weinberg law are rarely met, so allele frequencies in the gene pool of a population do change from one generation to the next, resulting in evolution. Any change of allele frequencies in a gene pool indicates that evolution has occurred. The Hardy-Weinberg law proposes those factors that violate the conditions listed cause evolution. The Hardy-Weinberg equilibrium provides a baseline by which to judge whether evolution has occurred. The Hardy-Weinberg equilibrium is a constancy of gene pool frequencies that remains across generations, and might best be found among stable populations with no natural selection or where selection is stabilizing.

2. Mechanisms of Change

   Evolution occurs when there are changes in the frequencies of alleles within a population of interbreeding organisms. Mechanisms that can lead to changes in allele frequencies include natural selection, genetic drift, mutation and gene flow.

   1) **Genetic drift(遗传漂变)**[18] is the random changes in allele frequencies of a gene pool due to chance or random events, which is the most evident in small populations.
      - The **founder effect(建立者效应)** is a type of genetic drift that occurs when the organisms in the founding group have different allele frequencies from those in the population they left. The resulting offspring will reflect the genetic makeup of the founders.

> 18. 遗传漂变:随机事件引起的基因库中等位基因频率的改变。遗传漂变包括以下两种情况:
> 建立者效应:当数量较小的种群从数量较大的种群中分离出来进入一个新区域时造成的等位基因频率的改变。
> 瓶颈效应:自然灾害随机地大量减少了种群数量,导致某些等位基因的消失,从而改变了等位基因频率。

- A **bottleneck effect**(瓶颈效应) is another type of genetic drift that occurs when the population undergoes a dramatic decrease in size. This may lead to the removal of some alleles from the gene pool if all the carriers of the alleles were wiped out.

2) **Gene flow**(基因流动)[19] is the addition or reduction of alleles when individuals enter and leave the population.

> 19. 基因流动：由个体的迁入和迁出造成的等位基因频率的改变。

- Gene flow moves alleles among populations through interbreeding as well as by migration of breeding individuals. Gene flow increases variation within a population by introducing new alleles produced in another population.
- Continued gene flow tends to decrease the diversity among populations, causing gene pools to become similar. Reduction or restriction of gene flow between populations is essential for the development of new species.

3) **Nonrandom mating**(选择性交配)[20] occurs when individuals choose mates based on certain traits, which involves individuals inbreeding and assortative mating.

> 20. 选择性交配是个体非随机地选择具有特定性状的个体进行交配。

4) Natural selection is the only mechanism that leads to adaptive evolution.[21] As the main point of Darwin's theory, natural selection is the process of differential survival and reproduction that inevitably leads to changes in allele frequencies over time as those individuals who are the most "fit" survive and leave more offspring. Selection acts on individuals in population, not their individual genes.

> 21. 自然选择是导致适应性进化的唯一机制。自然选择是生存和生殖差异导致等位基因变化的过程。自然选择并不改变个人的基因，但是自然选择会决定个体的基因能够持续在种群中出现。

3. Variation is the raw material on which natural selection operates. Without variation (which arises from mutations of DNA molecules to produce new alleles) natural selection would have nothing on which to act.[22]

All genetic variations in a population are generated by mutation. Mutation is any heritable change in DNA. Mutations can be changes of a single nucleotide base or may involve changes in the chromosome number. Whether a

> 22. 生物体变异的根本原因是突变，包括基因突变和染色体结构和数目的变化。有性生殖过程中发生的基因重组也能够增加生物多样性。

mutation is good, neutral, or harmful depends on how it affects survival and reproductive success. There are several types of mutations, both at the gene-level and the chromosome-level.[23]

- Gene mutations provide new alleles, making these mutations the ultimate source of variation. A gene mutation is an alteration in the DNA nucleotide sequence, producing an alternate sequence, termed an allele. Mutations occur at random, and can be beneficial, neutral, or harmful.

- Some chromosomal mutations are changes in the number of chromosomes inherited, while others are alterations in arrangement of alleles on chromosomes due to inversions and translocations.

- In sexually reproducing organisms, genetic recombination is the reallocation of alleles and chromosomes.[24] Recombination results from crossing-over during meiosis, the random segregation of chromosomes to gametes during meiotic division, and the random combination of gametes during fertilization. The entire genotype is subject to natural selection since new combinations of alleles may have improved the reproductive success of the organism. For polygenic traits, the most favorable combination may occur when the right alleles group recombine.

III. Speciation

As natural selection adapts populations occupying different environments, barriers to gene flow between populations isolate those populations, and then they will diverge into races, subspecies, and ultimately lead to the formation of new and separate species.[25] When populations no longer interbreed they are thought to be separate species. A **species** (物种)[26] is a group of organisms capable of interbreeding and producing fertile offspring. There are two main forms of speciation.

23. 遗传变异由突变造成。突变可以是单个碱基的改变，或者大段DNA序列的改变，也可能是染色体数目的改变。

24. 有性生殖会带来遗传变异。减数分裂形成配子时，同源染色体的非姐妹染色单体的交换以及第一次分裂中期非同源染色体随机组合都是变异的主要原因。

25. 处于不同环境中的种群为适应各自的环境加之隔离对于基因流动的影响，可能导致亚种的产生，甚至是导致两个独立的物种产生。当种群不能通过交配产生可育后代的时候，我们认为，两个独立的物种形成。同一物种的个体可进行繁殖并产生可育后代。

26. 物种是能够交配并产生可育后代的群体。

1. Allopatric Speciation(分区物种形成/异域物种形成)
   Populations begin to diverge when gene flow between them is restricted. **Geographic isolation(地理隔离)**[27] is often the first step in allopatric speciation. With no interbreeding occurring between the members of the separate populations, the genetic makeup of the two groups gradually changes through successive generations so that if the barrier were to be removed they would no longer be able to reproduce together. Other mechanisms may develop that further restrict reproduction between populations. These are the reproductive isolating mechanisms.

   > 27. 地理隔离的两个物种群,各自进化的最终结果是生殖隔离和新物种的形成。

2. Reproductive Isolating Mechanisms
   A reproductive isolating mechanism is a structural, functional, or behavioral characteristic that prevents successful reproduction from occurring. There are two main types of **reproductive isolation(生殖隔离)**[28].
   1) **Pre-zygotic reproductive isolation(合子前生殖隔离)** prevents fertilization of zygote.
      - **Habitat isolation(栖息地隔离)** occurs when organisms occupy different habitats, even within the same geographic range, so that they are less likely to meet and to attempt to reproduce.
      - **Temporal isolation(季节隔离)** occurs when the organisms live in the same location, but each reproduces at a different time of the year, preventing a successful mating.
      - **Behavioral isolation(行为隔离)** occurs when there are differences in mating behavior between two species.
      - **Mechanical isolation(机械隔离)** occurs when two species have differences in reproductive structures or other body parts, so that mating is prevented.
      - **Gamete isolation(配子隔离)** occurs when the male gametes cannot survive in the mating environment long enough to fertilize the female. If the gametes lack receptors to facilitate fusion, they cannot form a zygote.

   > 28. 生殖隔离是新物种形成的重要标志,包括合子前生殖隔离和合子后生殖隔离。合子前生殖隔离是指无法形成合子,包括栖息地隔离、季节隔离——交配时间的差异造成、行为隔离——交配行为的差异造成、机械隔离——交配结构的差异造成,以及配子隔离。

2) **Post-zygotic reproductive isolation**(合子后生殖隔离)[29] prevents the formation of fertile offspring.
- **Hybrid inviability**(杂交不亲和) occurs when the zygote fails to develop properly and dies.
- **Hybrid sterility**(杂交不育) occurs when the hybrid offspring are sterile that means they're unable to reproduce as adults.
- **Hybrid breakdown**(杂交衰退) occurs when the hybrids produce offspring that have limited reproductive capacity.

3. **Sympatric Speciation**(同域物种形成)[30]

Sympatric speciation the happens when the members of a population develop some genetic difference that prevents them from reproducing with the parent type.

1) This mechanism is best understood in plants, where failure to reduce chromosome number results in **polyploidy**(多倍体)[31] plants that reproduce successfully only with other polyploidy. Reproduction with their parent population (the diploids) produces sterile offspring.

2) Polyploidy and hybridization are important speciation mechanisms in plants. Whereas animals tend to be unisexual, plants often have both sexes functional in the same individual. Consequently, plants can reproduce with themselves both sexually and asexually, if they lack a self-incompatibility mechanism, establishing a reproductively isolated species very rapidly.

IV. Types of Evolution

1. Microevolution and Macroevolution
    1) Throughout most of the 20th century, researchers focused on **microevolution**(微观进化)[32], which is slight genetic change over a few generations in a population.

---

29. 合子后生殖隔离是指合子无法形成可育的后代,包括杂交不亲和、杂交不育和杂交衰退——杂种产生的后代生殖能力减弱。

30. 当种群中的某些个体因为其遗传物质的变化,而导致其与种群中的其他个体产生生殖隔离时,发生同域物种形成。

31. 同域物种形成的机制之一就是多倍体的形成,也就是因为染色体组的加倍导致多倍体个体不能与其他个体产生可育后代而导致新物种形成。

32. 微观进化,是指短时间内(几代)种群中发生小范围的变化,通常是指基因频率发生的变化。

- **Convergent evolution(趋同进化)**[33] occurs when dissimilar species gradually become more similar. This usually happens as a result of sharing similar lifestyles. Convergent evolution describes two or more unrelated species that have adopted similar adaptations to their environment.

> 33. 趋同进化是指不同的物种,为适应相同的环境,向着相似的方向进化。
> 　趋异进化是指具有共同祖先的物种,为适应不同的环境向不同的方向进化。
> 　有多个不同新物种产生的趋异进化称为适应辐射。

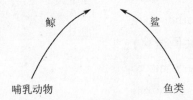

鲸与鲨各自祖先不同,但生活环境相似,长时间进化后使二者外形相似

- **Divergent evolution(趋异进化)** describes two or more species that evolved from a common ancestor. It occurs when closely related species gradually become very different. This most familiar form of evolution occurs when species compete with each other for resources. The formation of a number of diverse species from a single ancestral one is called **adaptive radiation(适应辐射)**.

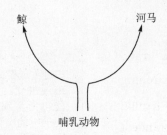

鲸与河马亲缘关系非常相近,但生活环境的不同使二者在外形上相差极大

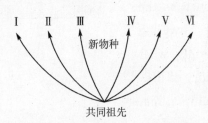

当某一物种迁移到新环境中,受地理多样性及适宜条件影响,可在短期内进化出多种新物种

- Some species evolve without converging on similar traits or diverging to different traits. These species undergo changes, but they maintain a constant level of similarity to each other. This process is known as **parallel evolution**(平行进化)[34]. Parallel evolution describes two or more species that have continued to evolve similar characteristics even after their divergence from a common ancestor.

- Species that live in a close relationship with each other often evolve adaptations to each other in a process called coevolution. **Coevolution**(共同进化) describes the evolution of one species in response to the evolution of another. Coevolution usually occurs in a predator-prey relationship. This evolution can escalate into rapid changes in offense and defense.

> 34. 平行进化是指两个物种虽都经历了一定程度的进化，但仍保持一个相对稳定的相似度。
> 　共同进化是指一个物种的进化，导致与其相关的另一个物种的进化。

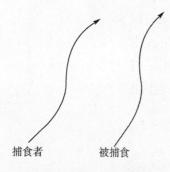

两种不同物种（如捕食者与被捕食者），当其中一种为增大生存几率而进化出新的性状（如被捕食进化出某些保护组织），另一物种为适应这种改变，自身也进化出对应的性状（如捕食者进化出可破坏这种保护组织的能力）

捕食者　　被捕食

2) **Macroevolution**(宏观进化)[35] is evolution on a grand scale — what we see when we look at the overarching history of life: stability, change, lineages arising, and extinction. Macroevolution encompasses the grandest trends and transformations in evolution, such as the origin of mammals and the radiation of flowering plants. Macroevolution patterns are generally what we see when we look at the large-scale history of life. It is not necessarily easy to "see" macroevolution history; there are no firsthand accounts to be read. Instead, we reconstruct the history of life using all available evidence: geology, fossils, and living organ-

> 35. 宏观进化是指长时间的进化过程。
> 　宏观进化的历史中可能包括生物群在化石记录中的突然出现、丢失的环节、物种长期停滞等。

isms. The basic evolutionary mechanisms — mutation, migration, genetic drift, and natural selection — can produce major evolutionary change if given enough time.

2. The Pace of Evolution
   1) The pace of evolution is often slow, so slow that all of the stages in species formation cannot be observed. The traditional, or Darwinian, view of evolution was that it was a very slow process, resulting from the gradual accumulation of small differences. Until the 1970's, it was generally thought that these changes from generation to generation indicated that past species evolved gradually into other species over millions of years. This model of long-term gradual change is usually referred to as **gradualism(渐变论)**[36] or phyletic gradualism.

   2) Recently, several alternative views on the pace and events in species formation have been proposed. Beginning in the early 1970's, this model was challenged by Stephen J. Gould, Niles Eldredge, and other leading paleontologists. They asserted that there is sufficient fossil evidence to show that some species remained essentially the same for millions of years and then underwent short periods of very rapid, major change. Gould suggested that a more accurate model in such species lines would be **punctuated equilibrium (骤变论)**.

36. 渐变论认为新物种的形成是变异逐渐积累的结果。
    骤变论则认为物种保持较长时间的稳定状态,然后经历一次非常迅速且剧烈的变化。

V. History of Life on Earth

Fossil evidence supports the origins of life on earth earlier than 3.5 billion years ago. The North Pole microfossils from Australia (the Apex Chert) are complex enough that more primitive cells must have existed earlier. From rocks of the Ishua Super Group in Greenland come possibly the earliest cells, as much as 3.8 billion years old. The oldest known rocks on earth are 3.96 billion years old and are from Arctic

Canada. Thus, life appears to have begun soon after the cooling of the earth and formation of the atmosphere and oceans.

1. Prebiotic Chemical Evolution and the Origin of Life
   Biochemically, living systems are separated from other chemical systems by three things.
   1) The capacity for replication from one generation to another. Most organisms today use DNA as the hereditary material, although recent evidence (ribozymes) suggests that RNA may have been the first nucleic acid system to form.
   2) The presence of enzymes and other complex molecules essential to the processes needed by living systems.
   3) A membrane that separates the internal chemicals from the external chemical environment. This also delimits the cell from not-cell areas.

2. Abiotic synthesis of organic monomers is a testable hypothesis.
   1) Until the mid-1800's scientists thought organic chemicals (those with a C-C skeleton) could only form by the actions of living things. A French scientist heated crystals of a mineral (a mineral is by definition inorganic), and discovered that they formed urea (an organic chemical) when they cooled.
   2) Russian scientist and academician A. I. Oparin, in 1922, hypothesized that cellular life was preceded by a period of chemical evolution. These chemicals, he argued, must have arisen spontaneously under conditions existing billions of years ago (and quite unlike current conditions). Oparin's original hypothesis called for:
      a) Little or no free oxygen (oxygen not bonded to other elements).
      b) C, H, O and N in abundance.
   3) Studies of modern volcanic eruptions support inference

of the existence of such an atmosphere. In 1950, then-graduate student Stanley Miller designed an experimental test for Oparin's hypothesis. Miller discharged an electric spark into a mixture thought to resemble the primordial composition of the atmosphere. From the water receptacle, designed to model an ancient ocean, Miller recovered amino acids. Subsequent modifications of the atmosphere have produced representatives or precursors of all four organic macromolecular classes.

3. Assembling Polymers
   1) The interactions of these organic molecules would have increased as their concentrations increased. Reactions would have led to the building of larger, more complex molecules.
   2) A pre-cellular life would have begun with the formation of nucleic acids. Chemicals made by these nucleic acids would have remained in proximity to the nucleic acids. Eventually the pre-cells would have been enclosed in a lipid-protein membrane, which would have resulted in the first cells.

4. Endosymbiosis
   1) The **endosymbiosis theory(内共生学说)**[37] postulates that:
      - The mitochondria of eukaryotes evolved from aerobic bacteria (probably related to the rickettsia) living within their host cell.
      - The chloroplasts of red algae, green algae, and plants evolved from endosymbiotic cyanobacteria.
   2) Evidences prove endosymbiosis theory.
      - Both mitochondria and chloroplasts can arise only from preexisting mitochondria and chloroplasts. They cannot be formed in a cell that lacks them because nuclear genes encode only some of the proteins of which they are made.

37. 真核生物的线粒体由与宿主细胞共生的好氧细菌进化而来,而藻类和植物细胞中的叶绿体则由内共生的蓝藻/蓝细菌进化而来。

- Both mitochondria and chloroplasts have their own genome, and it resembles that of bacteria not that of the nuclear genome. Both genomes consist of a single circular molecule of DNA. There are no histones associated with the DNA.
- Both mitochondria and chloroplasts have their own protein-synthesizing mechanism, and it more closely resembles that of bacteria than that found in the cytoplasm of eukaryotes.

本章词汇

survival of the fittest	适者生存	natural selection	自然选择
adaptation	适应	variation	变异
over-reproduction	过度繁殖	reproductive success	生殖成效
stabilizing selection	稳定选择	directional Selection	定向选择
disruptive selection	双歧选择/双向选择	sexual selection	性选择
artificial selection	人工选择	paleontology	古生物学
fossil	化石	biogeography	生物地理学
embryology	胚胎学	biochemistry	生物化学
comparative anatomy	比较解剖学	homologous structure	同源结构
analogous structure	同功结构	gene pool	基因库
allele frequency	等位基因频率	gene frequency	基因频率
genetic drift	遗传漂变	founder effect	建立者效应
bottleneck effect	瓶颈效应	gene flow	基因流动
nonrandom mating	选择性交配	species	物种
allopatric Speciation	分区物种形成/异域物种形成	geographic isolation	地理隔离
reproductive isolation	生殖隔离	pre-zygotic reproductive isolation	合子前生殖隔离
habitat isolation	栖息地隔离	temporal isolation	季节隔离
behavioral isolation	行为隔离	mechanical isolation	机械隔离
gamete isolation	配子隔离	post-zygotic reproductive isolation	合子后生殖隔离

hybrid inviability	杂交不亲和	hybrid sterility	杂交不育
hybrid breakdown	杂交衰退	sympatric speciation	同域物种形成
polyploidy	多倍体	microevolution	微观进化/种内进化
convergent evolution	趋同进化	divergent evolution	趋异进化
adaptive radiation	适应辐射	parallel evolution	平行进化
coevolution	共同进化	macroevolution	宏观进化/种外进化
gradualism	渐变论/渐进学说	punctuated equilibrium	骤变论/间断平衡学说
endosymbiosis theory	内共生学说		

本章重点

1. 达尔文自然选择理论与进化的关系。
2. 支持进化论的证据。
3. 种群基因频率与种群进化的关系。
4. 根据哈温公式判断特定种群基因频率的变化。
5. 自然选择与遗传漂变、基因流动对种群进化的影响的区别。
6. 物种形成的机制。
7. 不同进化方式的体现。

本章习题

1. Which of the following are necessary for evolution by natural selection to take place?
   i. Offspring resemble their parents more than other individuals in the population.
   ii. Differences among individuals exist and lead to different numbers of successful offspring being produced.
   iii. Individuals adjust their development depending on the environment.
   iv. Every individual has a desire to have many offspring.
   v. Populations tend to grow faster than their food suppliers.
   a. i and ii
   b. i and v
   c. ii, iii, and iv
   d. iii and v

2. Which of the following was a central point in Darwin's theory of evolution by natural

selection?
   a. The biological structures an organism is most likely to inherit from its parents are those that have become better suited to the environment through constant use.
   b. Mutations occur to help future generations adapt to their environment.
   c. Slight variations among individuals significantly affect the chance that a given individual will survive in its environment and be able to reproduce.
   d. Genes change in order to help organisms cope with problems encountered within their environment.

3. Which statement is FALSE?
   a. An adaptation is a trait that allows an organism to survive and reproduce better in its present environment.
   b. Different adaptive phenotypes can arise from the same genotype.
   c. A trait can be disadvantageous now even though it once had an adaptive function.
   d. Adaptation is a process that occurs within individuals within a single generation.

4. Which statement about natural selection is FALSE?
   a. Natural selection can lead to adaptation.
   b. Natural selection accounts for the resemblance between parent and offspring.
   c. Natural selection causes allele frequencies in a population to change.
   d. Natural selection is occurring today.

5. A study of cliff swallows on Prince Edward Island found that the smallest and largest adult birds contribute relatively fewer offspring to the next generation than those birds that are closer to the average size. These findings suggest that _____.
   a. this population is sexually dimorphic in body size
   b. artificial selection is acting on this population
   c. the mode of natural selection acting on this population is directional selection
   d. the mode of natural selection acting on this population is stabilizing selection

6. Which of the following gives sexual reproduction an advantage over asexual reproduction?
   a. It produces more offspring.
   b. It ensures the survival of the species.
   c. It increases the variation among the offspring of an individual.
   d. It preserves parental genotypes.

7. Which of the following statements best describes the effect of genetic drift on the gene frequencies of a population?

a. Genes enter a population through immigration, thus changing gene frequencies.
b. Genes leave a population through emigration, thus changing gene frequencies.
c. Chance alone can cause significant changes in gene frequencies of small populations.
d. Mutations over time cause gene frequencies to change.

8. In a population of humans, the frequency of a recessive allele causing a genetic disease is 0.01, or 1%. What proportion of the population would you expect to suffer from the disease?
    a. 0.000 1
    b. 0.001
    c. 0.002 5
    d. 0.01

9. For a trait that is controlled by two alleles at a single locus, the frequency of the dominant allele is 0.6. What is the genotype frequency of heterozygous individuals, assuming the population is at Hardy-Weinberg equilibrium?
    a. 0.16
    b. 0.24
    c. 0.36
    d. 0.48

10. A population is in genetic equilibrium when genotype and allele frequencies remain the same from one generation to the next. Genetic equilibrium will occur when _____.
    a. populations are small, thus more likely to be affected by genetic drift
    b. beneficial mutations arise
    c. there is no immigration and emigration
    d. there is mating between close relatives

11. Which of the following is necessary for speciation to occur?
    a. A large number of mutations accumulating within a population.
    b. Reproductive isolation of two populations of organisms.
    c. A reduction in the number of individuals in a population.
    d. Matings between two populations of organisms produce offspring with low survivorship.

12. Today there are many different breeds of dogs. What mechanism is responsible for most of this variation?
    a. Inbreeding.

b. Genetic drift.

   c. Natural selection.

   d. Artificial selection.

13. Although the seal and the penguin both have streamlined, fish-like bodies with a layer of insulating fat, they are not closely related. This similarity results from _____.

    a. homologous evolution

    b. convergent evolution

    c. adaptive radiation

    d. coevolution

14. If the fossil record has few or no intermediate forms, if there are long periods in which the fossils underwent no morphological change, and if new forms arose very quickly, then evolution of these new forms would be best described as _____.

    a. punctuated equilibrium

    b. adaptive radiation

    c. gradualism

    d. convergent evolution

15. An individual's fitness is best measured by _____.

    a. its ability to compete with other individuals for key resources

    b. its resistance to disease and parasites

    c. its ability to survive relative to other individuals

    d. its relative contribution to the gene pool of the next generation

16. What does the theory of endosymbiosis suggest about eukaryotic cells?

    a. Mitochondria and chloroplasts may have originated as independent prokaryotic cells that were engulfed by other cells.

    b. Eukaryotic cells can only survive in association with other cells, suggesting that they originated as a colony of prokaryotic cells.

    c. Because prokaryotic and eukaryotic mitochondria are very similar, they may share a common evolutionary origin.

    d. Vesicles containing enzymes, such as lysosomes, may bud off from the cell and become independently living cells.

Biological Diversity and Classification

CHAPTER 6

Ⅰ. Taxonomy

1. Linnaean System of Classification

   Taxonomy(分类学)[1] is that branch of biology dealing with the identification and naming of organisms. During the 1700s, Swedish botanist Carolus Linnaeus attempted to classify all known species of his time.

   1) Linnaean hierarchical classification was based on the premise that the species was the smallest unit, and that each species (or taxon) nested within a higher category.

      - Linnaeus classified all then-known organisms into two large groups: the kingdoms Plantae and Animalia. As scientists learned more about the biology of many organisms, this constraining into two kingdoms became less and less defensible.
      - Robert Whittaker in 1969 proposed five kingdoms: **Plantae(植物界)**, **Animalia(动物界)**, **Fungi(真菌界)**, **Protista(原生生物界)**, and **Monera(原核生物界)**. Other schemes involving an even greater number of kingdoms have lately been proposed, however most biologists employ Whittaker's five kingdoms.
      - Recent studies suggest that three **domains(域)** be employed: **Archaea(古细菌域)**, **Bacteria(细菌域)**, and **Eukarya(真核生物域)**. A simple phylogenetic representation of three domains of life is Archaea, Bacteria (Eubacteria), and Eukaryota (all eukary-

> 1. 分类学是生物学的分支之一,主要研究生物体的鉴定和命名。

otic groups: Protista, Plantae, Fungi, and Animalia).

2) Linnaeus also developed the concept of binomial nomenclature[2], whereby scientists speaking and writing different languages could communicate clearly. For example *Man* in English is *Hombre* in Spanish, *Herr* in German, *Ren* in Chinese, and *Homo* in Latin. Linnaeus settled on Latin, which was the language of learned men at that time. If a scientist refers today to *Homo*, all scientists know what organism/taxon he or she means. Hear are some general rules for nomenclature:

> 2. 双名法：物种的学名＝属名＋种加词（种名）

- Each species of plant and animal receives a two-term name; the first term is the genus, and the second is the species.
- All taxa must belong to a higher taxonomic group. Often a newly discovered organism is the sole species in a single genus, within a single family... etc.
- The first name to be validly and effectively published has priority. This rule has caused numerous name changes, especially with fossil organisms: *Brontosaurus* is invalid, and the correct name for the big sauropod dinosaur is *Apatosaurus*; *Eohippus* (the tiny "dawn horse") is invalid and should be referred to as *Hyracotherium*. Sometimes, however, names can be conserved if a group of systematists agree.
- All taxa must have an author. When you see a scientific name such as *Homo sapiens L*, the *L* stands for Linnaeus, who first described and named that organism. Most scientists must have their names spelled out, for example *Libopollis jarzenii Farabee* et al.
- Base on Linnaean system, the classification of a rose is shown below:

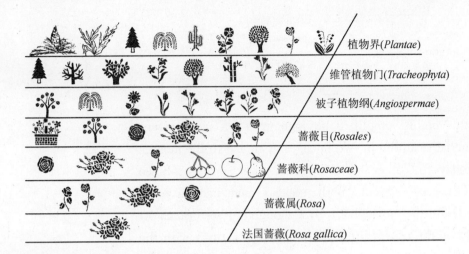

A **species**(种) is given a name consisting of a species name and a **genus** (plural, **genera** 属) name. For example, one kind of flower named French rose is categorized into the genus *Rosa* and is given the name *Rosa gallica*. Closely related plants are grouped in the same genus. Genera that share related features are grouped in a **family**(科). Plants like apple (*Malus domestica*), cherry (*Prunus pseudocerasus*), pear (*Pyrus serotina*), not all of them share the same genus name, but they have certain features and can be grouped in a family *Rosaceae*. Related families, in turn, are grouped in **orders**(目), which are grouped successively in **classes**(纲), **phyla** (singular, **phylum** 门) and **kingdoms**(界).

To summarize, the taxonomic hierarchy from most to least exclusive is as follows: Species, Genus, Family, Order, Class, Phylum, Kingdom[3].

2\. Phylogeny

Linnaean system was created long before scientists understood that organisms evolved. Because Linnaean system is not based on evolution, most biologists are switching to a classification system that reflects the organisms' evolutionary history. Determination of **phylogeny**(系统发生)[4] is a goal of systematics.

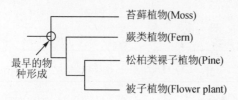

In this highly simplified phylogeny, a speciation event occurred resulting in two lineages. One led to the mosses of today; the other led to the fern, pine, and rose. Since that speciation event, both lineages have had an equal amount of time to evolve. So, although mosses branch off early on the tree of life and share many features with the ancestor of all land plants, living moss species are not ancestral to other land plants. Nor are they more primitive. Mosses are the cousins of other land plants.

1) Understanding phylogenies

- Understanding a phylogeny is a lot like reading a family tree. The root of the tree represents the ancestral lineage, and the tips of the branches represent the descendants of that ancestor. As you move from the root to the tips, you are moving forward in time.

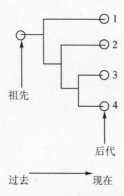

- When a lineage splits (speciation), it is represented as branching on a phylogeny. When a speciation event occurs, a single ancestral lineage gives rise to two or more daughter lineages.[5]

5. 系统发生树中的分支代表物种形成/分化。

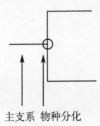

- Phylogenies trace patterns of shared ancestry between lineages. Each lineage has a part of its history that is unique to it alone and parts that are shared with other lineages.[6]

> 6. 每一世系/类群都有一段独一无二的进化史和一段与其他物种共享的进化史。

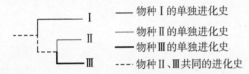

- Similarly, each lineage has ancestors that are unique to that lineage and ancestors that are shared with other lineages — common ancestors.[7]

> 7. 每一物种都有自己独一无二的祖先和与其他物种共享的共同祖先。

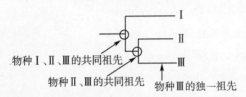

- When reading a phylogeny, it is important to keep three things in mind:
Evolution produces a pattern of relationships among lineages that is tree-like, not ladder-like.

Just because we tend to read phylogenies from left to right, there is no correlation with level of "advancement". Similarly, it's easy to misinterpret phylogenies as implying that some organisms are more "advanced" than others; however, phylogenies don't imply this at all.[8]

> 8. 系统发生并不涉及哪一个物种更加"高级"的问题。

≠ I < II < III < IV

For any speciation event on a phylogeny, the choice of which lineage goes to the right and which goes to the left is arbitrary.[9] The following phylogenies are equivalent:

9. 分支两端的地位相等。

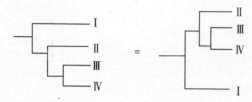

2) *A valid clade is monophyletic*[10], *consisting of an ancestral species and all descendants.*

- A **monophyletic group(单系群)**[11] is a grouping that includes a common ancestor and all the descendants (living and extinct) of that ancestor. Using a phylogeny, it is easy to tell if a group of lineages form a clade. Imagine clipping a single branch off the phylogeny — all of the organisms on that pruned branch make up a clade. Clades are nested within one another — they form a nested hierarchy. A clade may include many thousands of species or just a few.
- Some examples of clades at different levels are marked on the phylogenies below. Notice how clades are nested within larger clades. The tips of a phylogeny represent descendent lineages. Depending on how many branches of the tree you are including however, the descendants at the tips might be different populations of a species, different species, or different clades, each composed of many species.

10. 有效的进化支是单系的,由一个共同祖先及其所有后代组成。

11. 单系群包含一个共同的祖先,所有的后裔均进化自这一祖先。

Chapter 6 Biological Diversity and Classification   127

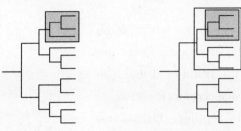
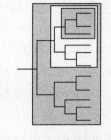

框内所含物种均各成一个单系群

3) Lacking information about some members of a clade, the result is a **paraphyletic group(并系群)**[12] that consists of some, but not all, of the descendants.

4) A **polyphyletic group(多系群)**[13] is any group other than a monophyletic group or a paraphyletic group, which like a paraphyletic group contains only some of the descendants of their closest common ancestor, but unlike a paraphyletic group is not characterized by the missing descendants forming one or more monophyletic groups. Such situations call for further reconstruction to uncover species that tie these groupings together into monophyletic clades.

12. 并系群是指一个生物类群,此类群中的成员都拥有"最近共同祖先",但该群中并不包含此"最近共同祖先"的所有后代。

13. 多系群是指一个分类群当中的成员,在演化树上分别位于相隔的其他分支的分支上;也就是说,该分类群并不包含其所有成员的最近共同祖先。

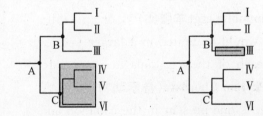

两图框内所含物种均为一个单系群。Ⅳ、Ⅴ、Ⅵ有最近的共同祖先C,且C演化为该三种物种。Ⅲ为一独立进化支,其最近祖先是其本身,没有发生演化

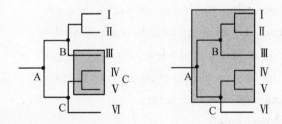

两图框内所含物种不是一个单系群
Ⅲ、Ⅳ、Ⅴ的最近祖先分别是B和C,无"最近共同祖先"
Ⅰ、Ⅱ、Ⅲ、Ⅳ、Ⅴ的最近共同祖先是A,但A演化出的所有后代还应包括Ⅵ

3. Construction of Phylogenetic Trees

To build these trees, we must have data, which come from the characteristics used in classification. There are two major methods of classification: traditional and cladistics.[14] They differ in how they value certain characters.

1) Traditional classification treats reptiles, birds, and mammals, as shown in below.

> 14. 传统分类方法源于林奈的分类系统,他根据物种共有的生理特征分类,并不把化石证据作为研究范围。

Data used in traditional systematics stress both common ancestry (monophylesis) and the amount of divergence among groups. The traditional, dating to Linnaean view, is that birds have feathers, reptiles have scales, and mammals have hair. Using this as a major character, a classification like that above has been constructed. Fossils, evidence of past life, are not included in this classification. Since all of these groups have the **amniotic egg(羊膜卵)**[15], or a modification of it, they would be united in a larger taxon. Linnaeus placed each of these groups in a separate class within the **Phylum Chordata(脊索动物门)**[16]. A primitive character is one present in the common ancestor and all members of the group, such as the amniotic egg. A derived character is one found only in a particular lineage within the larger group. In the example above, hair and feathers may be viewed as derived characters. A traditional view of our example group is that birds and mammals evolved from reptiles due to their unique derived characters.

2) Cladistics and cladograms
- **Cladistics(支序分类学)**[17] is a type of systematics developed by the late German biologist Willi Hennig, who attempted to formulate a more objective

> 15. 羊膜卵:具有羊膜的胚胎,是鸟类、爬行类和卵生的哺乳动物所产生的卵。在胚胎发育过程中,发生三层胚膜包围胚胎:外层称绒毛膜,内层称羊膜,另有尿囊膜。具有羊膜卵结构的动物称为羊膜动物。

> 16. 脊索动物门:在其个体发育全过程或某一时期具有脊索、背神经管和鳃裂。

> 17. 支序分类学:也称为系统发生分类学,只依据演化树分支的顺序,而不参考形态上的相似性来排列物种。分支里的所有生物体拥有属于此一分支的唯一祖先。每一分支都会有一些只共同出现在分支内每一个成员上,而不会出现在其他生命体上的特征。

method of classifying organisms. The value of cladistics lies in its capacity to generate (and provide a set of criteria for the evaluation) of multiple hypotheses (alternate cladograms) that can be evaluated with additional data. Almost always the "correct" cladogram employs the principle of parsimony, which proposes that the shortest number of steps or character state changes is most likely correct. Because the goal is to find evidence that will help us group organisms into less and less inclusive clades.

- Cladistics groups organisms based on the presence of shared **derived characters(衍征)**[18], not the overall similarity of potential group members. A shared character is one that two lineages have in common, and a derived character is one that evolved in the lineage leading up to a clade and that sets members of that clade apart from other individuals. Shared derived characters can be used to group organisms into clades. In the example cited above, for example, amphibians, turtles, lizards, snakes, crocodiles, birds and mammals all have, or historically had, four limbs. However, the presence of four limbs is not useful for determining relationships within the clade in green above, since all lineages in the clade have that character. To determine the relationships in that clade, we would need to examine other characters that vary across the lineages in the clade.

- The amniotic egg would be used to unite a group sharing common ancestry, since it would NOT be present in a group that was not in the lineage. The use of feathers and hair to separate birds and mammals from reptiles would NOT factor into a cladistic hypothesis, or cladogram, since these are characters unique to mammal clade in this group, and the lizard, pigeon, mouse-chimp clade is united by

> 18. 祖征是两个世系共同具有的特征；衍征是世系进化中产生的使其与其他个体有所区别的特征。

claws or nails, etc.

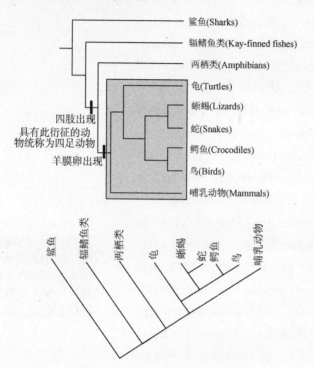

- The example used above, if treated cladistically, would produce a very different classification. Note that crocodiles have more in common (in a cladistic sense) with birds than they do with other reptiles. Birds and crocodiles form a clade, or monophyletic group united by shared derived characters not present in the other groups.

II. The Kingdoms of Life

Evolutionary theory and the cell theory provide us with a basis for the interrelation of all living things. We also utilize Linnaeus' hierarchical classification system, adopting (generally) five kingdoms of living organisms. Viruses, as discussed later, are not considered living. Recent studies suggest that there might be a sixth Kingdom, the Archaea.

1. Monera[19]
   Monera are the only kingdom composed of prokaryotic organisms, they have a cell wall, and lack both membrane-bound organelles and multicellular forms. The **Archaebacteria(古细菌)**, the most ancient of this kingdom, are so different that they may belong to a separate kingdom. Other groups of Monera include the cyanobacteria (autotrophic) and eubacteria (heterotrophic).

   19. 原核生物界包括所有的原核生物。现倾向于将古细菌分离出来作为单独的一界。

2. Protista[20]
   The most ancient eukaryotic kingdom, protists include a variety of eukaryotic body and nutritional heterotrophic, autotrophic, and both forms. Perhaps they are best defined as eukaryotes that are NOT fungi, animals, or plants.

   20. 原生生物界包括，除真菌、动物和植物外的单细胞真核生物。

3. Fungi[21]
   Fungi are a eukaryotic, heterotrophic, usually multicellular group having multinucleated cells enclosed in cells with cell walls. They obtain their energy by decomposing dead and dying organisms and absorbing their nutrients from those organisms. Some fungi also cause disease (yeast infections, rusts, and smuts), while others are useful in baking, brewing, as foods, drugs and sources for antibiotics.

   21. 真菌界由异养且有细胞壁的真核生物组成。

4. Plantae[22]
   Plants are immobile, multicellular eukaryotes that produce their food by photosynthesis and have cells encased in cellulose cell walls. Plants are important sources of oxygen, food, and clothing/construction materials, as well as pigments, spices, dyes, and drugs.

   22. 植物界由通过光合作用自养的、有细胞壁的多细胞真核生物组成。

5. Animalia[23]
   Animals are multicellular, heterotrophic eukaryotes that are capable of mobility at some stage during their lives,

   23. 动物界的生物均为多细胞、异养并能够移动的真核生物体。动物细胞不含细胞壁。

and that have cells lacking cell walls. Animals provide food, clothing, fats, scents, companionship, and labor.

Five kingdoms	Monera		Protista	Fungi	Plantae	Animalia
Six kingdoms	Archaebacteria	Eubacteria	Protista	Fungi	Plantae	Animalia
Domaine	Archaea	Bacteria	Eukarya	Eukarya	Eukarya	Eukarya
Prokaryote/eukaryote	Prokaryote	Prokaryote	Eukaryote	Eukaryote	Eukaryote	Eukaryote
Autotroph/heterotroph	Autotroph/heterotroph	Autotroph/heterotroph	Autotroph/heterotroph	Heterotroph	Autotroph	Heterotroph
Unicellular/multicellular	Unicellular	Unicellular	Unicellular	Unicellular/multicellular	Multicellular	Multicellular

III. Prokaryotes

1. Domain Bacteria

The old taxonomic Kingdom prokaryotes consisted of the bacteria (meaning the true bacteria and cyanobacteria, or photosynthetic bacteria) as well as the archea. The modern classification, seperates each of these groups to separate domain status.

1) Bacterial structure

- All bacteria also have a cell membrane, as well as a cell wall. Bacteria, since they are prokaryotes, lack a nuclear membrane and membrane-bound organelles, such as the nucleus and endoplasmic reticulum that typify the third domain, the Eukaryota. Biochemical processes that normally occur in a chloroplast or mitochondrion of eukaryotes will take place in the cytoplasm of prokaryotes. [24]
- Bacterial DNA is circular and arrayed in a region of the cell known as the nucleoid. Scattered within bacterial cytoplasm are numerous small loops of DNA known as **plasmids**(质粒)[25]. Plasmids are small DNA fragments known from almost all bacterial cells. These plasmids may carry between two and thirty genes. Some plasmids seem to have the

24. 细菌没有膜包裹的细胞器,所以细菌的光合和呼吸作用均在细胞质中进行。

25. 除拟核区的大型环状 DNA 外,细胞质中还有小型的环状 DNA——质粒。

ability to move in and out of the bacterial chromosome. As such they are important tools to the biotechnology arsenal. Bacterial genes are organized in by gene systems known as operons.
- The cytoplasm also contains numerous ribosomes, the structures where proteins are assembled.
- Bacteria have **flagella(鞭毛)**. The bacterial flagella have a different microtubule structure than the flagella of eukaryotes. Cell walls of bacteria contain the **peptidoglycan(肽聚糖)**[26] instead of the cellulose found in cell walls of plants and some algae.
- **Endospores(内生孢子)**[27] are a method of survival, not one of reproduction. Certain bacteria will form a spore inside their cell membrane (an endospore) that allows them to wait out deteriorating environmental conditions.

> 26. 细菌的细胞壁的组成成分为肽聚糖。

> 27. 内生孢子/芽孢是细菌应对极端环境的休眠体而非生殖方式。

2) Bacterial reproduction

Prokaryotes are much simpler in their organization than eukaryotes are. There are a great many more organelles in eukaryotes, as well as more chromosomes to be moved around during cell division. The typical method of prokaryote cell division is **binary fission(二分裂)**[28]. The prokaryotic chromosome is a single DNA molecule that first replicates, then attaches each copy to a different part of the cell membrane. When the cell begins to pull apart, the two chromosomes thus are separated. Bacteria have no sexual reproduction in the sense that eukaryotes do. They have:
- no alternation of diploid and haploid generations;
- no gametes;
- no meiosis.

> 28. 二分裂是原核生物典型的生殖方式,属于无性生殖。首先 DNA 进行复制,然后随着细胞的分裂,分别进入两个细胞。

But the essence of sex is genetic recombination, and bacteria do have three mechanisms to accomplish that:
- transformation;
- conjugation;
- transduction.

a) **Transformation(转化)**[29] involves a bacterium taking up free pieces of DNA secreted by live bacteria or released by dead bacteria into the surrounding environment. Recall that Griffith's experiment demonstrated this process.

> 29. 转化:细菌吸收来自其他细菌释放到环境中的DNA。

b) **Conjugation(接合)**[30] is the process where one bacterium passes DNA to another through a tube (the sex pilus) that temporarily joins the two conjugating cells. Conjugation occurs only between bacteria in the same or closely related species. Certain types of bacteria can "donate" a piece of their DNA to a recipient cell. The recombination is the bacterial equivalent of sexual reproduction in eukaryotes. Note that the entire DNA is not usually transferred, only a small piece. Some bacteria, E. coli is an example, can transfer a portion of their chromosome to a recipient with which they are in direct contact. As the donor replicates its chromosome, the copy is injected into the recipient. At any time that the donor and recipient become separated, the transfer of genes stops. Those genes that successfully made the trip replace their equivalents in the recipient's chromosome.

> 30. 接合:细菌通过性菌毛将复制后的DNA,部分或者全部转移到另一细菌的过程;接合属于有性生殖。

c) The third process, **transduction(转导)**[31], happens when bacteriophage transfer portions of bacterial DNA from one cell to another.

> 31. 转导:噬菌体将细菌的DNA转移到另一个细菌中。

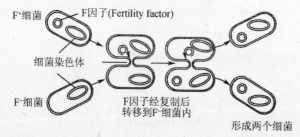

3) Classification of bacteria

Bacteria are classified on the basis of their method of energy acquisition. Traditional classifications include chemosynthetic, photosynthetic, and heterotrophic groups. Molecular and cladistic studies are reshaping these groups.

- **Chemosynthetic bacteria(化能合成细菌)**[32] are autotrophic, and obtain energy from the oxidation of inorganic compounds such as ammonia, nitrite (to nitrate), or sulfur (to sulfate).
- **Photosynthetic bacteria(光能合成细菌)**[33] carry out conversion of sunlight energy into carbohydrate energy. Cyanobacteria are the major group of photosynthetic bacteria. Some early cyanobacteria may have formed the oxygen released into the early atmosphere, transforming our planet from one with an oxygen-free atmosphere, to the modern one that has a significant amount of oxygen present. In addition to chlorophyll a, cyanobacteria also have the blue pigment phycocyanin and the red pigment phycoerythrin.
- Members of **heterotrophic bacteria(异养菌)**[34] must derive their energy from another organism by feeding. Two main types: saprophytic and symbiotic. **Saprophytes(腐生菌)** feed on dead or decaying material and are important nutrient recyclers. **Symbiotic bacteria(共生菌)** live within a host multicellular organism and contribute to the health of the host. Examples include cows and other grazing animals: the bacteria convert cellulose from plant leaves and stems eaten by the animal into glucose for digestion by the animal.

4) Roles in ecosystem[35]
- Plants need nitrogen for many important biological molecules including nucleotides and proteins. However, the nitrogen in the atmosphere is not in a form that plants can utilize. Many plants have a symbiotic relationship with bacteria growing in their roots: organic nitrogen as rent for space to live. These plants tend to have root nodules in which the nitrogen-fixing bacteria live. A vital symbiosis that bacteria seem to have participated in

> 32. 化能合成细菌是能够捕获无机化合物中的能量的自养细菌。

> 33. 光能合成细菌是能够捕获光能合成碳水化合物的细菌。

> 34. 异养菌：能量来自于捕食其他生物体。
> 腐生菌：能量来自于分解死亡腐败的生物体。
> 共生菌：与多细胞宿主共生。

> 35. 细菌的作用：豆科植物的根瘤中的固氮菌能够将空气中的氮气转化为可供植物利用的含氮化合物，固氮菌参与了氮元素的循环。细菌是重要的分解者，参与多种元素的循环过程。细菌可以通过发酵为人类提供丰富的食物，工程菌可生产多种医药产品，如抗生素、疫苗等。

for hundreds of millions of years is their relationship with plants, both as soil nitrogen-fixing bacteria, as well as internal guests in the root nodules of plants of the pea family. Most organisms cannot use atmospheric nitrogen (N_2) directly. Some bacteria have the metabolic pathways to convert inorganic N_2 into various forms of organic nitrogen. Mutualistic nitrogen-fixing bacteria, such as rhizobium, live in nodules on the roots of soybean, clover, and alfalfa plants, where they reduce N_2 to ammonia (NH_4) to the benefit of both themselves as well as their host. These bacteria also benefit by using some of a plant's photosynthetically produced organic molecules.

- Some bacteria are photosynthetic autotrophs, while others are heterotrophs. Bacteria play important ecological roles as decomposers, as well as important elements of phytoplankton at the base of many food chains.

2. Archea

The most primitive group, the archaebacteria[36], are today restricted to marginal habitats such as hot springs or areas of low oxygen concentration. Archaebacteria (now more commonly referred to as the Archaea) are considered among the oldest and most primitive types of organisms known. They have significant differences in their cell walls and biochemistry when compared to the bacteria. These differences are sufficient in most schemes, to place the Archaea into a separate kingdom or domain. Under the three domain model, they are the taxonomic equivalents of the other bacteria and the eukaryotes. It is thought that since bacteria and Archaea inhabit some of the modern environments thought by paleontologists to resemble what the early Earth was like, that both are descended from a common ancestor. The Eukarya later split

36. 古细菌是较为原始的生命体，古细菌的细胞壁成分与真细菌不同。

from the Archaea.

There are three groups of Archaea. The **methanogens**(产甲烷菌)³⁷ live under anaerobic environments (e. g. , marshes) where they produce methane. **Halophiles**(嗜盐菌) require high salt concentrations (such as in Utah's Great Salt Lake). **Thermophiles**(嗜热菌) live under hot, acidic environments (like those found in geysers).

> 37. 产甲烷菌为专性厌氧菌,可产生甲烷。
> 嗜盐菌需要高盐浓度的生存环境。
> 嗜热菌:很多嗜热菌同时也是嗜酸菌。

Ⅳ. Viruses

Viruses(病毒)³⁸ are obligate intracellular parasites that can be maintained only inside living cells. Since viruses are obligate intracellular parasites, the term conveys the idea that viruses must carry out their reproduction by parasitizing a host cell. They cannot multiply outside a living cell; they can only replicate inside a specific host. Viruses, unlike cells, carry genetic information encoded in their nucleic acid, and can undergo mutations and reproduce; however, they cannot carry out metabolism, and thus are not considered alive.

> 38. 病毒无细胞结构且必须寄生在活细胞内,利用宿主细胞中的物质完成自身繁殖。

1. Structure of Virus

All viruses have at least two parts. An outer **capsid**(衣壳)³⁹ composed of protein subunits. Surrounds is an inner core of either DNA or RNA, or neither. The viral genome has at most several hundred genes. In contrast, a human cell contains over thirty thousand genes. A viral particle may also contain various proteins, especially enzymes, needed to produce viral DNA or RNA.

> 39. 病毒由核酸(DNA或RNA)和衣壳构成。衣壳是由蛋白质亚单位构成的蛋白质外壳。

2. Replication of Virus

Bacteriophages can infect a host and insert their DNA into the host DNA. Under certain conditions the viral DNA can detach and direct replication of new virus, eventually killing the host cell. Once inside the cell, the nucleic acid follows one of two paths: lytic or lysogenic.

1) The **lytic cycle**(裂解循环)⁴⁰ is one in which the virus takes over operation of the bacterium immediately up-

> 40. 裂解循环:病毒进入宿主后会进行复制并最终裂解宿主细胞。

on entering it, with the production of new viruses and their subsequent release destroying the bacterium.

2) The **lysogenic cycle(溶源性循环)**[41] is seen when the virus incorporates its DNA into that of the bacterium, with some delay until the production of new viruses. Following attachment and penetration, viral DNA becomes integrated into bacterial DNA with no destruction of host DNA. When this occurs, the phage is latent, and the viral DNA is called a **prophage(前噬菌体)**. This prophage is replicated along with host DNA, so all subsequent cells produced by the infected but latent cells (lysogenic cells) carry a copy of the prophage. Certain environmental factors (for example, ultraviolet radiation) induce the prophage to enter the biosynthesis stage of the lytic cycle, followed by maturation and release.

> 41. 溶源性循环：病毒进入宿主细胞后会先与宿主细胞的DNA整合，随着宿主细胞的复制而复制。整合入宿主DNA的噬菌体的DNA称为前噬菌体。

3. Retroviruses

Still other viruses invade animal cells and replicate without killing the host cell immediately. New viruses are released by budding off the host cell's plasma membrane, turning the host cell for a time into a viral factory. The human immunodeficiency virus (HIV), the retrovirus that causes AIDS, replicates in this way.

1) **Retroviruses(逆转录病毒)**[42] use RNA instead of DNA as their nucleic acid core. They contain the enzyme **reverse transcriptase(逆转录酶)**, which will reverse transcribe the RNA sequence into a DNA strand. Once the retroviral RNA and reverse transcriptase are inside the host cell, the enzyme reverses transcription by making a single stranded DNA from the retroviral RNA. Viral DNA can be integrated into the host DNA. It remains in the genome and is replicated whenever the host DNA replicates. If viral DNA is transcribed, new viruses are produced by biosynthesis, maturation, and release by budding.

> 42. 逆转录病毒的遗传物质为RNA，其进入宿主细胞后，在逆转录酶的作用下，以RNA为模板合成双链DNA，再整合到宿主DNA上。

2) Retroviruses include HIV and also cause certain forms of cancer.

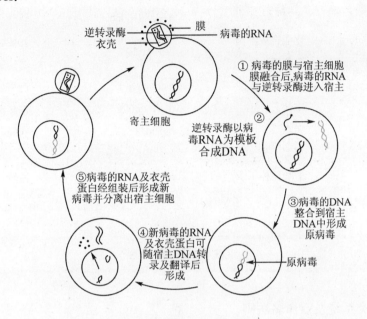

本章词汇

taxonomy	分类学	plantae	植物界
animalia	动物界	fungi	真菌界
protista	原生生物界	monera	原核生物界
domain	域	archaea	古细菌域
bacteria	细菌域	eukarya	真核生物域
species	种	genus	属
family	科	order	目
class	纲	phylum	门
kingdom	界	phylogeny	系统发生
monophyletic group	单系群	paraphyletic group	并系群
polyphyletic group	多系群	amniotic egg	羊膜卵
phylum Chordata	脊索动物门	cladistics	支序分类学
derived characters	衍征	archaebacteria	古细菌
plasmid	质粒	flagella	鞭毛

peptidoglycan	肽聚糖	endospore	内生孢子
binary fission	二分裂	transformation	转化
conjugation	接合	transduction	转导
chemosynthetic bacteria	化能合成细菌	photosynthetic bacteria	光能合成细菌
heterotrophic bacteria	异养菌	saprophyte	腐生菌
symbiotic bacteria	共生菌	methanogen	产甲烷菌
halophile	嗜盐菌	thermophile	嗜热菌
virus	病毒	capsid	衣壳
lytic cycle	裂解循环	lysogenic cycle	溶源性循环
prophage	前噬菌体	retrovirus	逆转录病毒
reverse transcriptase	逆转录酶		

本章重点

1. 了解林奈分类系统及双命名法则。
2. 区分林奈分类系统与支序分类法。
3. 根据数据及遗传信息判断物种进化关系,构建系统发生图。
4. 生物三域五界分类层次及各界生物的特点。
5. 细菌的结构、繁殖方式及适应性特征。
6. 病毒的结构及繁殖方式。

本章习题

1. Which important aspect of the classification of all organisms is attributed to Carolus Linnaeus?
   a. The use of Latin.
   b. The use of branching diagrams (trees) to depict relationships among groups.
   c. The use of two-part names (binomials).
   d. The use of standardized common names.

2. Of the following taxonomic categories which is the most inclusive (i. e. is the highest in the hierarchy)?
   a. Order.
   b. Subspecies.

c. Class.
d. Genus.

3. Two different animals are classified into the same Family. This means they would be classified in _____.
   a. the same Phylum, but different Classes
   b. the same Class, but different Species
   c. different Kingdoms and different Phylums
   d. different Classes and different Orders.

4. Which statement about taxonomic relationships is CORRECT?
   a. A class can contain more than one phylum.
   b. A genus can contain more than one order.
   c. A family can contain more than one class.
   d. An order can contain more than one family.

5. A lineage composed of two or more groups of organisms which includes the common ancestral group and all descendants are called a monophyletic group. The branching diagram (cladogram) below depicts the relationships of seven species. Which of the following is not a monophyletic group?

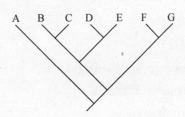

   a. B+C
   b. F+G
   c. B+C+E
   d. A+B+C+D+E+F+G

6. A monophyletic group is defined as including an ancestor and all of its descendants. The cladogram (branching diagram) below depicts the relationships between eight species. Which of the following represents a monophyletic group?

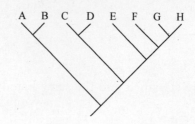

a. A+B+C
b. B+C+D+E
c. C+D+E
d. F+G+H

7. The phylogenetic tree below is a hypothesis of the evolutionary relationships between four species. Which statement is CORRECT?

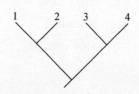

a. Species 1 evolved first.
b. Species 3 and 4 are more highly evolved than species 1 and 2.
c. Species 4 evolved last.
d. All four species share a common ancestor.

8. Which statement is CORRECT?
a. Viruses can grow in food in your refrigerator.
b. All viruses are dangerous to humans.
c. Viruses are prokaryotic organisms.
d. Viruses can take over control of eukaryotic cells.

9. It is generally agreed that prokaryotes constituted the first life on Earth. It is also generally accepted that the early eukaryotes were _____.
a. photosynthetic
b. chemosynthetic
c. heterotrophs
d. unicellular

10. All fungi _____.
    a. are parasitic
    b. are capable of carrying out photosynthesis
    c. are heterotrophic
    d. live on dead organic matters

11. A biologist discovered a new species of microorganism in a soil sample taken from a marsh. The organism required hydrogen sulphide gas as a source of energy and released methane gas. In addition, the organism was unicellular and none of its organelles were bounded by membranes. The biologist also found that the RNA polymerase of this organism was more similar to yeast than to E. COLI. To which group does the species belong?
    a. Animals.
    b. Bacteria.
    c. Fungi.
    d. Archaea.

12. Which of the following taxonomic classifications for the poisonous mushroom *Amanita muscaria* is CORRECT?
    a. species: muscaria; genus: Amanita; kingdom: Plantae; domain: Eukarya
    b. species: Amanita; genus: muscaria; kingdom: Fungi; domain: Eukarya
    c. species: muscaria; genus: Amanita; kingdom: Plantae; domain: Archaea
    d. species: muscaria; genus: Amanita; kingdom: Fungi; domain: Eukarya

CHAPTER 7

Responding to Environment and Maintaining Homeostasis

Ⅰ. Introduction to Homeostasis

Homeostasis(内稳态)[1] is the maintenance of a stable internal environment such as temperature, pH, water concentrations, etc. It is a term coined to describe the physical and chemical parameters that an organism must maintain to allow proper functioning of its component cells, tissues, organs, and organ systems.

Homeostasis frequently incorporates feedback loops. There are two kinds of feedback, positive and negative. **Negative feedback(负反馈)**[2] control mechanisms (used by most of the body's systems) are called negative because the consequence caused by the feedback leads to a reverse of the response while positive feedback control will increase or accelerate the response.

Unicellular organisms are completely immersed in their environment, and need only move materials across their cell membrane to regulate internal conditions and functions. Multicellular organisms are encased in multiple protective layers, and most of their cells are far removed from the outside world, having them surrounded by an aqueous internal environment. They maintain homeostasis through the close coordination of organs and organ systems. Whatever the organisms consist of, in order to maintain homeostasis, they must detect and communicate with other cells and external environment. Cell-to-cell communication or called cell signaling, we have already learned, is ubiquitous in biological systems, from unicellular to multicellular organisms.[3]

1. 内稳态是维持稳定内环境的过程,包括对于温度、pH 和水分的维持过程。

2. 负反馈是指反馈调节的结果会抑制反馈过程。

3. 单细胞个体直接面对周围环境,所以对它们来说,维持细胞内环境相对较为容易。而对于多细胞个体来说,细胞浸润在细胞外液当中。多细胞个体稳态的维持就需要各个器官、系统间的相互配合。为保持内环境的相对稳定,细胞间、细胞和外部环境之间也要进行信息交流。动物细胞稳态的维持是神经系统和内分泌系统协同作用调节的结果。

The ultimate control of homeostasis in animals is accomplished by the nervous system for rapid responses such as reflexes to avoid picking up a hot pot off the stove and the endocrine system for longer-term responses, such as maintaining the body levels of calcium, etc.

II. Rapid Control from Nervous System

The nervous system is the organ system specializing in coordinating the actions of an animal and rapid transmitting signals between different parts of its body. The basic unit of the nervous system through which all these signals move is the neuron, or nerve cell.

1. Neuron

   Neuron(神经元)[4] is the functional unit of the nervous system. Humans have about 100 billion neurons in their brain alone. While variable in size and shape, all neurons consist of a cell body, dendrites, an axon and a synaptic terminal.
   1) **Cell body(细胞体)** contains the nucleus and other cellular organelles typical of eukaryotic cells such as mitochondria and endoplasmic reticulum.
   2) **Dendrite(树突)** is typically a short, abundantly branched, slender extension of cell body, and receives information from another cell.
   3) **Axon(轴突)** is typically along, slender extension of the cell body that conducts messages away from the cell body. The length of some axons is so great that it is remarkable that the cell body controls them all the way to their tip.
   4) Many axons are covered with a glistening fatty sheath, **myelin sheath(髓鞘)**. Myelin sheath itself is maintained by **Schwann cells(施万细胞/神经鞘细胞)**, their plasma membrane wrapped around and around the axon forming the myelin sheath and periodically interrupted by **nodes of Ranvier(朗飞氏节)**, which plays an important part in the propagation of the nerve impulse.

> 4. 神经元,也就是神经细胞,是神经系统的基本功能单元。由细胞体、树突和轴突三部分构成。
> 　　细胞体包含细胞核和细胞器,如线粒体和内质网等。
> 　　树突为胞体周围较短且分支较多的突起,接受来自其他细胞的信号;轴突为胞体周围较长的突起,将信号传至其他细胞。
> 　　许多神经元的轴突由一层脂质鞘包裹,称为髓鞘;髓鞘由施万细胞产生;轴突上的髓鞘并不是连续不断的,髓鞘中断的部分称为朗飞氏节。

Chapter 7 Responding to Environment and Maintaining Homeostasis

A nerve impulse begins at the tips of the dendrite branches, passes through the dendrites to the cell body, then through the axon, and finally terminates at branches of the axon. Signals are transmitted between neurons across a synapse, the space between the synaptic terminal of one neuron and the dendrites of the next.

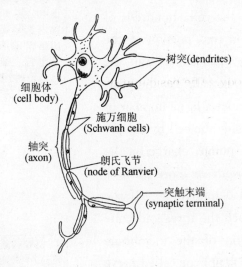

2. Mechanisms of Impulse Transmission in a Neuron

Nerves conduct information in the form of electrical signals. These signals contain information about the state of affairs both within and outside of the animal.

1) When nerve cells aren't sending signals, they're busy maintaining cross-membrane voltage called a **resting potential(静息电位)**[5]. The plasma membrane of neurons, like all other cells, has an unequal distribution of ions and electrical charges between the two sides of the membrane. The outside of the membrane has a positive charge; inside has a negative charge.

- The membrane voltage[6] is maintained by the active transport of ions to reset the membrane known as the sodium potassium pump. This pump pushes only two potassium ions (K^+) into the cell for every three sodium ions (Na^+) it pumps out of the cell.
- Meanwhile, some potassium channels in the plasma membrane are "leaky" allowing a slow facilitated

5. 当神经元不传递神经冲动时,细胞膜两侧的跨膜电位称为静息电位。细胞膜外带正电荷,细胞膜内带负电荷。

6. 膜电位由主动运输的钠-钾泵维持,它可以在将两个钾离子运输到膜内的同时,将三个钠离子运输到膜外。与此同时,部分钾离子通道允许少量钾离子扩散至膜外。

diffusion of K^+ out of the cell.

- Both activities result in a net loss of positive charges within the cell. Large amounts of negatively charged nucleic acids and proteins within the cell also help main the resting potential. In this state, we say that the neuron is polarized.[7]

2) If a signal stimulates a spot on the cell, hundreds of voltage-gated sodium channels in that portion of the plasma membrane will suddenly open and permit the Na^+ on the outside to rush into the cell. As the positively charged Na^+ rush in, because a large number of Na^+ have been accumulated outside the cell by the activities of the sodium potassium pump, charge on the cell membrane becomes depolarized, or more positive on the inside (from 70 toward 0 millivolts). If the stimulus is strong enough to reach the threshold voltage, the complete depolarization of the membrane leads to an **action potential(动作电位)**[8] or called **nerve impulse(神经冲动)**. This, in turn, stimulates neighboring Na^+ gates to open, further down the neuron, and the whole process repeats itself, spreading the depolarization along the length of the axon.

- The action potential is an **all-or-non(全或无)**[9] event: when the stimulus fails to produce a depolarization that exceeds the threshold value, no action potential results, but when threshold potential is exceeded, complete depolarization occurs. As long as stimuli can reach the threshold of the cell, strong stimuli produce no stronger action potentials than weak ones.
- When the membrane is depolarized, and the neuron is in its **refractory period(不应期)**[10]. During this refractory period, this spot will not respond to a new stimulus. Refractory period of neuron forces nerve impulse to transmit forward.
- The myelin sheath, separated by nodes of Ranvier, speeds up transmission of the signal by restricting the

> 7. 主动运输使膜外的正电荷多于膜内,另外膜内其他带负电的物质也帮助细胞维持静息电位。细胞处于静息电位时,我们认为细胞是极化的。

> 8. 信号刺激神经元后,电压门控钠离子通道打开,带正电荷的钠离子流进膜内,降低细胞膜电势的极化状态,此时称为去极化。如果膜电势变化超过阈值,细胞完全去极化便产生动作电位,也称为神经冲动。

> 9. 动作电位的特征是"全或无":如果刺激产生的去极化没有超过阈值,则不会产生其他效应;如果超过阈值,细胞完全去极化,神经冲动将传递下去。

> 10. 细胞膜在去极化时不能对新的刺激产生反应,这一时期称做不应期。不应期能够保证神经冲动向前传递。

Chapter 7   Responding to Environment and Maintaining Homeostasis

points at which ions can rush across the membrane. In effect, the signal jumps from node to node.

3) In response to the inflow of Na⁺, another kind of gated channel opens up allowing potassium ions to rush outside the cell. The movement of K⁺ out of the cell causes **repolarization(复极化)**[11] to reestablish the original membrane polarization. Unlike the resting potential, however, the K⁺ are on the outside and the Na⁺ are on the inside.

4) Before potassium gated channel closes, more K⁺ have moved out of the cell than is actually needed to establish the original resting potential. Thus, the membrane is in a state of **hyperpolarization(超极化)**[12].

5) After that the neuron begins to pump the ions back to their original sides of the membrane. When the membrane voltage is restored to original resting potential, neuron is ready for the new stimuli.

11. 钠离子大量进入细胞内后,门控钾离子通道打开,钾离子流向膜外,使细胞恢复外正内负的电荷分布,称为复极化。

12. 在钾离子门控通道关闭前,过量的钾离子流出细胞,称为超极化。

Steps in an Action Potential can be summarized as:

- Polarization. Neuron establishes negative membrane voltage named resting potential.
- Depolarization. Sodium ions move inside the cell causing an action potential, the influx of positive sodium ions makes the inside of the membrane more positive than the outside.
- Repolarization. Potassium ions flow out of the cell, restoring the resting potential net charges.

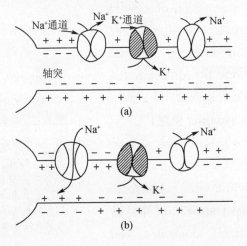

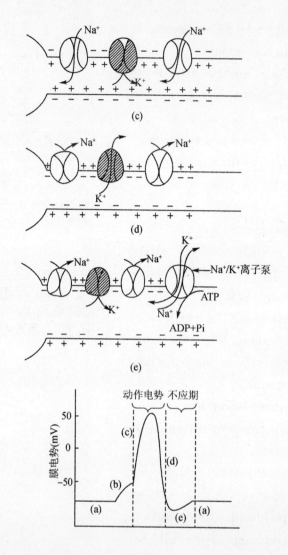

3. Impulse Transmission between Two Neurons

 Action potentials account for the transmission of signals along neurons, not for the transmission of signals between neurons. To move from neuron to neuron, a signal must cross the synapse separating one neuron from the next. The junction between the axon terminals of a neuron and the receiving cell is called a **synapse(突触)**[13].

1) Action potentials travel down the axon of the neuron to its ends, the axon terminals. Each axon terminal is swollen forming a synaptic sac filling with membrane-enclosed vesicles containing a **neurotransmitter(神经递质)**[14]. Neurotransmitters are small molecules that

13. 轴突末端与另一个细胞的结点称为突触。

14. 神经元细胞间并不直接接触,信号的传递需要神经递质的作用。神经递质是促进细胞间信息传递的小分子物质,位于突触末端的囊泡中。

promote transmission of the message along that cell's membrane.

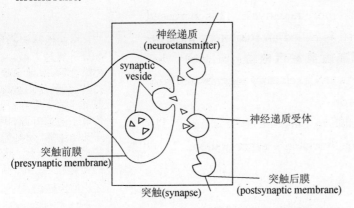

2) Neurotransmitter is released into the synaptic cleft and then binds to receptors on the postsynaptic membrane. These receptors are ligand-gated ion channels. Depending upon the kind of neurotransmitters and the kind of membrane receptors, there are two possible outcomes for the postsynaptic membrane.

- Acetylcholine is called **excitatory depolarizing neurotransmitter(兴奋性神经递质)**[15]. It binds to receptors on the postsynaptic cell opening up ligand-gated sodium channels. These allow an influx of Na^+, and depolarize membrane potential. This reduced membrane potential is called an **excitatory postsynaptic potential(兴奋性突触后电位) or EPSP**[16]. If depolarization of the postsynaptic membrane reaches threshold, an action potential is generated in the postsynaptic cell.
- Gamma amino butyric acid is inhibitory (hyperpolarizing) neurotransmitter. The GABA-A receptor is a ligand-gated chloride channel. Binding of GABA to the receptors increases the influx of chloride (Cl^-) ions into the postsynaptic cell. Binding of GABA to GABA-B receptors activates an internal G protein and a second messenger that leads to the opening of nearby potassium (K^+) channels, moving K^+ out of cell. In both cases, the resulting

15. 兴奋性神经递质，如乙酰胆碱，与受体结合后，使突触后膜的钠通道打开，发生膜电位去极化。

16. 降低的膜电位成为兴奋性突触后电位。如果兴奋性突出后电位超过阈值，动作电位将在突触后细胞产生。

facilitated diffusion of ions (chloride in; potassium out) increases the membrane potential (makes membrane potential more negative). This increased membrane potential is called an **inhibitory postsynaptic potential**（抑制性突触后电位）or **IPSP**[17] because it counteracts any excitatory signals that may arrive at that neuron.

3) The receiving cell is able to integrate these signals. The diagram shows how this works in a motor neuron.

17. 抑制性神经递质，如伽马氨基丁酸，与受体结合后，氯离子通道打开，突触后细胞内的氯离子浓度升高；同时钾离子通道打开，钾离子流出细胞，使细胞膜的电位差增大。增大的膜电位称为抑制性突出后电位。

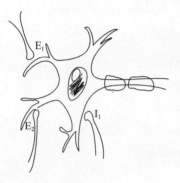

突触 E_1 在突触后膜形成兴奋性突触后电位 $EPSP_1$
突触 E_2 在突触后膜形成兴奋性突触后电位 $EPSP_2$
突触 I_1 在突触后膜形成抑制性突触后电位 $IPSP_1$

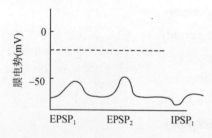

$EPSP_1$ 与 $EPSP_2$ 均可使突触后膜电势去极化
$IPSP_1$ 使突触后膜电势超极化

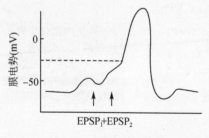

$EPSP_1$ 与 $EPSP_2$ 若在极短时间内同时形成，可产生叠加效果，叠加后若达到动作电位的域值，便可使突触后神经元产生动作电位

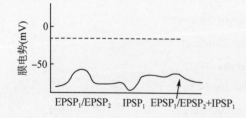

$EPSP_1$ 或 $EPSP_2$ 与 $IPSP_1$ 同时形成，会产生抵消的效果

4. Movement under Nerve System Control

Movement is a major characteristic of animals. This movement involves the action of muscles on skeletal elements. Some invertebrates employ hydrostatic skeletons, in which skeletal elements are created by filling cavities with fluid, making those cavities stiff with **hydrostatic pressure** (液体静压)[18]. This type of skeleton is used by several kinds of worms, and by simpler animals living in watery environments. Other invertebrates, like crabs and insects, have an **exoskeleton**(外骨骼)[19], or a hard outer shell. Vertebrates like humans have an **endoskeleton**(内骨骼), in which bones are encased within softer tissues like muscle and skin. All three types of skeleton give an animal shape, provide protection, and enable movement.

- **Cardiac muscle**(心肌)[20], also called heart muscle, is unique to the heart, makes up the wall of the heart.
- **Skeletal muscle**(骨骼肌) as its name implies, is the muscle attached to the skeleton and contract to create movement about skeletal joints.
- **Smooth muscle**(平滑肌) is not striated, nor is it as strong as skeletal or cardiac muscle. It is found in the walls of all the hollow organs of the body, such as arteries, gastrointestinal tract and urinary bladder.

1) Anatomy of skeletal muscles[21]

Skeletal muscles are the body's most abundant tissue consisting of thousands of cylindrical muscle fibers. Each muscle fiber contains an array of myofibrils and many nuclei (thus each skeletal muscle fiber is multinucleate). Because a muscle fiber is not a single cell, its parts are often given special names such as:

- The **sarcolemma**(肌纤维膜) for plasma membrane of the muscle cell is highly in vaginated by transverse tubules (or T tubules) that permeate the cell.
- The **sarcoplasm**(肌浆) for cytoplasm of the muscle cell contains calcium-storing sarcoplasmic reticulum (SR), the specialized endoplasmic reticulum of a muscle cell.

Sarcomeres(肌节) are the basic functional units (i.e. the individual structures that actually contract) within the myofibrils of skeletal and cardiac muscle. Myofibrils are built from two types of myofilament:

- Thin filaments are made of two strands of the globular protein **actin(肌动蛋白)** arranged in a double helix. Along the length of the helix are **troponin(肌钙蛋白)** and **tropomyosin(原肌球蛋白)** molecules that cover special binding sites on the actin.
- Thick filaments are made of groups of the filamentous protein **myosin(肌球蛋白)**. Each molecule of myosin in the thick filaments contains a globular subunit called the myosin head. The myosin heads have binding sites for the actin molecules in the thin filaments and ATP.

The two kinds of myofilaments overlap one another in a repeating pattern that produces the striated appearance of these muscles. Each repeating unit is a sarcomere, and a contraction consists of thin and thick filaments sliding over one another, as detailed in sliding filament theory.

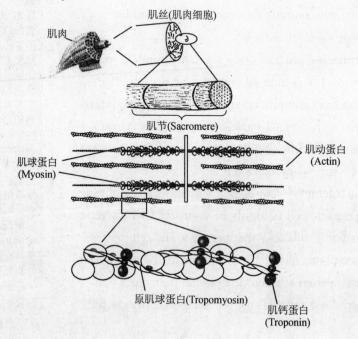

2) **Sliding filament theory(肌丝滑动学说)**[22]
Muscles contract by shortening each sarcomere. The sliding filament theory of muscle contraction states thin filaments on each side of myosin slid past myosin head until they meet in the middle.

Calcium ions and ATP are required for each cycle of myosin-actin interaction.[23]

- When the muscle fiber is stimulated, Ca^{2+} are released and bind to the troponin molecule causing tropomyosin to expose positions on the actin filament for the attachment of myosin heads.
- ATP molecules bind to myosin heads and are hydrolyzed by activate actin. Energy from ATP powers the myosin heads to attach to actin and swivel toward the center of the sarcomere. ADP and Pi remain attached to the myosin head till a new ATP replaces them and starts a new cycle.

Ca^{2+} links action potentials in a muscle fiber to contraction.[24]

- In resting muscle fibers, Ca^{2+} is stored in the sarcoplasmic reticulum. An impulse from a nerve cell causes calcium release and brings about a single, short muscle contraction.
- Acetylcholine, an important neurotransmitter, is released from the axon end of the nerve cell when a nerve impulse reaches the neuromuscular junction, the point where a motor neuron attaches to a muscle. It then depolarizes sarcolemma. A wave of action potential is produced in the muscle cell when the acetylcholine binds to receptors on its surface.
- The arrival of the action potential at the ends of the T tubules triggers the release of Ca^{2+}. The Ca^{2+} diffuses among the thick and thin filaments where it binds to troponin. This turns on the interaction between actin and myosin and the sarcomere contracts.
- When the process is over, the calcium is pumped back

22. 肌丝滑动学说认为肌肉收缩是肌动蛋白丝与肌球蛋白丝的相对滑动所致。

23. 钙离子和ATP为肌动蛋白和肌球蛋白相互作用所必需的。当肌纤维受到刺激时，钙离子释放，与肌钙蛋白结合，释放出肌动蛋白丝与肌球蛋白头部相互作用的位置。ATP与肌球蛋白头部结合，ATP的能量使肌球蛋白头部与肌动蛋白结合并向肌小节中心弯曲。

24. 钙离子将动作电位与肌纤维收缩联系起来。肌肉在放松状态时，钙离子储存在肌浆网中，神经冲动时钙离子释放，引发肌肉收缩。乙酰胆碱是一种非常重要的神经递质，当神经冲动到达神经肌肉节点（运动神经与肌肉连接处）时从神经细胞轴突末端释放。乙酰胆碱使肌纤维膜去极化。动作电位到达T小管末端引发钙离子的释放，随后钙离子与肌钙蛋白结合。这将开启肌动蛋白与肌球蛋白的相互作用并引起肌小节的收缩。随后钙离子将被重新泵回肌浆网。

into the sarcoplasmic reticulum using a Ca^{2+} ATPase.

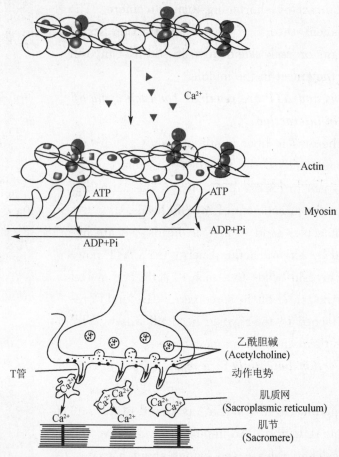

乙酰胆碱在突触末端释放后与肌肉纤维细胞膜上的受体结合,激发肌肉纤维产生动作电位。动作电位顺 T 管抵达肌肉纤维的肌质网,刺激肌质网释放 Ca^{2+}。Ca^{2+} 随即与肌钙蛋白结合,使肌动蛋白与肌球蛋白发生上图的变化。

III. Slow Control under Endocrine System

The essence of multicellular organism is the coordinated interaction of various kinds of cells that make up the body. The **endocrine system(内分泌系统)**[25] is all about this kind of coordination, ensuring that cells, tissues, organs and organ systems of the animal use materials and energy in the most appropriate ways.

> 25. 内分泌系统包含一系列能够分泌化学信号物质的腺体。内分泌腺分泌的化学物质称为激素或荷尔蒙。

The endocrine system is a collection of glands that secrete chemical messages we call **hormones(荷尔蒙/激素)**. These signals are passed through the blood to arrive at a target organ, which has cells possessing the appropriate receptor.

Receptors on target cell membranes bind only to one type of hormone. The binding hormone changes the shape of the receptor causing the response to the hormone. We have already discussed signal pathway in cell communication in Chapter 2, and hormone is the most vital chemical signal in organisms.

1. Hormones

    Hormones are classified into three types based on their structure: steroids, peptides and amines.[26]

    1) Steroids are lipids derived from cholesterol. Being hydrophobic molecules, these hormones diffuse freely through the plasma membrane, into nucleus and to the nuclear membrane receptors, producing an activated hormone-receptor complex. The hormone-receptor complex acts as a transcription factor turning target genes "on" (or "off").

    2) Peptides are short chains of amino acids and amines are derived from the amino acid tyrosine. Both of them are hydrophilic, so they do not enter the cell but bind to plasma membrane receptors, stimulating the production of a chemical signal (second messenger) inside the target cell. Second messengers activate other intracellular chemicals to produce the target cell response that may alter the behavior of the cell (such as by opening or closing membrane channels) or stimulate (or repress) gene expression in the nucleus by turning on (or off) the promoters and enhancers of the genes.

    Hormones in endocrine system can trigger one after another by using cycles and negative feedback to regulate physiological functions. Negative feedback regulates hormone pathways can be summarized as follows:[27]

    Endocrine cell secretes a hormone in response to a stimulus.
    ↓
    The hormone travels to target cells.
    ↓
    Signal transduction produces a response.
    ↓
    Consequence of response reduces the stimulus.
    ↓
    Pathway shuts off.

> 26. 固醇类激素能够直接通过细胞膜,与受体形成复合体。
> 多肽类激素及氨类激素不能直接透过细胞膜,而是与膜上的受体结合,激活第二信使,进一步影响细胞内活动。

> 27. 负反馈调控途径可总结如下:
> 内分泌细胞对刺激进行反应,分泌荷尔蒙
> ↓
> 荷尔蒙到达靶细胞
> ↓
> 信号转导引起靶细胞的反应
> ↓
> 反应的结果降低刺激
> ↓
> 途径关闭

For example, pituitary gland makes TSH. TSH, in turn, has effect on thyroid gland, so cells in thyroid gland are the target cells of TSH. When thyroid gland detects TSH, it secrets **thyroxin(甲状腺素)**. Once TSH excesses peak level in blood stream, thyroxin can signal pituitary gland to stop producing TSH. Besides controlling release of TSH in negative regulation, thyroxin controls development of animal body and regulates metabolism. All most of body cells are the target cells for thyroxin. 28

> 28. 垂体产生促甲状腺激素(TSH)，TSH 刺激甲状腺，所以甲状腺细胞是 TSH 的靶细胞。甲状腺受到 TSH 影响后会释放甲状腺激素。一旦血液中的 TSH 超过峰值，甲状腺激素可以影响垂体使 TSH 的分泌停止。

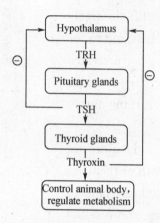

2. Coordination with Nerve System

The endocrine system's effects are slow to initiate, and prolonged in their response, lasting from a few hours up to weeks. So it needs some quick signal to response to the internal changes. Generally, endocrine system interacts with nervous system to maintain homeostasis. The master gland, **pituitary gland(脑垂体)**[29], is located in a small bony cavity at the base of the brain. A stalk links the pituitary to the **hypothalamus(下丘脑)**. The hypothalamus contains neurons that control releases from the pituitary. Certain hypothalamic hormones are released into a portal system connecting the hypothalamus and pituitary, and cause targets in the pituitary to release hormones.

The nervous and endocrine systems work as partners, each helping to regulate the other's activity as they guide the systems of the body toward appropriate responses.

> 29. 内分泌系统与神经系统协同作用，维持内环境的稳定。下丘脑将神经系统与内分泌系统联系起来。下丘脑释放激素刺激位于脑下骨腔的脑垂体，从而进一步影响其他靶器官或靶细胞。

Chapter 7 Responding to Environment and Maintaining Homeostasis

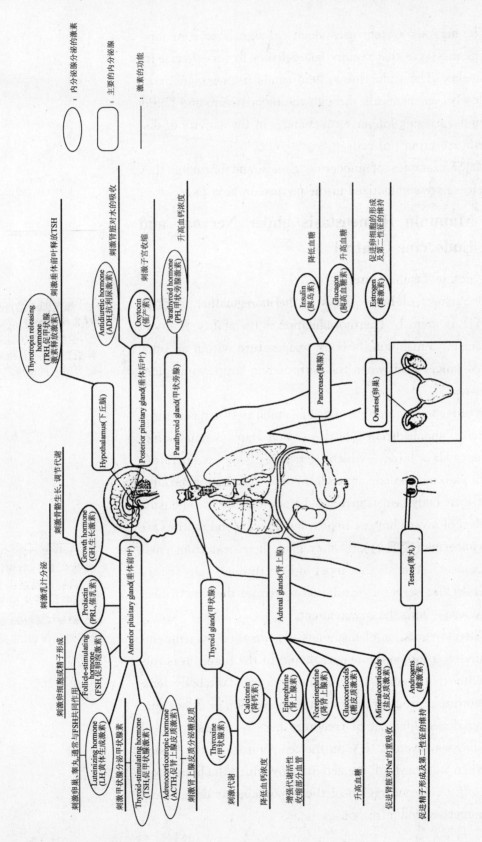

The nervous system uses electrical signals to communicate messages that require fast delivery to very precise locations. The endocrine system sends its messages more slowly, as chemicals through the bloodstream and bodily fluids, causing longer-term changes in the activity of distributed groups of cells.

Major examples of endocrine glands and hormone they release are summarized in the picture on next page.

IV. Maintain Homeostasis under Nervous and Endocrine Control

1. Maintain Temperature Stable

One aspect of homeostasis is **thermoregulation**(温度调节)[30] in animal. Thermoregulation is the ability of an organism to maintain its body temperature within an optimal range, even when the surrounding temperature fluctuates.

In order to maintain the dynamic stability of temperature, animal should balance heat loss and gain. Animals, like mammals, birds, which generate body temperature through metabolism are endothermic. The major resource of their body heat is generated from internal metabolism. Most of invertebrates, fishes, amphibians and reptiles are **ectothermic**(变温的).[31] They gain their heat from environment. Animals lose most of heat through skin or fur, which also serves as insulation to reduce the rate of heat exchange with the environment.

Thermoregulation of mammals is controlled by temperature receptors in the hypothalamus of the brain. It is this center that enables us to maintain a constant body temperature during periods of extreme exertion or in hot surroundings. One set of receptors here responds to small increases, even 0.01 ℃ in the temperature of the blood. When triggered, all the activities by which the body cools itself. A second region of the hypothalamus detects and triggers warming responses.

30. 温度调节是指尽管外部环境温度变化剧烈，生物体仍然能够使体温处在一个相对稳定且适宜的范围内。

31. 无脊椎动物、鱼类、两栖类、爬行动物都是外温性，也就是说它们要依赖环境中的热量来维持自身温度。

- When body temperature rises above normal range, sweating is a good option for endotherms to decrease body heat. Considerable heat is carried away from body surface with **water evaporation(水分蒸发)**[32], which results from property of water learned before.
- Endotherms also can shunt blood vessels to the skin and extremities by **vasodilation(血管舒张)**, which elevates blood flow to increase heat loss from body.
- Shivering, the muscle activity that uses glucose and fat as fuel to produce heat is effective to warm animal body.
- **Vasoconstriction(血管收缩)**[33], a reverse process, prevents blood from losing heat to the environment.
- Thyroxin, a hormone produced in thyroid gland can increase mitochondrial metabolism and signal mitochondria to produce more heat instead of ATP.

32. 当外界温度高于正常值时,流汗即利用水分蒸发可以带走身体部分热量。恒温动物的皮肤和四肢的血管舒张,增加血流量,从而使热量散失增加。

33. 当外界温度低于最适温度时,血管收缩,减少血液流经皮肤时的热量散失。同时甲状腺素的分泌增加热量的产生。

2. Water and Salts Balance

Osmoregulation(渗透调节)[34] is the active regulation of the chemical composition of body fluid by control the moving of water and other solutions out of or into the cell.

1) Water and Na$^+$

- Unicellular organism, like Ameba and Paramecium have contract vacuole to collect or push water based on the osmotic pressure.
- Kidneys help control the osmotic balance of the mammal blood by controlling the concentrations of water and solutes, especially Na$^+$ within it.

  ADH(抗利尿激素) (antidiuretic hormone), a hormone acts on the collecting ducts of the kidney to facilitate the reabsorption of water into the blood.

  Dropping levels of fluid in the blood signal the hypothalamus to cause the pituitary to release ADH into the blood. ADH acts to increase water absorption in the kidneys. This puts more water back in the blood, increasing the concentration of the urine.

34. 渗透调节是生物体通过对水分和其他液体的摄入与排出,对体液中的化学组成进行主动调节的过程。

When too much fluid is present in the blood, sensors in the heart signal the hypothalamus to cause a reduction of the amount of ADH in the blood. This increases the amount of water absorbed by the kidneys, producing large quantities of a more dilute urine.[35]

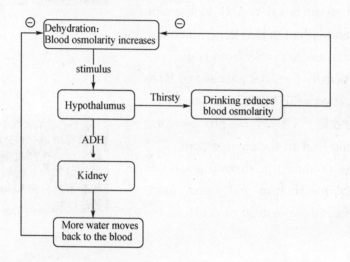

> 35. 当血液中的水分降低时，垂体会释放抗利尿激素（ADH）。ADH 会增加肾脏对于水分的重吸收，使更多的水分留在血液中。当血液中水分含量较高时，感受器刺激下丘脑，降低血液中 ADH 的含量。当肾脏对于水分的吸收增加时，排出体外的水分增加。

2) The balance of another important ion, Ca^{2+}, is controlled by calcitonin and PTH.

- The thyroid cells in **thyroid gland(甲状腺)**[36] that synthesize **calcitonin(降钙素)** have receptors that bind calcium ions (Ca^{2+}) circulating in the blood. A rise in its level, such as would occur with the absorption of calcium from a meal, stimulates the cells to release calcitonin. Calcitonin prevents a sharp rise in blood calcium by inhibiting the uptake of Ca^{2+} from the small intestine and enhances Ca^{2+} release by kidneys.

> 36. 甲状腺分泌的降钙素能够降低血液中钙离子的含量。

- **PTH(甲状旁腺激素/副甲状腺素)**[37] (parathyroid hormone), released from parathyroid gland, increases the concentration of Ca^{2+} in the blood by regulating how much calcium is absorbed from small intestine, how much calcium is excreted by kidneys, and how much calcium is stored in bones. PTH also increases the formation of active vitamin D, and it is active vitamin D that increases intestinal calcium and phosphorus absorption.

> 37. 甲状旁腺激素能够增加血液中钙离子的浓度，同时增加肠道对于磷的吸收。

Chapter 7 Responding to Environment and Maintaining Homeostasis

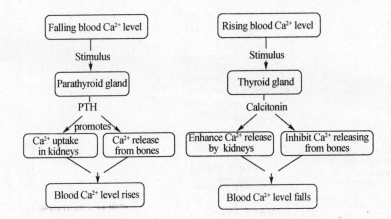

3. Sugar Balance in Blood

Sugar, especially glucose, is the major energy resource for organism metabolism. Groups of pancreatic endocrine cells are known as **islets of langerhans(胰岛)**[38] that produce these two. Working together, **insulin(胰岛素)** and **glucagon(胰高血糖素)** regulate glucose level in blood. After a meal, blood glucose levels rise, prompting the release of insulin, which causes cells to take up glucose. Triggered by insulin, liver and skeletal muscle cells convert glucose to glycogen. As glucose levels in the blood fall, further insulin production is inhibited. Glucagon causes the breakdown of glycogen into glucose, which in turn is released into the blood to maintain glucose levels within a homeostatic range. Glucagon production is stimulated when blood glucose levels fall, and inhibited when they rise.

Like PTH and calcitonin, insulin and glucagon are antagonistic hormones, which means opposite effects. But PTH and calcitonin are released from different glands, while insulin and glucagon are produced in different groups of cell in the same endocrine gland, insulin in β islets and glucagon in α islets.

38. 胰岛分泌的胰岛素和胰高血糖素共同参与血糖调节。胰岛素能够降低血糖浓度,而胰高血糖素能够增加血糖浓度。

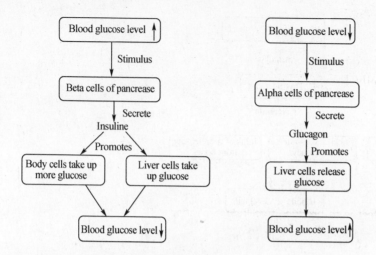

Ⅴ. How Plant Respond to Environment

1. Maintain Water Balance

   Water is one of the most widely used compounds in biological processes, and organisms need to maintain a proper water concentration in order to carry out reactions and transport nutrients and wastes around the body, and in some cases to provide internal support.

   Plants move water and dissolved nutrients upwards from the roots to the remainder of the plant mainly by transpiration. **Transpiration(蒸腾作用)**[39] is a process that water evaporates from leaves via pores called **stomata(气孔)**. Each stoma is surrounded by two kidney-shaped **guard cells(保卫细胞)**. The cell walls of guard cells are not of uniform thickness. Instead, the cell wall that borders the stomata is thicker than the rest of the cell wall, which makes inner part more flexible comparatively. In addition, the cellulose microfibrils are arranged radially, that is, they encircle the guard cell from the stoma side to the outside. Water vapor flows into and out of plants primarily through the stomata. The opening and closing of the stomata is controlled by the movement of water into and out of the guard cells accompanied by a movement of potassium ions (K^+).

   1) Light activate a blue-light receptor that stimulates po-

> 39. 蒸腾作用是指植物中的水分通过叶片上的气孔蒸发的过程。
> 气孔由两个肾形的保卫细胞包围。

tassium pumps on the plasma membrane of guard cell with active transport of K^+ out of the guard cell.

2) Uptake of K^+ decreases guard cell water potential so H_2O is taken up, cells become turgid, and stomata open. When water diffuses into a guard cell, the guard cell expands. But because of the non uniform and radially constructed cell wall, the expansion is distorted in such a way that most of the expansion is realized by the bulging out of the thinner wall, the wall away from the stoma. The overall effect is to produce two kidney-shaped guard cells that create an opening, the stoma, between them.

3) Closing of the stomata results when K^+ exits in the guard cells and creates an osmotic loss of water. When water diffuses out of the guard cells, the kidney shape collapses and the stoma closes.

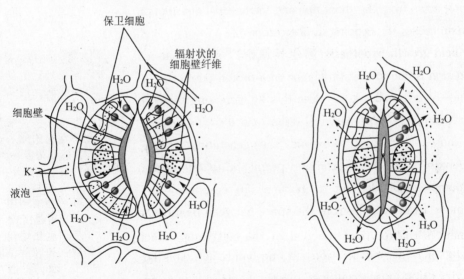

K^+进入液泡后降低保卫细胞的水势，从而使得细胞周围的水分子进入细胞，保卫细胞因此变得膨胀并且通过辐射状排布的纤维拉动细胞内壁，打开气孔

2. Phototropism

A **tropism(向性运动)**[40] is a growth movement whose direction is determined by the direction from which the stimulus strikes the plant. **Positive phototropism(正趋光性)**[41] is growth towards light and negative is away light.

40. 向性运动是指植物的生长运动方向受到其所接受刺激的方向影响。

Plants arch towards sunlight enables plants to expose their leaves so that photosynthesis can occur.

Charles Darwin and his son Francis in 1880 discovered that the phototropic stimulus was detected at the tip of the coleoptile, and the tip was, in some way, communicating with the cells in the region of elongation. In 1913, Danish plant physiologist Boysen Jensen showed that certain chemical signal was passing down from the tip of the coleoptile, so that connected tip and stem. F. W. Went then extracted this chemical and named it auxin.

Phototropism of plant stem is really a clever use of hormones and sunlight to promote the growth of cells in specific areas of the plant in such a way that the plant grows in a specific direction. It is generally accepted that cells on the dark side of a grass coleoptile elongate faster than cells on the bright side due to asymmetric distribution of auxins moving down from the shoot tip, and the unequal distribution of auxin causes the bending in phototropism.

The **acid-growth hypothesis(酸生长理论)**[42] states that cell elongation is due to the stimulation of a proton pump that acidifies the cell wall. Auxin does this by increasing the concentration of H^+ in primary cell walls, and then turgor pressure causes the cell wall to expand, thus generating growth.

- Auxin signals to promote permeability of proton pumps embedded on membrane. In response, H^+ move from cytoplasm to the space between membrane and cell wall.
- Higher acid concentration, in one hand, activates enzymes that loosen cellulose fibers. The result is an increase in cell wall plasticity. In another hand, more H^+ decrease water potential in the space allowing water uptake, which results in elongation of the cell.

3. Photoperiods

Many angiosperms flower at about the same time every year. Their flowering is a response to the photoperiod, a

> 41. 正趋光性是指植物朝向有光一侧生长。正趋光性的适应性特征在于能使植物尽可能多地接触阳光。

> 42. 酸生长理论是指细胞伸长是因为受到使细胞壁酸化的质子泵的刺激。
> 生长素通过增加氢离子在细胞膜与细胞壁之间的浓度,改变膨压使细胞壁向外扩张,从而促进增长。生长素可增加细胞膜上质子泵的通透性,使氢离子从细胞质中流入到细胞膜和细胞壁的间隙中。较高的酸浓度激活了能够使纤维素纤维变得松弛的酶,增加了细胞壁的可塑性。另外,较高浓度的氢离子减少了间隙中的水势,从而导致细胞的伸长。

Chapter 7 Responding to Environment and Maintaining Homeostasis

changing of relative lengths of night and day as the season progresses. The phenomenon is called **photoperiods(光周期)**[43] referring to the responses a plant makes to photoperiods. It helps plants perform photosynthesis as efficiently as possible and promotes cross pollination.

W. W. Garner and H. A. Allard in 1920 postulated that the amount of day length controls flowering. Based on their studies, they classified flowering plants into three categories[44]:

1) Short-day plants, typically chrysanthemum, flower in late summer and early fall when daylight is decreasing.
2) Long-day plants, like tulip, flower only in the spring and early summer when daylight is increasing.
3) Day-neutral plants, like rose, are unaffected by photoperiod and flower when they reach a certain stage of maturity, such as appropriate temperature or water.

It was discovered in the 1940s that night length, not day length, actually controls flowering and other responses to photoperiod, which means **critical night length(临界夜长)**[45] determines plant flowering.

- If the daytime period is broken by a brief exposure to darkness, there is no effect on flowering.
- If the nighttime period is interrupted by short exposure to light, photoperiodic responses are disrupted and the plants do not flower.
- Therefore, short-day plants flower if night is longer than a critical length, and long-day plants need a night shorter than a critical length.

Note that plants make both daily decisions and seasonal decisions based on photoperiods. The daily period is critical to deciding when to open and close stomata, and daily responses are enforced by a "circadian rhythm", a sort of built-in, daily biological clock. The seasonal period is important for deciding when to flower or perform other major life-cycle events.

> 43. 被子植物的开花受到光周期,也就是每天光照时长的影响。

> 44. 短日照植物,如菊花,在夏末秋初日照时间逐渐减少时开花;长日照植物,如郁金香,在春季和夏初日照时间逐渐增长时开花;中日照植物,如玫瑰,不受光周期的影响,在达到一定的成熟阶段,如遇到适宜的温度和水分时开花。

> 45. 植物开花受到临界夜长的影响,即持续无光照的时间。
> 　如果白天光照时长被短时间的黑暗无光状态破坏,对植物开花无影响;如黑暗时长被短时间光照扰乱,则光周期被破坏,植物不开花;当黑暗时长高于临界值时,短日照植物开花;当黑暗时长低于临界值时,长日照植物开花。

4. Phytochromes Function as A Photoreceptor

Pigments named **phytochromes**（光敏色素）[46] in many plants response to light and photoperiod. Phytochrome, a protein containing a light-absorbing component, responsible for a plant's response to photoperiod, functions as a photodetector that tells plants if light is present and helps plants measure the length of darkness in a photoperiod.

1) There are two forms of phytochromes[47], P_r (or P660) and P_{fr} (or P730), depending upon which wavelength of light the phytochrome absorbs. P_{fr} is the active form of phytochrome and appears to maintain photoperiod accuracy. It absorbs far-red light (wavelength 730 nm) while P_r absorbs red light (wavelength 660 nm). The two forms are photoreversible; that is, when P_r is exposed to red light, it is converted to P_{fr}.

2) P_r is synthesized in the leaves of plants[48]. During daylight, P_r is converted to P_{fr}, since red light is present in sunlight. Some far-red light is also present in sunlight, so some of P_{fr} is converted back into P_r. By measuring the red to far-red light ratio, the phytochrome system evaluates the quality of light reaching the plant which would adjust a plant's growth and development in response to some environmental changes.

> 46. 光敏色素是植物中的蛋白色素。植物通过光敏色素接收外界光信号来调节本身的生长发育。

> 47. 有两种形式的光敏色素，根据它们对于光的吸收波长的不同，分别叫做 P_r 和 P_{fr}。P_r 吸收红光，P_{fr} 吸收远红光。这两种光敏色素是光可逆的，也就是说 P_r 可以通过吸收红光转化为 P_{fr}。P_{fr} 是一种活跃的光敏色素，它能够保持光周期的精确性。

> 48. P_r 在植物叶片中生成。白天，P_r 在日光中红光的作用下变成 P_{fr}；因为日光中也包含红外线，所以部分 P_{fr} 也会变成 P_r。通过测量红光与远红光的比值，光敏色素系统将评估照射在植物上的光的质量，并调节植物的生长和发育，以适应环境的变化。

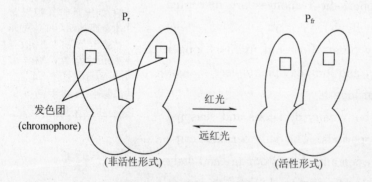

Chapter 7 Responding to Environment and Maintaining Homeostasis

本章词汇

homeostasis	内稳态	negative feedback	负反馈
neuron	神经元	cell body	细胞体
dendrite	树突	axon	轴突
myelin sheath	髓鞘	Schwann cell	施万细胞/神经鞘细胞
nodes of Ranvier	朗飞氏节	resting potential	静息电位
action potential	动作电位	nerve impulse	神经冲动
all-or-non	全或无	refractory period	不应期
repolarization	复极化/再极化	hyperpolarization	超极化/过极化
synapse	突触	neurotransmitter	神经递质
excitatory depolarizing neurotransmitter	兴奋性神经递质	excitatory postsynaptic potential	EPSP, 兴奋性突触后电位
inhibitory postsynaptic potential	IPSP, 抑制性突触后电位	hydrostatic pressure	液体静压
exoskeleton	外骨骼	endoskeleton	内骨骼
cardiac muscle	心肌	skeletal muscle	骨骼肌
smooth muscle	平滑肌	sarcolemma	肌纤维膜
sarcoplasm	肌浆	sarcomere	肌节
actin	肌动蛋白	troponin	肌钙蛋白
tropomyosin	原肌球蛋白	myosin	肌球蛋白
sliding filament theory	肌丝滑动学说	endocrine system	内分泌系统
hormone	荷尔蒙/激素	thyroxin	甲状腺素
pituitary gland	脑垂体	hypothalamus	下丘脑
thermoregulation	温度调节	ectothermic	变温的
water evaporation	水分蒸发	vasodilation	血管舒张
vasoconstriction	血管收缩	osmoregulation	渗透调节
ADH	抗利尿激素	thyroid gland	甲状腺
calcitonin	降钙素	PTH	甲状旁腺激素/副甲状腺素
islets of langerhans	胰岛	insulin	胰岛素
glucagon	胰高血糖素	transpiration	蒸腾作用

stomata	气孔	guard cell	保卫细胞
tropism	向性运动	positive phototropism	正趋光性
acid-growth hypothesis	酸生长理论	photoperiod	光周期
critical night length	临界夜长	phytochrome	光敏色素/植物色素

本章重点

1. 生物维持内稳态的意义及负反馈调节机制。
2. 神经元的结构及传递信号的机制。
3. 神经系统对动物生理功能的调控。
4. 结合细胞信号传递机制,理解内分泌系统的主要激素及功能。
5. 神经系统与内分泌系统对动物水、温、盐、糖的调控方式。
6. 植物水分调控的方式。
7. 植物向性运动的原理。
8. 植物的光周期。

本章习题

1. Which of the following is FALSE?
    a. In vertebrates' sensory neurons, nerve impulses normally travel both away from and toward the cell body.
    b. The resting potential of a neuron is maintained by membrane "pumps" actively transporting sodium into and potassium out of the cell.
    c. Neurons operate with two main types of electrical signals: slow graded potentials and fast action potentials.
    d. Saltatory conduction involves nerve impulses "jumping" between regions of the axon where the myelin sheath is missing.

2. As a nerve impulse passes along an axon _____.
    a. the membrane potential changes from positive to negative and then back again
    b. sodium ions flow out through ion channels and potassium ions flow in
    c. sodium channels open as the membrane potential becomes less negative
    d. the sodium-potassium pump moves sodium ions into the cell

3. The figure below shows two nerve action potentials recorded intracellularly in response to stimulating an axon. What experimental manipulation would most likely have caused the change from curve A (solid line) to curve B (dashed line)?

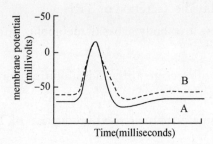

   a. A decrease in stimulus intensity.
   b. A decrease in sodium concentration in the extracellular fluid.
   c. A decrease in the potassium concentration inside the neuron.
   d. The presence of a low concentration of tetrodotoxin, a sodium-channel blocker.

4. In a laboratory experiment, a scientist applies a drug that opens sodium channels to a neuron. Two millilitres of the drug barely brings the membrane to threshold potential, at which time the scientist removes the drug by washing it away. After the neuron returns to stable resting potential, 10ml of the same drug is applied. Which statement about the experiment is most likely to be CORRECT?
   a. The first application of the drug will not produce an action potential, as it is washed away quickly.
   b. No action potential will be produced because opening sodium channels will hyperpolarize the membrane.
   c. The action potential produced by the second application of the drug will be much greater than the first.
   d. Both applications will produce action potentials of similar magnitude.

5. What is responsible for the rapid depolarization of the axon (i.e. the rising phase of an action potential)?
   a. Voltage-gated sodium channels open allowing Na^+ into the cell.
   b. Voltage-gated potassium channels open allowing K^+ into the cell.
   c. The Na^+/K^+ pump actively moves Na^+ out of the cell and K^+ into the cell.
   d. Voltage-gated potassium channels open allowing K^+ ions out of the cell.

6. The human's thyroid gland is controlled by a negative feedback mechanism. The hy-

pothalamus secretes thyrotropin-releasing hormone (TRH). TRH stimulates the anterior pituitary to secrete thyroid-stimulating hormone (TSH). TSH induces the thyroid gland to secrete thyroxine. What is the next step in the control system?
   a. Thyroxine will inhibit the secretion of TRH.
   b. Thyroxine will cause the body's basal metabolic rate and body temperature to drop.
   c. The hypothalamus will secrete a thyroid-inhibiting hormone that slows down production of thyroxine.
   d. Thyroxine will stimulate the increased production of TSH.

7. Suppose you are developing a new drug, and have found that when it is administered in humans there is a substantial increase in the volume of urine produced. When you administer antidiuretic hormone (ADH, or vasopressin) at the same time, the volume of urine returns to normal. Which hypothesis best fits these observations? The new drug _____.
   a. blocks the receptors for ADH on the collecting ducts of kidneys
   b. blocks the release of ADH from the pituitary
   c. mimics the action of ADH
   d. damages kidneys

8. If you were outside for a long time on a hot, dry day, without anything to drink, which of the following would happen?
   a. The production of thyroxin by your thyroid gland would increase.
   b. The osmotic pressure of your blood would decrease.
   c. The reabsorption of fluids from your kidney tubules would decrease.
   d. The secretion of anti-diuretic hormone from your pituitary gland would increase.

9. Thermoregulation in mammals is a balance between heat gain and heat loss. All of the following can affect both heat gain and heat loss EXCEPT _____.
   a. activity of the sweat glands
   b. thickness of the fat layer under the skin
   c. air movement near the body surface
   d. blood flow in the skin

10. Suppose you were working in a diagnostic laboratory and had measured high levels of glucagon and low levels of insulin in a blood sample from a patient. What would

be the most likely explanation?

a. The patient had consumed a large soft drink on the way to the lab.

b. The patient was suffering from diabetes.

c. The patient had not eaten anything for several hours.

d. You had made an error in one or both of the measurements.

11. When you become cold, your body has a number of control mechanisms to maintain homeostasis. Which of the following is NOT a physiological response to a drop in body temperature?

a. Contraction of piloerector (hair) muscles.

b. Involuntary contraction of skeletal muscles (shivering).

c. An increase in fat metabolism.

d. Vasodilation (increased diameter) of the blood vessels near the skin.

12. Charles Darwin and his son Francis experimented with phototropism of grass seedlings by placing a metal foil "blindfold" over different parts of the seedling's coleoptile. A simplified version of their results is shown below. Which of the following statements best explains their results?

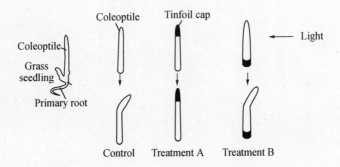

a. The light signal is perceived a few millimetres below the tip, and these cells cause the coleoptile to grow toward the light.

b. Both the seedling root and coleoptile perceive and respond to light in the same manner.

c. A chemical messenger must travel from the base of the coleoptile to the tip.

d. The light signal is perceived at the tip of the coleoptile, but the growth response occurs a few millimetres below the tip.

13. Which of the following changes would DECREASE the rate of water loss (transpiration) from the leaves of a sugar maple tree?

a. Light breeze.
b. Bright sunshine.
c. An afternoon rain shower.
d. A plentiful supply of soil water.

14. The graphs below show the relationship between the rate of water loss by transpiration and leaf temperature. Based on these results, which plant is best adapted for conserving water in a hot dry environment?

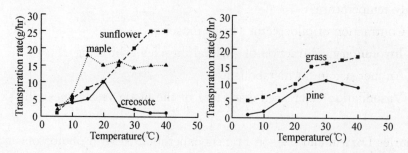

a. Sunflower.
b. Maple.
c. Creosote.
d. Grass.

CHAPTER 8

Defense against Disease

Homeostasis in an organism is constantly threatened. Failure to respond effectively can result in disease or death. Disease is a disturbance of homeostasis or steady state within an organism. Living organisms that cause disease are known as **pathogens**(病原体)[1]. Some viruses, bacteria, fungi, and parasites are examples of living things which are pathogens causing disease. Other factors may be involved which contribute to or cause the body to develop disease. Some of these factors include heredity, exposure to poisonous (toxic) substances, poor nutrition, organ failure or malfunction, and poor personal behavior and choices.

Defense against pathogens' invasion is the province of the **immune system**(免疫系统)[2]. It also protects people from many cancer cells that arise within our bodies. The immune response includes both **specific**(特异性) and **nonspecific**(非特异性) components. Human immune system possess a three-pronged strategy in this ongoing battle.

1. 病原体是能够导致疾病的生物体,包括病毒、细菌、真菌和寄生生物等。

2. 人体的免疫系统能够保护我们免受病原体和癌细胞的侵袭。免疫反应包括特异性免疫反应和非特异性免疫反应。

I. Nonspecific Immune Responses

1. Skin

   Physical barriers are the first line of defense, which prevent pathogens from entering the body and include skin, mucous membranes, cilia, and stomach acid. The skin is a passive barrier to infectious agents such as bacteria and viruses. The organisms living on the skin surface are unable to penetrate the layers of dead skin at the surface.
   Tears and saliva secrete enzymes that break down bacterial cell walls. Skin glands secrete chemicals that retard the

growth of bacteria. Mucus membranes lining the respiratory, digestive, urinary, and reproductive tracts secrete mucus that forms another barrier.

These initial defenses are nonspecific in that they defend generally against all forms of invaders.

2. **Inflammation(炎症)**

The second line of defense is also nonspecific, and includes the inflammatory response, phagocytes, and interferon.[3]

When microorganisms penetrate skin or epithelium lining respiratory, digestive, or urinary tracts, inflammation results. Damaged cells release chemical signals such as **histamine(组胺/组织胺)** that increase capillary blood flowing into the affected areas (causing the areas to become heated and reddened). The heat makes the environment unfavorable for microbes, promotes healing, raises mobility of white blood cells, and increases the metabolic rate of nearby cells. Capillaries pass fluid into interstitial areas, causing the infected or injured area to swell. Clotting factors trigger formation of many small blood clots. Finally, monocytes, a type of white blood cell clean up dead microbes, cells, and debris.

The inflammatory response is often strong enough to stop the spread of disease-causing agents such as viruses, bacteria, and fungi. The response begins with the release of chemical signals and ends with cleanup by monocytes. If this is not enough to stop the invaders, the phagocytes and interferon act.

3. Phagocytosis

Many different kinds of white blood cells exist which are able to help the body fight foreign invaders in various ways. A class of white blood cells called **phagocytes(巨噬细胞)**[4] is attracted to the inflamed area, concentrating their attack at the site of invasion. They recognize and at-

> 3. 皮肤和分泌物等物理屏障构成人体的第一道防线；炎症反应、巨噬细胞和干扰素构成人体的第二道防线。炎症反应是人体局部红肿热痛的反应，由化学物质组胺引起。

> 4. 巨噬细胞是能够识别和通过内吞作用吞噬异物颗粒的细胞。

tack foreign particles, and engulf invaders to form food vacuoles. Lysosomes in phagocytes then digest these engulfed vacuoles.

4. **Interferon(干扰素)**[5]

Interferon is a species-specific chemical produced by cells that are against viral attack. It alerts nearby cells to prepare for a virus. The cells that have been contacted by interferon resist all viral attacks.

> 5. 干扰素是能够帮助细胞抵御病毒感染的化学物质,具有种群特异性。

Ⅱ. Specific Immune Responses

The immune system also generates **specific immune responses (特异性免疫反应)**[6] to specific invaders. It is more effective than the nonspecific methods, and has a memory component that improves response time when an invader of the same type (or species) is again encountered.

> 6. 特异性免疫反应只针对一种抗原;相对于非特异性免疫来说,特异性免疫显得更为高效;当机体再次被同种抗原感染时,特异性免疫能够迅速做出反应。

Lymphocytes(淋巴细胞)[7] are primary components of specific immune response. During fetal development, red bone marrow releases lymphocytes into circulation. Undifferentiated lymphocytes that reach the **thymus(胸腺)** become **T cells(T 细胞)**; **B cells(B 细胞)** are thought to mature in the **bone marrow(骨髓)**. Both B and T cells reside in lymphatic organs, like spleen, thymus and tonsil. When B or T cells become activated the first time encountering a new antigen, their actions constitute a **primary immune response(初次免疫应答)**, after which some cells remain as **memory cells(记忆细胞)**.

> 7. 淋巴细胞是特异性免疫的主要组成成分。在骨髓中成熟的淋巴细胞称为 B 细胞;在胸腺中成熟的淋巴细胞称为 T 细胞。B 细胞和 T 细胞参与初次免疫应答,并产生记忆细胞。

Specific immune response (or acquired immune response) differs from nonspecific immune response (or innate immune response) in that it targets specific antigens. An **antigen(抗原)**[8] is any molecule, usually a protein or polysaccharide, which can trigger a specific response by lymphocytes. It can be components of the coats of viruses, capsules and cell walls of bacteria, or surface molecules of other cell types. Molecules on the cell surface of transplanted tissues and organs or blood cells from other individuals are also recognized

> 8. 抗原是能够引起淋巴细胞发生特异性免疫反应的物质,通常其成分为蛋白质或者多糖。

as antigens.

Antigen receptors on the plasma membranes of lymphocytes recognize and distinguish among antigens. Each antigen activates only a small number of the diverse group of lymphocytes by binding to the membrane receptor of lymphocyte. The binding, like that between an enzyme and its substrate depends on complementarity of the surface of the receptor and the surface of the antigen molecule. The activated cells proliferate to produce a clone of millions of effector cells that are specific for the original antigen. If the same antigen is encountered again, more numerous memory cells can mount a more rapid response, known as the **secondary immune response(二次免疫应答)**[9].

Specific immunity branches into **humoral immune response (体液免疫应答/体液免疫)** and **cell-mediated response(细胞介导的应答/细胞免疫)**. **Helper T cells(辅助 T 细胞)**, one type of T lymphocytes mediate both responses. [10]

1. Helper T Cells: Help Other Lymphocytes
   In many cases, the antigen or antigen-bearing pathogen must first be engulfed by a macrophage. Helper T cells then bind to the macrophage in a cell-mediated response called **antigen presenting(抗原递呈)**[11].
   Antigen presenting occurs when **antigen-presenting cells (抗原递呈细胞)** like macrophages, B cells or other cells that have already encountered the antigen. Engulfing or being infected by pathogens, antigen-presenting cells display the antigen on its **major histocompatibility complex (MHC) molecules(主要组织相容性复合体分子)**.
   - The MHC molecules are glycoproteins expressed at the plasma membrane of almost all vertebrate cells. They get their name because they are responsible for the compatibility —distinguish between self and nonself — of the tissues of genetically different individuals. Their normal function is to display antigens so that they can be recognized by T lymphocytes. The

> 9. 对于再次出现的抗原,记忆细胞可迅速发挥作用,称为二次免疫应答。

> 10. 特异性免疫包括体液免疫和细胞免疫。辅助 T 细胞既参加体液免疫也参加细胞免疫。

> 11. 巨噬细胞能够吞噬抗原或病原体,并将部分抗原递呈至细胞表面的主要组织相容性复合体上。此过程称为抗原递呈。能够进行抗原递呈的细胞称为抗原递呈细胞。

most rapid and severe rejection of foreign tissue occurs when there is a failure to properly match the donor and recipient for the MHC molecules. There are two categories: Class Ⅰ and Class Ⅱ.[12]

- **Class Ⅰ MHC molecules(Ⅰ类主要组织相容性复合体分子)** are transmembrane proteins expressed at the all nucleated cell surface, which facilitate antigen binding to **cytotoxic T cells(细胞毒性 T 细胞)**, effector cells in cell-mediate immunity.
- Class Ⅱ MHC molecules consist of two transmembrane polypeptides, and are found only on specialized cells, such as macrophages, B cells, and activated T cells. They facilitate antigen binding to helper T cells. Helper T cells recognize Class Ⅱ MHC and proliferate into both activated helper T cells and memory helper T cells. Activated helper T cells release cytokines to activate B cells and cytotoxic T cells.

> 12. 主要组织相容性抗原Ⅰ类分子为跨膜蛋白,帮助细胞毒性T细胞结合抗原。细胞毒性T细胞可释放穿孔素,使受到感染的靶细胞裂解。
> 主要组织相容性抗原Ⅱ类分子由两个跨膜多肽构成,主要存在于巨噬细胞、B细胞、活化T细胞表面,帮助辅助T细胞结合抗原。

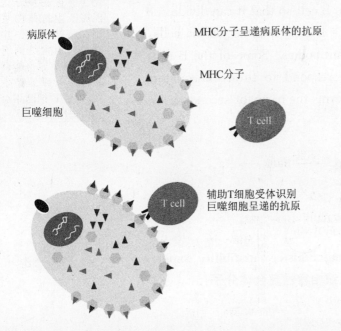

Type	Structure	Expressed at	Binding to
MHC Ⅰ	α chain(transmembrane) and β2 microglobulin	All nucleated cells	Cytotoxic T cells
MHC Ⅱ	α chain and β chain (both transmembrane)	Antigen-presenting cells	Helper T cells

2. Humoral Immunity: A Response to Extracellular Pathogens
The humoral response also called **antibody-mediated response(抗体介导的反应)**[13] refers to responds to antigens or pathogens that are circulating in the lymph or blood. **Antibodies(抗体)**[14], an **antigen-binding immunoglobulin(抗原结合免疫球蛋白)** produced by B cells, function as the effector in this immune response.

The humoral response occurs when an antigen binds to B cell receptors that are specific for the **antigen epitopes(抗原表位)**[15]—a localized region on the surface of an antigen. Then B cells differentiate into a clone of plasma cells to secrete antibodies. The specific antibodies help eliminate the foreign invaders from the body.

Most of the time, B cells need helper T cells for activation.[16] When a helper T cell encounters a B cell that has itself encountered an antigen, the helper T cell releases cytokines that activate the B cell so that it can divide and form a clone. Some of the B cells become plasma cells, producing and secreting antibodies. Some of the B cells become memory cells to respond to future encounters with the antigen, which forms the basis for secondary immune responses.

> 13. 体液免疫也称为抗体介导的免疫反应,主要针对淋巴和血液循环中的抗原或者病原体。

> 14. 抗体也称为抗原结合免疫球蛋白,由B细胞产生。

> 15. 抗原表位,也称为抗原决定簇,是抗原表面上决定抗原特异性的区域。B细胞上的受体结合可与之结合。

> 16. 大多数情况下细胞需要被辅助T细胞活化才能进一步分化为能够产生抗体的浆细胞和记忆细胞。除了这类较为常见的通路外,部分抗原也能够直接刺激B细胞产生抗体,但是B细胞不会分化为记忆细胞。

```
病原物        识别
(第一次感染) ←------ B细胞
                    ↓  ↘
病原物        识别
(第二次感染) ---→ 记忆B细胞 --→ 浆细胞
              (Memory B cell)   ↓ 分泌
                                抗体
                                ↓
                            清除病毒物

——— 初次免疫应答
------ 二次免疫应答
```

Besides this regular pathway, a few number of antigens can trigger B cells to secrete antibodies directly. But no memory cells are generated and antibody production is usually much weaker.

3. Cell-mediated Immunity: A Response to Infected Cells

The cell-mediated response mainly uses T cells and responds to cells infected by pathogens and cancer cells.[17] This is a very useful function if the target cell is infected with pathogens, especially viruses, because the cell is usually destroyed before it can release a fresh crop of viruses able to infect other cells.

Once infected by viruses and other pathogens, host cells display antigens episode with Class I MHC molecules on their surfaces. Cytotoxic T cells[18] have specific receptors that recognize and then bind to antigen-Class I MHC markers. When a cytotoxic T cell binds to the infected cell, it releases **perforin(穿孔素)** that is a protein that forms a lesion in the infected cell's membrane. Cytoplasm escapes through the lesion and eventually cell lysis occurs. Destroyed host cell not only removes the site where pathogens can reproduce, but also exposes the pathogens to circulating antibodies from the humoral response.

The cytotoxic T receptor can bind to any cell in the body displaying the antigen-Class I MHC marker since Class I MHC is present on all nucleated cells. Note that this differs from helper T cells that bind to antigen-Class II MHC complexes because cytotoxic T cells carry a surface molecule called CD8, which has an affinity for Class I MHC molecules, and facilitates the interaction between an antigen presenting cell and the cytotoxic T cell.

> 17. 细胞介导的免疫反应也称为细胞免疫，主要针对被病原体感染的细胞或者是癌细胞。

> 18. 细胞免疫的效应细胞为细胞毒性T细胞。宿主细胞受到病毒或者其他病原体感染后，会将抗原表位通过MHC I 类分子递呈到细胞表面，细胞毒性T细胞上的特殊受体会与之结合，并释放穿孔素，破坏受感染细胞的细胞膜。

Cytotoxic T cells also function to destroy cancer cells, which develop periodically in the body. Cancer cells possess distinctive markers not found on normal cells, known as **tumor antigen(肿瘤抗原)**[19]. Cytotoxic T cells recognize these markers as non-self and attach and lyse the cancer cells.

> 19. 癌细胞会在细胞表面表达一些有别于正常细胞的分子标记, 称为肿瘤抗原。

III. Immune System and Health

1. Immunity can be achieved naturally or artificially.

   Active immunity(主动免疫)[20] is the immunity conferred by recovery from an infectious disease. It depends on response by the person's own immune system. It may be acquired naturally from an infection to the body or artificially by immunization, also known as **vaccination(预防接种)**.

   > 20. 主动免疫是通过感染病原体后产生而获得的免疫过程。人工主动免疫, 也就是预防接种, 是通过注射疫苗的方式, 使机体获得对病原体的免疫力。疫苗可以是灭活的细菌毒素或者微生物, 微生物的部分结构, 或者减毒的微生物。它能够刺激机体产生免疫力, 但是不会致病。

   - **Vaccines(疫苗)** can be inactivated bacterial toxins, killed microbes, parts of microbes, or viable but weakened microbes. In all cases the organisms can no longer cause the disease but can act as antigens and stimulate an immune response.
   - A person vaccinated against an infectious agent who encounters the pathogen will show the same rapid, memory-based secondary immune response as someone who has had the disease.

   Passive immunity(被动免疫)[21] is the immunity that has been transferred from one individual to another by the transfer of antibodies.

   > 21. 被动免疫是通过直接得到抗体而获得免疫的过程。胎儿通过胎盘、婴儿通过母亲的乳汁获得抗体的方式称为自然被动免疫; 直接注射抗血清或者抗体的方式称为人工被动免疫。

   - It naturally occurs when IgG antibodies, most abundant circulating antibody, cross the placenta from a pregnant woman to her fetus. Some antibodies are transferred to nursing infants through breast milk. It provides temporary protection to newborns whose immune systems are not fully operational at birth. Persisting as long as the antibodies last (a few weeks or months), it can provide protection from infections until a baby's own immune system has matured.
   - It may also be transferred artificially from an animal or

human already immune to the disease. Rabies is treated by injecting antibodies from people vaccinated against rabies; produces an immediate immunity important to quickly progressing infections. Artificial passive immunity is of short duration but permits the body's own immune system to begin to produce antibodies against the rabies virus.

2. Blood Types, Rh, and Antibodies

There are 30 or more known antigens on the surface of blood cells. These form the blood groups or blood types. In a transfusion, the blood groups of the recipient and donor must be matched. If improperly matched, the recipient's immune system will produce antibodies causing clotting of the transfused cells, blocking circulation through capillaries and producing serious or even fatal results.

- ABO blood types are determined by a gene, I[22]. There are three alleles, I^A, I^B and i. Proteins produced by the I^A and I^B alleles are antigenic. Individuals with type A blood have the A antigen on the surface of their red blood cells, and antibodies to type B blood in their plasma. People with type B blood have the B antigen on their blood cells and antibodies against type A in their plasma. Individuals with type AB blood have antigens for A and B on their cell surfaces and no antibodies for either type A or B blood in their plasma. Type O individuals have no antigens on their red blood cells but antibodies to both A and B are in their plasma.

- People with type AB blood can receive blood of any type. Those with type O blood can donate to anyone.[23] If a transfusion is made between the incompatible donor and recipient, the recipient's blood will undergo a cascade of events. Reaction of antigens on cells and antibodies in plasma will produce clumping

22. 与 ABO 血型相关的等位基因为 I^A、I^B 和 i。I^A 和 I^B 分别指导 A、B 抗原的产生。A 型血的血细胞上带有 A 抗原,血清中含有抗 B 抗体;B 型血的血细胞上带有 B 抗原,血清中含有抗 A 抗体;AB 型血的血细胞上带有 A 和 B 两种抗原,血清中没有抗体;O 型血的血细胞上没有抗原,血清中含有抗 A 和抗 B 两种抗体。

23. 通常情况下,输血者血液中的血清会被分离,仅仅把红细胞供给受血者。因此,O 型输血者的血液可以供给所有血型的受血者(因为此血液中已不含抗体)。AB 型受血者的血液中没有抗体,因此可以接受任何输血者的血液。

that clogs capillaries, other cells burst, releasing hemoglobin that can crystallize in the kidney and lead to kidney failure.

The Rh (for the rhesus monkey in which it was discovered) blood group is made up of those Rh positive (Rh$^+$) individuals who can make the Rh antigen and those Rh negative (Rh$^-$) who cannot. [24]

- Hemolytic disease of the newborn results from Rh incompatibility between an Rh$^-$ mother and Rh$^+$ fetus. Rh$^+$ blood from the fetus enters the mother's system during birth, causing her to produce Rh antibodies. The first child is usually not affected, however subsequent Rh$^+$ fetuses will cause a massive secondary immune reaction of the maternal immune system. To prevent HDN, Rh$^-$ mothers are given an Rh antibody during the first pregnancy with an Rh$^+$ fetus and all subsequent Rh$^+$ fetuses.

24. Rh 阳性个体血液中的血细胞上有 Rh 抗原，血清中没有抗 Rh 抗体；Rh 阴性个体的血细胞上没有抗原。Rh 阴性的母亲如果第一胎怀的婴儿是 Rh 阳性，那么分娩时，Rh 抗原就会进入母体，使母亲产生抗 Rh 抗原。如果母亲再次怀孕，婴儿依然是 Rh 阳性，那么母体内的抗 Rh 抗原就会通过胎盘进入婴儿体内造成溶血。

3. Allergies and Disorders of the Immune System

   The immune system can overreact, causing allergies or autoimmune diseases. Likewise, a suppressed, absent, or destroyed immune system can also result in disease and death. Allergies result from immune system hypersensitivity to weak antigens that do not cause an immune response in most people. Allergens, substances that cause allergies, include dust, molds, pollen, cat dander, certain foods, and some medicines (such as penicillin).

4. **Acquired Immunodeficiency Syndrome (AIDS, 获得性免疫缺陷综合征)** [25]

   AIDS is a collection of disorders resulting from the destruction of T cells by the **Human Immunodeficiency Virus (HIV, 人类免疫缺陷病毒)**, a retrovirus. When HIV replicates in the human T cells, it buds from the T cell plasma membrane encased in a coat derived from the T cell plasma membrane. HIV selectively infects and kills T4

25. 获得性免疫缺陷综合征，即艾滋病，是指人感染艾滋病病毒，也就是人类免疫缺陷病毒（HIV）后，因辅助 T 细胞的损伤而导致的一系列症状。HIV 为 RNA 病毒，能够通过自身携带的逆转录酶利用 RNA 上的遗传信息产生双链 DNA，并整合入人体细胞的染色体数月或者数年之久。

helper cells. The viral RNA is converted into DNA by the enzyme reverse transcriptase; this DNA can become incorporated into a human chromosome for months or years.

When the infected T cell is needed in the immune response, the viral genes are activated and the virus replicates, killing the infected cell and producing a new round on T4 cell infection. Gradually the number of T4 cells, the master on switch for the immune system, decline. The immune response grows less powerful, eventually failing. Premature death results from a series of rare diseases such as fungal pneumonia and Kaposi's sarcoma, a rare cancer that overwhelms the body and its compromised immune system.

本章词汇

pathogen	病原体	immune system	免疫系统
specific	特异性	nonspecific	非特异性
inflammation	炎症	histamine	组胺/组织胺
phagocyte	巨噬细胞	interferon	干扰素
specific immune response	特异性免疫反应	lymphocyte	淋巴细胞
thymus	胸腺	T cell	T 细胞
B cell	B 细胞	bone marrow	骨髓
primary immune response	初次免疫应答	memory cell	记忆细胞
antigen	抗原	secondary immune response	二次免疫应答
humoral immune response	体液免疫应答/体液免疫	cell-mediated response	细胞介导的应答/细胞免疫
helper T cell	辅助 T 细胞	antigen presenting	抗原递呈
antigen-presenting cell	抗原递呈细胞	major histocompatibility complex (MHC) molecule	主要组织相容性复合体分子

Class Ⅰ MHC molecule	Ⅰ类主要组织相容性复合体分子	cytotoxic T cell	细胞毒性T细胞
antibody-mediated response	抗体介导的反应	antibody	抗体
antigen-binding immunoglobulin	抗原结合免疫球蛋白	antigen epitope	抗原表位
perforin	穿孔素	tumor antigen	肿瘤抗原
active immunity	主动免疫	vaccination	预防接种
vaccine	疫苗	passive immunity	被动免疫
Acquired Immunodeficiency Syndrome(AIDS)	获得性免疫缺陷综合征	Human Immunodeficiency Virus（HIV）	人类免疫缺陷病毒

本章重点

1. 特异性免疫的种类。
2. 细胞免疫及体液免疫的作用方式。
3. 区分B细胞和T细胞在免疫应答过程中的异同。
4. 免疫应答与血型的关系。
5. 免疫系统与人体健康的关系。

本章习题

1. A patient can produce antibodies against some bacterial pathogens, but he does not produce antibodies against viral infections. This is probably due to a disorder in which cells of the immune system?
    a. B cells.
    b. Plasma cells.
    c. Natural killer cells.
    d. T cells.

2. All of the following are nonspecific defense mechanisms except _____.
    a. acid secretions of the stomach
    b. inflammation

c. antibodies

d. mucus in the respiratory tract

3. Cytotoxic T cells recognize _____.
   a. receptors on B cells
   b. fragments of self proteins of infected cells
   c. viral antigens and Class I MHC
   d. viral antigens and Class II MHC

4. When a doctor gives you an antibiotic when you are sick, he/she always tells you to keep taking the antibiotic until it is all finished. The reason he/she tells you this is because _____.
   a. it is wasteful not to finish all the antibiotic
   b. viruses require high doses of antibiotics to kill them
   c. allowing the more antibiotic-tolerant bacteria to survive may encourage a population of antibiotic-resistant bacteria to evolve
   d. a long period of antibiotic use is required to prevent secondary virus infection

5. A doctor discovers her patient can resist many bacterial infections by producing appropriate antibodies, but the patient is highly susceptible to viral infections. The most likely diagnosis is a disorder of the patient's _____.
   a. T cells
   b. macrophages
   c. plasma cells
   d. erythrocytes

6. Which cells are NOT normally involved in the functioning of the immune system in humans?
   a. White blood cells.
   b. Red blood cells.
   c. Lymphocytes.
   d. B cells.

7. Multiple sclerosis is an autoimmune disorder in which the body's immune system attacks and destroys the myelin sheath of its own nervous system. What implications does this damage have for the nervous system?

a. The cell bodies of nerve cells can no longer reach action potential because the receptors that take up sodium have been damaged.
b. Degraded myelin molecules block receptor proteins in the postsynaptic membrane.
c. Lack of myelin decreases production of acetylcholine (a neurotransmitter), disrupting muscular coordination.
d. Axons conduct nervous impulses less effectively because their insulating sheaths have been damaged.

CHAPTER 9

Ecology

Ecology is the scientific study of the interactions of organisms and their environments. It is a complex and critical area of biology. Individual organisms are grouped into populations, which in turn form communities, which form ecosystems.

***Population*(种群)**[1]: Groups of similar individuals who tend to mate with each other in a limited geographic area.

***Community*(群落)**: The relationships between groups of different species.

***Ecosystem*(生态系统)**: The relationships of smaller groups of organisms with each other and their environments.

> 1. 种群是指一群属于同一物种且在一定地理区域内活动的生物。
> 群落由同一地理区域内的不同的种群构成。
> 生态系统由群落与其周围的非生物因素构成。

Ⅰ. Population Ecology

A population is a group of individuals of the same species living in the same geographic area. The study of factors that affect growth, stability, and decline of populations is population dynamics. All populations undergo three distinct phases of their life cycle:

- *Growth*: Population growth occurs when available resources exceed the number of individuals able to exploit them. Reproduction is rapid, and death rates are low, producing a net increase in the population size.
- *Stability*: Population stability often proceeds by a "crash" since the growing population eventually outstrips its available resources. Stability is usually the longest phase of a population's life cycle.
- *Decline*: Decline is the decrease in the number of individuals in a population, and eventually leads to population extinction.

1. Checks on Population Growth
   Nearly all populations will tend to grow exponentially as long as there are resources available. Most populations have the potential to expand at an exponential rate, since reproduction is generally a multiplicative process. Two of the most basic factors that affect the rate of population growth are the birth rate, and the death rate. The intrinsic rate of increase is the birth rate minus the death rate.
   1) Two modes of population growth
      The **exponential curve(指数曲线)**[2], also known as a J-curve occurs when there is no limit to population size. The **logistic curve(逻辑曲线)**, also known as an S-curve shows the effect of a limiting factor.
   2) The mathematics of population growth
      Rate of natural increase (r) = Birth Rate (b) − Death Rate (d)
      Birth Rate expressed as the number of births per 1 000 per year.
      Death Rate expressed as the number of deaths per 1 000 per year.

      The rate of population growth at any instant is given by the equation[3]
      $$\frac{dN}{dt} = rN$$
      r is the rate of natural increase rate.
      t is some stated interval of time.
      N is the number of individuals in the population at a given instant.
      This graph shows the growth of a yeast population in culture. After a period of exponential growth, the size of the population begins to level off and soon reaches a stable value. This type of growth curve is S-shaped.

> 2. 指数曲线也叫做 J 型曲线,种群数量呈指数型不受限制地增长。
> 　　逻辑曲线也为 S 型曲线,种群数量增长后期受到限制因素的影响。

> 3. r 代表自然增长率,t 代表给定的时间间隔,N 代表给定时间的人口数目。

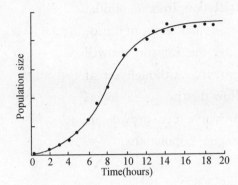

When $r=0$, $dN/dt=0$ and the population ceases to grow.[4] The yeasts have reached zero population growth or ZPG. It might be caused by running out of food and accumulation of toxic waste like ethanol (when its concentration reaches 12%~14%, the yeast die).

The limiting value of the population that can be supported in a particular environment is called its **carrying capacity**(环境容量)[5] and is designated as K. When the population is far below K, its growth is exponential, but as the population approaches K, it begins to encounter ever-stronger "environmental resistance".

$(K\text{-}N)/K$ is used as a "growth realization factor" that represents the degree to which the population can actually realize its maximum possible rate of increase.[6] Introducing this factor into original (exponential) growth equation, we get

$$\frac{dN}{dt}=rN\left(\frac{K-N}{K}\right)$$

The equation tells us that if the size of population (N) is far below the carrying capacity of environment (K), the growth realization factor will be close to 1, and the population will show exponential growth.

But as N begins to approach K, the growth realization factor approaches zero, and the rate of population growth drops to zero:[7]

$$\frac{dN}{dt}=0$$

4. 当增长率降为0时，种群停止增长，种群个体数目恒定。

5. 环境容量定义为K，是指特定环境能容纳某种群最极限的数量。当种群数量远低于K时，种群呈现指数增长；当种群数量接近K时，环境容量的作用越明显。

6. $(K-N)/K$也称做生长实现因子，代表种群实现最大可能生长率的程度。当种群数量N远小于环境容量K时，$(K-N)/K=1$，种群经历指数增长。

7. 当种群数量达到环境容量时，$K-N=0$，增长率也就为0，种群停止增长。

Plotting the growth of a population from an initial growth realization factor of 1 to a final factor of 0 produces a curve like this, called the logistic growth curve or S-shaped curve of growth. Although actual populations are unlikely to follow the theoretical logistic growth curve exactly, the curve can provide us with valuable guidance in managing populations.

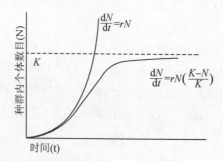

3) r-Strategists and K-Strategists

Weeds, many insects, and many rodents grow rapidly and produce a huge number of offspring. Their approach to continuing survival is through rapid reproduction, i.e. a high value of r, it is called an **r-strategists(r 策略生物)**[8]. In general r-strategists share a number of features:

- They are usually found in disturbed and/or transitory habitats.
- They have short life spans. The house mouse, with a maximum life span of 3 years, is an r-strategist.
- They begin breeding early in life.
- They usually have short generation times; that is, they have short gestation periods and are soon ready to produce another crop of young. The housefly can produce 7 generations each year, each of about 120 young.
- They produce large numbers of offspring. The American oyster, releasing a million eggs in one season, is an r-strategist. Most of its offspring will die, but the sheer size of its output increases the likelihood that some offspring will disperse to new habitats.

> 8. 生长快速并产生大量后代的个体,它们的种群增长率较快,也就是 r 值较高,所以称做 r 策略生物。
> r 策略生物的特点是:生命周期短、妊娠时间短、后代数目多、幼体死亡率高。

- They take little care of their offspring, and infant mortality is huge.

For r-strategists, alleles that enhance any of the traits listed above will be favored by natural selection. Hence, r-strategists are said to be the product of **r-selection(r 选择)**[9].

When a habitat becomes filled with a diverse collection of creatures competing with one another for the necessities of life, the advantage shifts to **K-strategists(K 策略生物)**[10]. K-strategists have stable populations that are close to K. There is nothing to be gained from a high r. The species will benefit most by a close adaptation to the conditions of its environment. Typically, K-strategists share these qualities:

- They are usually found in stable habitats. Most of the species in a mature forest will be K-strategists.
- They have long life spans. The elephants and the tortoises are K-strategists.
- They begin breeding later in life.
- They usually have long generation times. It takes 9 months to produce a human baby.
- Most produce small numbers of offspring. Birds are K-strategists, most species producing fewer than a dozen young each year.
- They take good care of their young. Infant mortality tends to be low.

For K-strategists, alleles that enhance their ability to exploit the resources of their habitat; that is, to increase the carrying capacity, K, of their environment, will be favored by natural selection. Hence, K-strategists are said to be the product of **K-selection(K 选择)**.

> 9. r 策略生物为 r 选择的产物。也就是说它们的等位基因进化均加强了它们的对策生物特征。

> 10. K 策略生物能够使种群数量稳定并接近环境容量。它们的特点是：栖息地稳定、生命周期长、性成熟周期长、妊娠时间长、后代数量少、后代死亡率低。加强 K 策略生物特征的选择称为 K 选择。

2. Several Basic Controls Governing Population Size

The environment is the ultimate cause of population stabilization. Two categories of factors are commonly used: physical environment and biological environment.

1) The vagaries of the physical environment include drought, freezes, hurricane, floods, forest fires, soil and light. These factors are described as **density-independent(与种群密度无关的)**[11] because they exert their effect irrespective of the size of the population when the catastrophe strikes.

2) Density-dependent or biological factors are mainly competition, predation, and symbiosis.

- **Interspecific competition(种间竞争)**[12] is a density-dependent factor limiting the growth of one or both populations. All the ecological requirements of a species constitute its ecological niche. The dominant requirement is usually food, but others, such as nesting sites and a place in the sun. When two species share overlapping ecological niches, they may be forced into competition for the resource(s) of that niche. Organisms or populations in competition have a niche overlap of a scarce resource for which they compete. Competitive exclusion occurs between two species when competition is so intense that one species completely eliminates the second species from the area. In nature this is rather rare. **Intraspecific competition(种内竞争)**[13] is the competition between members of the same species.
- As a population increases, its predators are able to harvest it more easily. **Predators(捕食者)**[14] kill and consume other organisms. Carnivores prey on animals; herbivores consume plants. Predators usually limit the **prey(被捕食者)** population, although in extreme cases they can drive the preys to extinction. There are three major reasons why predators rarely kill and eat all the preys:

Prey species often evolve protective mechanisms such as camouflage, poisons, spines, or large size to deter predation.

11. 环境因素多为与种群密度无关的限制因素，这些因素对于种群的影响与种群密度无关。

12. 竞争、捕食和共生是与种群密度相关的限制因素，也就是说，随着种群密度的增加，这些因素对于种群数量的影响作用将更加明显。

13. 种内竞争发生在同一个物种的个体间；种间竞争发生在两个物种的个体间。如果两个物种的生态位存在交叉，那么这两个物种的个体就可能因为争夺资源而发生竞争。根据竞争排斥原理，其中一个物种将最终被淘汰。

14. 在捕食关系中，捕食者以被捕食者为食物来源。捕食者不会使被捕食者完全灭绝。

Prey species often have refuges where the predators cannot reach them.

Often the predator will switch its prey as the prey species becomes lower in abundance: prey switching.

- **Symbiosis(共生)**[15] has come to include all species interactions besides predation and competition. **Mutualism(互利共生)** is a symbiosis where both parties benefit, for example algae inside reef-building coral. **Parasitism(寄生)** is a symbiosis where one species benefits while harming the other. Parasites act more slowly than predators and often do not kill their host. **Commensalism(共栖)** is a symbiosis where one species benefits and the other is neither harmed nor gains a benefit.

> 15. 共生是指除捕食和竞争外的其他种间关系。
> 互利共生是两个物种均受益的共生关系。
> 寄生是一方受益一方受害的共生关系,但寄生生物通常不杀死寄主。
> 共栖是一方受益而对另一方无影响的共生关系。

3) Human impact

Human populations have continued to increase, due to the use of technology that has disrupted natural populations.

- Pollutants generally are releases of substances into the air and water. Many lakes often have nitrogen and phosphorous as limiting nutrients for aquatic and terrestrial plants. Runoff from agricultural fertilizers increases these nutrients, leading to runaway plant growth, or eutrophication. Increased plant populations eventually lead to increased bacterial populations that reduce oxygen levels in the water, causing fish and other organisms to suffocate.

- Removal of a competing species can cause the ecological release of a population explosion in that species competitor. Pesticides sprayed on wheat fields often result in a secondary pest outbreak as more-tolerant-to-pesticide species expand once less tolerant competitors are removed.

- Predator release is common where humans hunt, trap, or otherwise reduce predator populations, allowing the prey population to increase. Introduction of exotic or alien non-native species into new areas is perhaps the greatest single factor to affect natural populations.

II. Community Ecology

A community is the set of all populations that inhabit a certain area. Communities can have different sizes and boundaries.

1. Classification of Communities

There are two basic categories of communities: terrestrial (land) and aquatic (water). These two basic types of community contain eight smaller units known as biomes. A biome is a large-scale category containing many communities of a similar nature, whose distribution is largely controlled by climate.

- **Tropical rain forest(热带雨林)**[16] biome occurs in regions near the equator. The climate is always warm (between 20℃ and 25℃) with plenty of rainfall (at least 190 cm per year). The rain forest is probably the richest biome, both in diversity and in total biomass. The tropical rain forest has a complex structure, with many levels of life. More than half of all terrestrial species live in this biome. While diversity is high, dominance by a particular species is low.

  > 16. 热带雨林终年温度高、雨水丰沛,是生物多样性和生物量最丰富的生物群系。

- **Temperate forest(温带森林)**[17] biome occurs south of the taiga in eastern North America, eastern Asia, and much of Europe. Rainfall is abundant (75~150 cm per year) and there is a well-defined growing season of between 140 and 300 days. Dominant plants include beech, maple, oak, and other deciduous hardwood trees. Trees of a deciduous forest have broad leaves, which they lose in the fall and grow again in the spring.

  > 17. 温带森林多为落叶林。

- **Shrubland(灌丛带)**[18] biome is dominated by shrubs with small but thick evergreen leaves that are often coated with a thick, waxy cuticle, and with thick underground stems that survive the dry summers and frequent fires. This Mediterranean-type shrubland lacks an understory and ground litter, and is also highly flam-

  > 18. 灌丛带的代表植物为常绿灌木,且叶表被蜡质覆盖,以减少水分散失。

mable. The seeds of many species require the heat and scarring action of fire to induce germination.

- **Grasslands(草原)**[19] occur in temperate and tropical areas with reduced rainfall (25～75 cm per year) or prolonged dry seasons. Grasslands occur in the Americas, Africa, Asia, and Australia. Soils in these regions are deep and rich and are excellent for agriculture. Grasslands are almost entirely devoid of trees, and can support large herds of grazing animals. Natural grasslands once covered over 40 percent of the earth's land surface. In temperate areas where rainfall is between 10 and 30 inches a year, grassland is the climax community because it is too wet for desert and too dry for forests.

> 19. 草原的气候为季节性干旱。同时草原的气候和土壤非常适合农耕。

- **Deserts(沙漠)**[20] are characterized by dry conditions (usually less than 25 cm per year) and a wide temperature range. The dry air leads to wide daily temperature fluctuations from freezing at night to over 120 degrees during the day. Plants in this biome have developed a series of adaptations such as succulent stems, and small, spiny, or absent leaves to conserve water and deal with these temperature extremes. Photosynthetic modifications like CAM plants are another strategy to life in the drylands.

> 20. 沙漠降水少,昼夜温差大。植物的叶子特化以适应干旱的气候。

- **Taiga(针叶林带)**[21] is a coniferous forest extending across most of the northern area of northern Eurasia and North America. The taiga receives between 25 and 100 inches of rain per year and has a short growing season. Winters are cold and long, while summers tend to be cool. The taiga is noted for its great stands of spruce, fir, hemlock, and pine. These trees have thick protective leaves and bark, as well as needlelike (evergreen) leaves can withstand the weight of accumulated snow. Conifers, alders, birches and willows are common plants; wolves, grizzly bears, moose, and caribou are common animals.

> 21. 针叶林带的代表植物为松、柏、杉。

- **Tundra(苔原带)**[22] covers the northernmost regions of

> 22. 苔原带的特征之一就是土壤为永久冻土;降水少,但夏天土壤中水分含量较高。

North America and Eurasia, about 20% of the Earth's land area. This biome receives about 20 cm of rainfall annually. Snow melt makes water plentiful during summer months. Winters are long and dark, followed by very short summers. Water is frozen most of the time, producing frozen soil, permafrost. Vegetation includes no trees, but rather patches of grass and shrubs; grazing musk oxen, reindeer, and caribou exist along with wolves, lynx, and rodents. A few animals highly adapted to cold live in the tundra year-round.

- **Freshwater biome(淡水生物群系)**[23] is subdivided into two zones: running waters and standing waters. Larger bodies of freshwater are less prone to stratification (where oxygen decreases with depth). The upper layers have abundant oxygen; the lowermost layers are oxygen-poor. Mixing between upper and lower layers in a pond or lake occurs during seasonal changes known as spring and fall overturn.

  > 23. 淡水生物群系分为两个区域：流动水和静水。上层氧含量高，下层氧含量较低。

- **Oceans(海洋)**[24] cover about three-quarters of the Earth's surface. Oceanic organisms are placed in either pelagic (open water) or benthic (ocean floor) categories. Pelagic division is divided into neritic and three levels of pelagic provinces. Neritic province has greater concentration of organisms because sunlight penetrates; nutrients are found here. Epipelagic zone is brightly lit, has much photosynthetic phytoplankton, which support zooplankton that are food for fish, squid, dolphins and whales. Mesopelagic zone is semi-dark and contains carnivores; adapted organisms tend to be translucent, red colored, or luminescent; for example: shrimps, squids, lantern and hatchet fishes. The bathypelagic zone is completely dark and largest in size; it has strange-looking fish. Benthic division includes organisms on continental shelf (sublittoral), continental slope (bathyal), and the abyssal plain.

  > 24. 海洋覆盖了地球表面四分之三的面积。生物体分为浮游生物和底栖生物两种。有光带中的浮游植物可进行光合作用，是浮游动物和其他生物体的食物来源。

- **Estuaries**(河口湾)[25] are bays where rivers empty into the sea. Erosion brings down nutrients and tides wash in salt water; forms nutrient trap. Estuaries have high production for organisms that can tolerate changing salinity. Estuaries are called "nurseries of the sea" because many young marine fish develop in this protected environment before moving as adults into the wide open seas.

> 25. 河口湾是指河流和海洋交汇处,长有丰富的耐盐植物,海洋动物的幼年期也在此处度过。

Biome	Abiotic factors			Biotic factors		Remark
	Soil	Climate		Plant	Animal	
		Temperature	Precipitation			
Tropical rain forest	Nutrient-poor	Hot	2 m	Canopies; understory	Camouflage	
Tropical dry forest		Warm	Long period of drought	Deciduous	Estivation	
Tropical grassland/ savanna/shrubland	Compact	Warm	Seasonal rainfall	Deciduous; waxy leaf covering	Migration / inactive	Fire
Desert		Extreme daily temperature change	25 cm	Store water in tissue; minimize leaf surface area	Get water from food active at night	
Temperate grassland	Fertile; ideal for agriculture	Warm summer; cold winter	Seasonal rainfall	Grass; resist of fire and grazing	Small animals; camouflage and borrowing	Fire
Temperate woodland and shrubland	Nutrient-poor	Hot summer; cold winter	Dry summer; moist winter	Adapt to drought; waxy leaves	Browers	Fire
Temperate forest	Fertile & humus	Warm summer; cold winter	Year-round	Deciduous / coniferous		
Temperate rain forest / NW coniferous forest		Mild; cool summer	Dry summer	Lush vegetation	Camouflage	
Boreal forest / taiga	Acidic nutrient-poor	Mild summer; cold winter	Moderate; high humidity	Conifers; wax-covered needlelike leaves	Small limb and ear; fat; downy feather	
Tundra	Nutrient-poor	Cold winter	Low; permafrost; soggy summer	Moss; low-growing	Migrate; natural antifreeze	Wind

2. Changes in Communities over Time

Biological communities like the organisms that comprise them, can and do changes over time. Ecological time focuses on community events that occur over decades or centuries.

Community succession(群落演替)[26] is the sequential replacement of species by immigration of new species and local extinction of older ones following a disturbance that creates unoccupied habitats for colonization. The initial rapid colonizer species are the pioneer community. Eventually a **climax community(顶级群落)**[27] of more or less stable but slower growing species eventually develops.

During succession productivity declines and diversity increases. These trends tend to increase the biomass (total weight of living tissue) in a community. Succession occurs because each community stage prepares the environment for the stage following it.

Primary succession(初生演替)[28] begins with bare rock and takes a very long time to occur. Weathering by wind and rain plus the actions of pioneer species such as lichens and mosses begin the buildup of soil. Herbaceous plants, including grasses, grow on deeper soil and shade out shorter pioneer species. Pine trees or deciduous trees eventually take root and in most biomes will form a climax community of plants that are stabile in the environment. The young produced by climax species can live in that environment, unlike the young produced by successional species.

Secondary succession(次生演替)[29] occurs when an environment has been disturbed, such as by fire, geological activity, or human intervention (farming or deforestation in most cases). This form of succession often begins in an abandoned field with soil layers already in place. Compared to primary succession, which must take long periods of time to build or accumulate soil, secondary succession occurs rapidly. The herbaceous pioneering plants give way to pines, which in turn may give way to a hardwood deciduous forest.

> 26. 群落演替是指老物种消亡新物种潜入的一系列的变化过程。

> 27. 群落演替的最终结果是一个稳定而复杂的群落,称为顶级群落。

> 28. 初生演替始于裸露的岩石,且经历的时间较长。地衣和苔藓等先锋物将在初生演替过程中最先出现。

> 29. 如果生物群落没有被彻底破坏,土壤依旧存在,那么将发生次生演替。次生演替的时间较短。

Ⅲ. Ecosystems Ecology

Ecosystems include both living and nonliving components. These living, or **biotic(生物的)**[30], components include habitats and niches occupied by organisms. Nonliving, or **abiotic(非生物的)**, components include soil, water, light, inorganic nutrients, and weather. An organism's place of residence, where it can be found, is its habitat. A niche is often viewed as the role of that organism in the community, factors limiting its life, and how it acquires food.

Producers(生产者)[31], a major niche in all ecosystems, are autotrophic, usually photosynthetic organisms. In terrestrial ecosystems, producers are usually green plants. Freshwater and marine ecosystems frequently have algae as the dominant producers.

Consumers(消费者)[32] are heterotrophic organisms that eat food produced by another organism. **Herbivores(食草动物)** are a type of consumers that feed directly on green plants (or another type of autotroph). Since herbivores take their food directly from the producer level, we refer to them as primary consumers. **Carnivores(食肉动物)** feed on other animals (or another type of consumers) and are secondary or tertiary consumers. **Omnivores(杂食动物)**, the feeding method used by humans, feed on both plants and animals.

Decomposers(分解者)[33] are organisms, mostly bacteria and fungi that recycle nutrients from decaying organic material. Decomposers break down detritus, nonliving organic matters, into inorganic matters. Small soil organisms are critical in helping bacteria and fungi shred leaf litter and form rich soil.

Even if ecosystems do differ in structure, they have some common uniting processes such as **energy flow(能量流动)** and **matter cycling(物质循环)**.[34] Energy flow moves through feeding relationships. The term **ecological niche(生态位)**[35] refers to how an organism functions in an ecosystem. **Food chains(食物链)**, **food webs(食物网)**, and **food pyramids(食**

---

30. 生物因素是指生态系统中的生物体;非生物因素是指没有生命的物体,如土壤、水分、光照、无机营养素和天气等。

31. 生产者,也称为自养生物,多为可进行光合作用的生物体,如绿色植物和藻类等。

32. 消费者,也称为异养生物,以其他生物体为食物来源。消费者包括以植物为食的食草动物、以其他动物为食的食肉动物和以动植物为食的杂食动物。

33. 大多数的细菌和真菌为分解者,通过分解有机体来促进物质循环。

34. 尽管各个生态系统结构不同,但是它们的能量流动和物质循环都是相似的。我们常用食物链、食物网和食物金字塔来描述能量流动。

35. 生物体在生态系统中的功能就是其生态位。

物金字塔) are three ways of representing energy flow.

1. Energy Flowing
   1) Food chains indicate who eats whom in an ecosystem, representing one path of energy flow through an ecosystem. Natural ecosystems have numerous interconnected food chains. Each level of producers and consumers is a **trophic level**(营养级)[36]. Some primary consumers feed on plants and make grazing food chains; others feed on detritus.

      > 36. 食物链中的每级生物体都可称做一个营养级。

      - At each trophic level, **net production**(净产量)[37] is only a fraction of **gross production**(总产量) because the organisms must expend energy to stay alive. Only a certain amount of food is captured and eaten by organisms on the next trophic level. Some of food that is eaten cannot be digested and exits digestive tract as undigested waste. Only a portion of digested food becomes part of the organism's body; the rest is used as source of energy. Substantial the portion of food energy goes to build up temporary ATP in mitochondria that is then used to synthesize proteins, lipids, carbohydrates, fuel contraction of muscles, nerve conduction, and other functions.

        > 37. 每一个营养级的净产量都只是总产量的很小的一部分。并不是食物中的所有成分都能被消化吸收,不能被消化的部分将排出体外;被消化的食物只有部分用于构建生物体本身的结构,剩下的被用作能量来源。

      - Note that the difference between gross and net production is greater for animals than for the producers — reflecting their greater activity. **Net primary productivity** (**NPP**,净初级生产力)[38] is the rate at which producer biomass is formed. Tropical forests and swamps are the most productive terrestrial ecosystems. Reefs and estuaries are the most productive aquatic ecosystems. All of these productive areas are in danger from human activity. Humans redirect nearly 40% of the net primary productivity and directly or indirectly use nearly 40% of all the land food pyramid. This energy is not available to natural populations.

        > 38. 生产者产生的生物量称为净初级生产力。

- Much of the energy stored in net production was lost to the system by decay and being carried downstream.
- Note the substantial losses in net production as energy passes from one trophic level to the next.
- The ratio of net production at one level to net production at the next higher level is called the conversion efficiency. Here it varied from 17% from producers to primary consumers (147 8/8 833) to 4.5% from primary to secondary consumers (67/1 478). From similar studies in other ecosystems, we can take 10% as the **average conversion efficiency**(平均转化/转换效率)[39] from producers to primary consumers.

2) Most food chains are interconnected. Animals typically consume a varied diet and, in turn, serve as food for a variety of other creatures that prey on them. These interconnections create food webs.

The population size in an undisturbed ecosystem is limited by the food supply, competition, predation, and parasitism. Food webs help determine consequences of perturbations: if titmice and vireos fed on beetles and earthworms, insecticides that killed beetles would increase competition between birds and probably increase predation of earthworms, etc.

3) The trophic structure of an ecosystem forms an **ecological pyramid**(生态金字塔)[40]. The food pyramid provides a detailed view of energy flow in an ecosystem. The first level consists of the producers (usually plants). All higher levels are consumers. The shorter the food chain the more energy is available to organisms.

The base of this pyramid represents the producer trophic level. At the apex is the highest level consumer, the top predator. Other pyramids can be recognized in an ecosystem.

- A **pyramid of numbers**(数量金字塔)[41] is based on how many organisms occupy each trophic level.

---

39. 上下两营养级之间的净产量之间的比值称为转化效率。生产者到初级消费者的平均转化效率为10%。

40. 生态系统中的营养结构构成生态金字塔。生态金字塔的最底层为生产者，上层为消费者。

41. 数量金字塔基于每个营养级中的生物体数目。
　　生物量金字塔可通过每一营养级中生物体的个数乘以生物体的平均重量来计算。
　　能量金字塔用于描述每一营养级中利用能量的数量。

- Since all organisms are made of roughly the same organic molecules in similar proportions, a measure of their dry weight is a rough measure of the energy they contain. The **pyramid of biomass(生物量金字塔)** is calculated by multiplying the average weight for organisms times the number of organisms at each trophic level.
- An **energy pyramid(能量金字塔)** illustrates the amount of energy available at each successive trophic level. The energy pyramid always shows a decrease moving up trophic levels because energy transfered between trophic levels are so inefficient.

2. Biogeochemical Cycles

   More than thirty chemical elements are cycled through the environment by biogeochemical cycles. There are six important biogeochemical cycles that transport carbon, hydrogen, oxygen, nitrogen, sulfur, and phosphorous. Recall that these six elements comprise the bulk of atoms in living things. Carbon, the most abundant element in the human body, is not the most common element in the crust, silicon is.

   1) Water cycle

      Saltwater evaporates from sun's energy producing fresh water in clouds, leaving salts in the ocean. Water vapor cools and condenses to precipitation over oceans and land. Runoff forms freshwater lakes, streams, ponds, groundwater, and is held in plants and transpired. Some water infiltrates the ground, becoming part of the groundwater, returning very slowly to the oceans. Water may be polluted or inadequate for human populations concentrated in specific areas.

   2) Phosphorus cycle

      Weathering of rocks makes phosphate ions available to plants through uptake from the soil. The mineral apatite contains a small amount of phosphorous, although this is enough for all living things to utilize. Runoff returns phosphates to aquatic systems and sediment. Organisms use phosphate in phospholipids, ATP, teeth, bones, and shells. Phosphate is a limiting nutrient because most of it is being currently used in organisms. The inorganic source, apatite, is a rare mineral, further limiting the input of this essential nutrient.

3) The nitrogen cycle

Atmospheric nitrogen gas (N_2), the major portion of our modern atmosphere, is unfortunately in a form that is not usable by plants and most other organisms. Plants therefore depend on various types of nitrogen-fixing bacteria to take up nitrogen gas and make it available to them as some form of organic nitrogen. Nitrogen fixation occurs when nitrogen gas is chemically reduced and nitrogen is added to organic compounds. Atmospheric nitrogen is converted to ammonium (NH_4^+) by some cyanobacteria in aquatic ecosystems and by nitrogen-fixing bacteria in the nodules on roots of legume plants (beans, peas, clover, etc.) in terrestrial ecosystems. Plants take up both NH_4^+ and nitrate (NO^{3-}) from soil. The nitrate (NO^{3-}) is enzymatically reduced to ammonium (NH_4^+) and used in the production of both amino acids and nucleic acids.

4) The carbon cycle

There is a relationship between the two major metabolic processes of photosynthesis and cellular respiration.

- Cellular respiration releases carbon dioxide, which is used as a raw material in photosynthesis. Photosynthesis in turn releases oxygen used in respiration. Animals and other heterotrophs depend on green organisms for organic food, energy, and oxygen. In the carbon cycle, organisms exchange carbon dioxide with the atmosphere.

- On land, plants take up carbon dioxide via photosynthesis and incorporate it into food used by themselves and heterotrophs. When organisms respire,

some of this carbon is returned to the atmosphere in the molecules of carbon dioxide.
- In aquatic ecosystems, carbon dioxide from air combines with water to give carbonic acid, which breaks down to bicarbonate ions. Bicarbonate ions are a source of carbon for algae. When aquatic organisms respire, they release carbon dioxide that becomes bicarbonate (HCO_3^-). The amount of bicarbonate in water is in equilibrium with the amount of carbon dioxide in air.

本章词汇

population	种群	community	群落
ecosystem	生态系统	exponential curve	指数曲线
logistic curve	逻辑曲线	carrying capacity	环境容量
r-strategist	r策略生物	r-selection	r选择
K-strategist	K策略生物	K-selection	K选择
density-independent	与种群密度无关的	interspecific competition	种间竞争
intraspecific competition	种内竞争	predator	捕食者
prey	被捕食者	symbiosis	共生
mutualism	互利共生	parasitism	寄生
commensalism	共栖	tropical rain forest	热带雨林
temperate forest	温带森林	shrubland	灌丛带
grassland	草原	desert	沙漠
taiga	针叶林带	tundra	苔原带
freshwater biome	淡水生物群系	ocean	海洋
estuary	河口湾	community succession	群落演替
climax community	顶级群落	primary succession	初生演替
secondary succession	次生演替	biotic	生物的
abiotic	非生物的	producer	生产者
consumer	消费者	herbivore	食草动物
carnivore	食肉动物	omnivore	杂食动物

decomposer	分解者	energy flow	能量流动
matter cycling	物质循环	ecological niche	生态位
food chain	食物链	food web	食物网
food pyramid	食物金字塔	trophic level	营养级
net production	净产量	gross production	总产量
net primary productivity (NPP)	净初级生产力	average conversion efficiency	平均转化/转换效率
ecological pyramid	生态金字塔	pyramid of numbers	数量金字塔
pyramid of biomass	生物量金字塔	energy pyramid	能量金字塔

本章重点

1. 种群增长模式及影响因子。
2. 利用数据或其他信息判断种群间的关系。
3. 利用数据或其他信息阐述环境对群落组成、分布的影响。
4. 生态系统的基本形态。
5. 能量及物质对食物链或食物网结构的影响。
6. 人类活动对种群、群落、生态系统的影响。
7. 负调控机制对生态系统的作用。

本章习题

1. Which of the following is least likely to result in density-dependent effects on the growth of natural populations?
    a. Interspecific competition.
    b. Parasitism.
    c. Disease.
    d. Increased rainfall.

2. In ecology, which of the following would most likely be considered as a K-selected trait?
    a. Excellent dispersal ability.
    b. Short lifespan.
    c. Short generation times.

d. A few, large offspring.

3. Which statement best describes the difference between exponential and logistic growth?
   a. Exponential growth depends on birth and death rates; logistic growth does not.
   b. Emigration and immigration are not important for logistic growth and are important for exponential growth.
   c. Exponential growth depends on density; logistic growth depends on the carrying capacity.
   d. Logistic growth reflects density-dependent effects of birth and death rates; exponential growth is independent of density.

4. Of the following species interactions, which one does NOT reduce population size?
   a. Commensalism.
   b. Predation.
   c. Competition.
   d. Brood parasitism.

5. Some plants contain nitrogen-fixing bacteria (of the genus *Rhizobium*) in their root nodules. This relationship is known as _____.
   a. an amensalism (one participant harms the other)
   b. a commensalism (one participant benefits but has no effect on the other)
   c. a mutualism (both participants benefit)
   d. interspecific (between species) competition

6. Two insect species were used in a laboratory experiment. For one treatment, both species were grown by themselves (in separate chambers) on a suitable food source. For the second treatment, the two species were grown together (in the same chamber) on the same type and amount of food as in the first treatment. The figure below shows the results (the number of individuals of each species in the two treatments) at the end of the experiment. Based on these results the two species should be classified as:

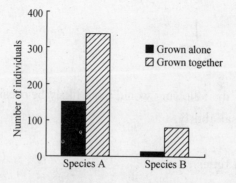

a. competitors
b. antagonists
c. mutualists
d. predators or pathogens

7. Which of the following statements about food chains and energy flow through ecosystems is FALSE?
   a. A single organism can feed at several trophic levels.
   b. Detritivores feed at all trophic levels except the producer level.
   c. The lower the trophic level at which an organism feeds, the more energy available.
   d. Food webs include two or more food chains.

8. The diagram below shows the feeding interactions between nine species (A to I) of a food web with four trophic levels. Which statement about this food web is CORRECT?

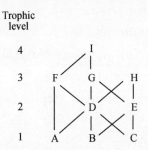

   a. Species A is a herbivore.
   b. Species D is a carnivore.
   c. Species G is an omnivore.
   d. Species H is a predator.

9. The total biomass in a terrestrial ecosystem will be the greatest for which trophic level?
   a. Herbivores.
   b. Producers.
   c. Primary consumers.
   d. Tertiary consumers.

10. A study of a freshwater community revealed the following food chain:
    phytoplankton→zooplankton→perch→trout→osprey.
    The amount of energy in phytoplankton in this community is 1,000,000 joules.

How much of this energy would most likely appear in the tertiary consumer given a 10% efficiency transfer between trophic levels?

a. 100,000 joules.

b. 10,000 joules.

c. 1,000 joules.

d. 100 joules.

11. The diagram below shows the feeding interactions between four species.

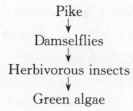

Which statement about the species interactions is CORRECT?

a. The damselflies are secondary carnivores.

b. The algae are chemoautotrophs.

c. If the pike were removed, the algae and damselfly populations would increase and herbivorous insects would decrease.

d. The pike are on the first (bottom) trophic level.

12. Energy enters an ecosystem via photosynthesis and moves up through the ecosystem's trophic levels. All of this energy will be _____.

a. used as fuel by the top predators in the ecosystem

b. converted into glucose by the primary producers

c. translated into the net primary productivity (NPP) of the ecosystem

d. converted into heat, a type of energy unusable by life on the Earth

13. Which of the following pairs does NOT match?

a. Tropical rainforest—high species diversity.

b. Ozone shield depletion—increased radiation reaching the surface of the Earth.

c. Greenhouse effect—rise in atmospheric CO_2.

d. Eutrophication—decreased net primary productivity.

CHAPTER 10

Labs, Equations and Formulas

Ⅰ. Labs Review

1. 对实验的考查方式仍以考题形式进行,不会要求实际操作。实验题可能会涉及实验设计,答题过程中需要包括以下内容:
   a. 实验假设(Hypothesis),用"IF... THEN..."的形式。
   b. 自变量(Independent Variables)和应变量(Dependent Variables),如有需要分别在 X 轴和 Y 轴上表示。
   c. 对自变量的处理,如:
      5 temperatures will be tested.
      5 individual wavelengths of light will be tested.
      3 environmental conditions (dry, wet, and normal) will be tested.
      Blood pressure will be taken while lying down, sitting up and standing.
   d. 实验组与对照组结果的比较,对照组的设计如:
      Room temperature
      Using white light
      Normal pressure conditions
      Normal humidity
      Blood pressure while sitting
   e. 列出实验步骤及材料。
   f. 说明实验重复的次数。
   g. 描述实验的结果。
   h. 如有需要绘制表格及坐标图。
   i. 用生物学领域的知识解释结果。

2. 若不需要设计实验,则会要求对一个已有实验进行描述,其中会要求解释:
   What was the hypothesis tested?
   实验假设的内容是什么?
   What were the independent and dependent variables?

自变量和应变量分别是什么？

How was the independent variable manipulated?

自变量如何处理？

What was the control group?

对照组是什么？

Why was there a control group?

为什么需要对照组？

If they used a certain material/setup, which process was being tested?

用该材料或设备是为了测定什么？

How could the experiment be improved?

该实验如何改进？（措施：repeated, larger samples, apply to other samples, use statistical analysis)

Be able to design a graph, complete a Chi-squared analysis, or a Hardy Weinberg equation if given data.

利用已知数据绘制图表、进行卡方测验或哈温公式计算。

下表总结了各知识点会涉及的实验及实验相关知识。

Lab	Process tested	Be sure to understand	Procedures to know	Materials to know
1	Diffusion and Osmosis (Plasmolysis and water potential)	• Factors that affect the movement of water across a membrane • How water & solutes will move across a membrane under different osmotic conditions • How to measure osmotic concentration of an unknown tissue or solution using solutions of known concentrations	Dialysis tubing setup(透析管)：体液内的成分(溶质或水分)通过半透膜排出 Red onion wet mount(红色洋葱细胞涂片)：用于观察质壁分离及复原 Potato core setup：通过测量并计算土豆小块浸于不同浓度溶液中前后质量变化的百分数并绘制曲线图，利用曲线图确定土豆细胞水势(曲线与X轴相交处对应的X轴数值即为土豆细胞水势)	Dialysis tubing Iodine（Lugols, IKI）—tests for starch Benedicts solution—must be heated and tests for simple sugars

2	Enzyme Catalysis Action	• Factors that influence enzyme action: *salt concentration, pH, temperature, and activators/inhibitors*
		• How to set up a similar experiment
		  • Enzyme extraction
		  • Enzyme dilution
		  • Altering enzyme pH
		  • Altering temperature
			Filter paper float method：将浸有过氧化氢酶的纸片放入不同浓度的 H_2O_2 溶液中，反应生成的 O_2 会聚集在纸片上使纸片上浮，比较不同溶液中纸片上升快慢可确定酶的催化效率	Catalase（过氧化氢酶）—enzyme (protein) used
				H_2O_2 (hydrogen peroxide)—substrate used

3	Mitosis and Meiosis	• How chromosomes are distributed during mitosis • The products of mitosis	Onion root tip squash(洋葱根尖细胞压片)：用于观察细胞有丝分裂	

Chapter 10　Labs, Equations and Formulas　213

(Continued)

Lab	Process tested	Be sure to understand	Procedures to know	Materials to know
4	Photosynthesis	• Factors that affect the rate of the photosynthesis • How to set up a similar experiment 　• What was being measured? 　• What was DPIP's role? • How to test for starch production (stored glucose)	Cuvette setup：用于分离从植物叶片中提取的色素 Spectrophotometer（分光光度计）：用于测定溶液的透光率，与 DPIP 共同使用可测定光合作用率	DPIP：随光合作用的进行可被还原，溶液逐渐从蓝色变成无色，结合分光光度计，透光率越高，光合作用越强烈 Phosphate buffer：用于维持溶液的 pH 值 Lugol's solution：淀粉指示剂，用于检验溶液中是否有淀粉存在 Bromthymol blue（溴百里酚蓝）：吸收 CO_2 后呈黄色，在封闭容器中若有光合作用发生则变蓝
5	Cellular Respiration	• Factors that affect the rate of respiration • How to set up a similar experiment 　• What was being measured? 　• How was generated CO_2 dealt with?	Respirometer setup（呼吸计）：留有通水口的半密封容器，内置豌豆及 KOH 溶液。容器浸入水中因植物呼吸作用消耗 O_2 形成负压，根据入水量换算成 O_2 的消耗量以测定呼吸率。KOH 溶液用于吸收反应生成的 CO_2	
6	Genetic Engineering	How to interpret gel electrophoresis results in restriction analysis	Electrophoresis（电泳）：经限制性内切酶酶切后的 DNA 样品带有电荷，在通电的凝胶电泳装置上 DNA 小片段可从负极移动到正极（小片段移动快于大片段），以此进行分离 DNA 样品并测定 DNA 片段的大小 Bacterial transformation：普通细菌无法在含有特定抗生素的培养基上生长，但细菌突变重组率极高，利用自然突变或人为干扰后筛选突变菌种	Restriction enzyme（限制性内切酶）：该酶可识别特定 DNA 位点，并在识别位点处剪切 DNA。不同 DNA 片段被同一限制性内切酶酶切后会形成不同长度的 DNA 小片段。常见的限制性内切酶如 EcoR1, HindIII, 具有不同的酶切位点。 Ampicillin plates（氨苄青霉素培养基）：正常细菌无法在该培养基上生长，若有突变菌种则生成抗性菌种（ampicillin resistance）
7	Genetic Analysis	• How to determine the genotype of individuals through crosses (P crosses, F_1 crosses with F_2 results) • Know how to calculate Chi-squared for P, F_1, and F_2 results to see if the null hypothesis can be accepted • Life cycle of *Drosophilae*		*Drosophilae*/fruit flies（果蝇）：遗传实验的模式生物，具有生命周期短、繁殖最大、染色体数目少等特点
8	Population Genetics and Evolution	• Factors that affect evolution (changes in allele frequency) in populations • How and when to use both Hardy Weinberg equation • Compare expected frequencies to actual to test for evolution • Heterozygote advantage		

Lab	Process tested	Be sure to understand	Procedures to know	Materials to know
9	Transpiration	• Factors that affect the rate of transpiration	Potometer setup(蒸腾计)：U型管填充水后，一端放置带茎叶的植物，另一端放置带刻度的毛细管，开口端用橡皮塞封住。根据反应前后毛细管水位变化测定蒸腾速率	Leaf mass and surface area needed for all set-ups to keep controlled conditions Normal conditions are control group
10	Circulatory System	• Factors that affect heart rate	Sphygmomanometer(血压计) Stethoscope(听诊器)	

11	Aquatic Dissolved Oxygen and Primary Productivity	• Factors that affect primary productivity
		• How to set up a similar experiment
		  • What was being measured?
		  • How was respiration measured?
		  • How was photosynthesis measured?
		  • How was gross productivity calculated?
		  • How was net productivity calculated?
		• How does this relate to health/stability of ecosystems?		

Ⅱ. Equations and Formulas

1. **pH**—用于计算溶液 pH 值。

    $pH = -\lg[H^+]$

2. **Gibbs Free Energy**—用于恒温、恒压下自发与平衡的判断

    $\Delta G = \Delta H - T\Delta S$　　　　ΔG：吉布斯自由能变化值

    　　　　　　　　　　　　ΔS：熵(Entropy)的变化值

    　　　　　　　　　　　　ΔH：焓(Enthalpy)的变化值

    　　　　　　　　　　　　T：绝对温度(Kelvin)

3. **Dilution**—用固定温度的溶液配制相同溶质不同浓度的新溶液

    $C_i V_i = C_f V_f$　　　　　i：起始/初始

    　　　　　　　　　f：终止

    　　　　　　　　　C：溶质的浓度

    　　　　　　　　　V：溶液的体积

4. **Surface Area-to-Volume Ratio**—用于计算细胞比表面积

(1) Sphere: $A/V = \dfrac{4\pi r^2}{4/3 \pi r^3} = \dfrac{3}{r}$

(2) Cube: $A/V = \dfrac{6a}{lwh}$

(3) Column: $A/V = \dfrac{2\pi r^2 + 2\pi rh}{\pi r^2 h} = \dfrac{2(r+h)}{r}$

l: 长
r: 半径
h: 高
w: 宽
A: 表面积
V: 体积

5. **Water Potential (ψ)**—用于计算及判断细胞水势

$\psi = \psi_p + \psi_s$
$\psi_s = -iCRT$

ψ_p: 压力势, 在开放容器中 $\psi_p = 0$
ψ_s: 溶质势, 渗透势
i: 电离常数, 蔗糖电离常数为1, 因其在水溶液中不电离
C: 摩尔浓度
R: 压力常数, $k = 0.0831$
T: 温度, 273℃ + t℃

6. **Law of Probability**—用于遗传概率的计算

(1) $P(A \text{ or } B) = P(A) + P(B)$
    性状 A 或性状 B 在个体上出现的概率

(2) $P(A \text{ and } B) = P(A) \times P(B)$
    性状 A 和性状 B 同时在个体上出现的概率

$P(A)$: 性状 A 单独出现的概率
$P(B)$: 性状 B 单独出现的概率

7. **Chi-Square Test**—在遗传学中用于测验所得结果是否与孟德尔遗传的分离比例相符

$\chi^2 = \sum \dfrac{(0-e)^2}{e}$

0: 具有某表现型的实际个体数
e: 具有某表现型的理论个体数
Degrees of freedom: 自由度 = 变量个体 - 1

P	Degrees of Freedom						
	1	2	3	4	5	6	7
0.05	3.84	5.99	7.82	9.49	11.07	12.59	14.07
0.01	6.64	9.32	11.34	13.28	15.09	16.81	18.48

(0.05 和 0.01 分别表示符合和概率, 0.05 的要求高于 0.01)

例: 有一豌豆遗传试验, 以黄色圆形种子(YYRR)品种与绿色皱皮种子(yyrr)品种杂交, F_2 代种子出现四种性状: 黄色圆形种子, 黄色皱皮种子, 绿色圆形种子, 绿色皱皮种子, 各有 491, 76, 90, 86 株。该遗传试验结果是否满足孟德尔自由组合定律?
按 9∶3∶3∶1 的理论比率算得各种表现型的理论值, 并得出以下数据:

表现型	黄圆	黄皱	绿圆	绿皱	点数
实际值(0)	491	76	90	86	743
理论值(e)	$417.94\left(743\times\frac{9}{16}\right)$	$139.31\left(743\times\frac{3}{16}\right)$	$139.31\left(743\times\frac{3}{16}\right)$	$46.44\left(743\times\frac{1}{16}\right)$	743
0−e	73.06	−63.31	−49.31	39.56	

$$\chi^2=\frac{73.06^2}{417.94}+\frac{(-63.31)^2}{139.31}+\frac{(-49.31)^2}{139.31}+\frac{39.56^2}{46.44}=92.696$$

Degrees of freedom＝4−1＝3

查表得 $\chi^2_{0.05,3}=7.82$，现实得 $\chi^2=92.696>\chi^2_{0.05,3}$，表示实际结果符合比率的概率小于5%，属小概率事件，认为结果不符合 9：3：3：1 的分离比例

若 $\chi^2<\chi^2_{0.05,3}$，表示结果符合。

8. **Hardy-Weinberg Equation**—种群未进化时，即基因频率未发生改变时，一对等位基因与其控制的相对性状的关系

$p+q=1$

p：种群中显性等位基因频率
q：种群中隐性等位基因频率
p^2：纯合显性个体比例

$p^2+2pq+q^2=1$

$2pq$：杂合显性个体比例
q^2：纯合隐性个体比例

9. **Growth Rate**—种群增长速率

Exponential Growth：$\dfrac{dN}{dt}=r_{max}N$

Logistic Growth：$\dfrac{dN}{dt}=r_{max}N\left(\dfrac{K-N}{K}\right)$

t：时间
N：种群个体数
K：环境容量
r_{max}：种群人均最大增长率

10. **Standard Error**—用于衡量抽样误差，推断样本是否对全体具有代表性

$SE\, \overline{x}=\dfrac{s}{\sqrt{n}}$

$s=\sqrt{\dfrac{\sum(xi\cdot\overline{x})^2}{n-1}}$

$\overline{x}=\dfrac{1}{n}\sum\limits_{x=1}^{n}xi$

$\overline{x}$：平均数
n：全体个体数

11. **Temperature Coefficient** Q_{10}—温度系数，温度每升高10℃所引起呼吸作用速率增加的倍数

$$Q_{10} = \left(\frac{k_2}{k_1}\right)^{\frac{10}{t_2-t_1}}$$

t_2:较高温度
t_1:较低温度
k_2:t_2 时的代谢速率
k_1:t_1 时的代谢速率

12. Primary Productivity Calculation

mg O_2/L×0.698=mL O_2/L

mL O_2/L×0.536=mg Carbon fixed/L

Vocabulary

Chapter 2

activation energy _____
active site _____
adenine _____
adhesion _____
ADP (adenosine diphosphate) _____
amine group _____
amino acid _____
amphipathic _____
amylopectin _____
amylose _____
anabolism _____
ATP (adenosine triphosphate) _____
carbohydrate _____
carboxyl group _____
catabolism _____
catalyst _____
cellulose _____
chitin _____
cholesterol _____
choline group _____
coenzyme _____
cofactor _____
cohesion _____
competitive inhibitor _____
condensation reaction _____
cytosine _____
dehydration reaction _____

denaturation _____
deoxyribose _____
disaccharide _____
electronegativity _____
endergonic reaction _____
energy coupling _____
enzyme _____
enzyme-substrate complex _____
exergonic reaction _____
fatty acid _____
free energy _____
fructose _____
glucose _____
glycerol _____
glycogen _____
glycosidic linkage _____
guanine _____
hydrogen bond _____
hydrolysis _____
hydrophilic _____
hydrophilic interaction _____
hydrophobic _____
induced fit model _____
isomer _____
lipid _____
metabolism _____
monomer _____

monosaccharide _____
negative feedback inhibition _____
nitrogenous base _____
noncompetitive inhibitor _____
nucleic acid _____
nucleoside _____
nucleotide _____
pentose sugar _____
peptide bond _____
phosphate group _____
phosphodiester bond _____
polar molecule _____
polarity _____
polymer _____
polypeptide _____
polysaccharide _____

primary structure _____
protein _____
quaternary structure _____
r group _____
ribose _____
saturated _____
secondary structure _____
sex hormone _____
specific heat capacity _____
starch _____
substrate _____
sucrose _____
tertiary structure _____
thymine _____
unsaturated _____
uracil _____

Chapter 3

active transport _____
alcoholic fermentation _____
amphipathic molecule _____
aquaporin _____
biosynthesis _____
bound ribosome _____
C_3 plant _____
C_4 plant _____
calcium ion _____
Calvin cycle _____
CAM pathway _____
carrier protein _____
cell wall _____
cellular respiration _____
central vacuole _____
centriole _____
centrosome _____
channel protein _____

chemiosmosis _____
chloroplast _____
cholesterol _____
cilia _____
contractile vacuole _____
cotransport _____
cristae _____
cyclic AMP _____
cyclic electron flow _____
cytochrome protein _____
cytoskeleton _____
cytosol _____
diffusion _____
electrochemical gradient _____
electrogenic pump _____
electron transport chain _____
endocytosis _____
endoplasmic reticulum _____

eukaryote _____
eukaryotic cell _____
exocytosis _____
extra cellular matrix _____
facilitated diffusion _____
fermentation _____
flagella _____
fluid mosaic model _____
food vacuole _____
free ribosome _____
gap junction _____
gated channel _____
glycolysis _____
Golgi apparatus _____
G-protein-coupled receptor _____
hypertonic _____
hypotonic _____
inner membrane _____
integral protein _____
intermediate filament _____
isotonic _____
Kreb's cycle _____
lactic acid fermentation _____
light reaction _____
light-harvest complex _____
lysosome _____
membrane potential _____
mesophyll cell _____
microfilament _____
microtubule _____
mitochondria _____
mitochondrial matrix _____
noncyclic electron flow _____
nuclear envelope _____
nuclear lamina _____
nucleoid region _____

nucleus _____
osmosis _____
outer membrane _____
oxidative phosphorylation _____
P680 _____
P700 _____
palisade layer _____
passive transport _____
peripheral protein _____
peroxisome _____
phagocytosis _____
phospholipid _____
photophosphorylation _____
photorespiration _____
Photosystem I _____
Photosystem II _____
pinocytosis _____
plasma membrane _____
plasmodesmata _____
plastid _____
prokaryote _____
prokaryotic cell _____
protein kinase _____
proton pump _____
proton-motive force _____
reaction center _____
reception _____
receptor-mediated endocytosis _____
receptor _____
response _____
ribosome _____
ribulose bisphosphate (RuBP) _____
rough endoplasmic reticulum _____
rubisco _____
second messenger _____
smooth endoplasmic reticulum _____

sodium-potassium pump _____   target cell _____
stroma _____   thylakoid _____
substrate-level phosphorylation _____   transduction _____

Chapter 4

acetylated _____   DNA ligase _____
allele _____   dominant _____
alternative splicing _____   double helix _____
anaphase _____   Duchenne muscular dystrophy _____
anaphase I _____   duplication _____
anaphase II _____   egg _____
aneuploidy _____   enhancer _____
asexual reproduction _____   euchromatin _____
bacteriophage _____   exon _____
Barr body _____   fertilization _____
cancer cell _____   frameshift mutation _____
catabolic activator protein (CAP) _____   gamete _____
Cdks _____   gametophyte _____
cell cycle _____   genotype _____
cell plate _____   haploid _____
checkpoint _____   helicase _____
chiasmata _____   hemophilia _____
cleavage furrow _____   heterochromatin _____
codominance _____   heterozygous _____
codon _____   histone _____
completely dominant _____   homologous chromosome _____
complimentary base pairing _____   homozygous _____
conservative replication _____   Huntington's disease _____
corepressor _____   incomplete dominance _____
cross over _____   inducer _____
cyclin _____   inducible operon _____
cystic fibrosis _____   intron _____
cytokinesis _____   inversion _____
deletion _____   kinetochore _____
diploid _____   lagging strand _____
dispersive replication _____ law of segregation _____

leading strand _____
linked gene _____
meiosis _____
meiosis I _____
meiosis II _____
metaphase _____
metaphase I _____
metaphase II _____
metaphase plate _____
methyl group _____
methylation of DNA sequence _____
missense mutation _____
mitosis _____
monohybrid cross _____
monosomy _____
multiple allele _____
negative control system _____
nonsense mutation _____
oncogene _____
operator site _____
operon _____
origin of replication _____
phenotype _____
phenylketonuria (PKU) _____
positive control _____
promoter _____
promoter site _____
prophase _____
prophase I _____
prophase II _____
recessive _____
regulatory sequence _____
repressible operon _____

repressor protein _____
RNA polymerase _____
RNA splicing _____
self-fertilization _____
semiconservative replication _____
sickle-cell disease _____
silent _____
single base substitution _____
sister chromatid _____
somatic cell _____
sperm _____
spore _____
sporophyte _____
start codon _____
stop codon _____
synapsis _____
Tay-Sachs disease _____
telomere _____
telophase _____
telophase I _____
telophase II _____
template strand _____
terminator _____
test Cross _____
tetrad _____
transcription _____
transformation _____
translation _____
translocation _____
trisomy _____
tumor repressor gene _____
zygote _____

Chapter 5

adaptation _____
adaptive radiation _____
allele frequency _____
allopatric Speciation _____
analogous structure _____
artificial selection _____
behavioral isolation _____
biochemistry _____
biogeography _____
bottleneck effect _____
coevolution _____
comparative anatomy _____
convergent evolution _____
directional selection _____
disruptive selection _____
divergent evolution _____
embryology _____
endosymbiosis theory _____
fossil _____
founder _____
gamete isolation _____
gene flow _____
gene frequency _____
gene pool _____
genetic drift _____
geographic isolation _____
gradualism _____

habitat isolation _____
homologous structure _____
hybrid breakdown _____
hybrid inviability _____
hybrid sterility _____
macroevolution _____
mechanical isolation _____
microevolution _____
natural selection _____
nonrandom mating _____
over-reproduction _____
paleontology _____
parallel evolution _____
polyploidy _____
post-zygotic reproductive isolation _____
Pre-zygotic reproductive isolation _____
punctuated equilibrium _____
reproductive isolation _____
reproductive success _____
sexual selection _____
species _____
stabilizing selection _____
survival of the fittest _____
sympatric speciation _____
temporal isolation _____
variation _____

Chapter 6

amniotic egg _____
animalia _____
archaea _____
archaebacteria _____
bacteria _____

binary fission _____
capsid _____
chemosynthetic bacteria _____
cladistics _____
class _____

conjugation _____
endospore _____
eukarya _____
family _____
flagella _____
fungi _____
genus _____
halophile _____
heterotrophic bacteria _____
lysogenic cycle _____
lytic cycle _____
methanogen _____
monera _____
monophyletic group _____
order _____
paraphyletic group _____
peptidoglycan _____
photosynthetic bacteria _____

phylogeny _____
phylum _____
phylum Chordata _____
plantae _____
plasmid _____
polyphyletic group _____
prophage _____
protista _____
retrovirus _____
reverse transcriptase _____
saprophyte _____
shared derived character _____
species _____
symbiotic bacteria _____
taxonomy _____
thermophile _____
transduction _____
transformation _____

Chapter 7

acid-growth hypothesis _____
actin _____
action potential _____
ADH _____
all-or-non _____
axon _____
calcitonin _____
cardiac muscle _____
cell body _____
critical night length _____
dendrite _____
endocrine system _____
endoskeleton _____
excitatory depolarizing neurotransmitter _____
excitatory postsynaptic potential _____

exoskeleton _____
glucagon _____
guard cell _____
homeostasis _____
hormone _____
hyperpolarization _____
hypothalamus _____
inhibitory postsynaptic potential _____
insulin _____
islets of langerhans _____
myelin sheath _____
myosin _____
negative feedback _____
nerve impulse _____
neuron _____

neurotransmitter _____
nodes of Ranvier _____
osmoregulation _____
photoperiod _____
phytochrome _____
pituitary gland _____
positive phototropism _____
PTH _____
refractory period _____
repolarization _____
resting potential _____
sarcolemma _____
sarcomere _____
sarcoplasm _____

Schwann cell _____
skeletal muscle _____
sliding filament theory _____
smooth muscle _____
stomata _____
synapse _____
thermoregulation _____
thyroid gland _____
transpiration _____
tropism _____
tropomyosin _____
troponin _____
vasoconstriction _____
vasodilation _____

Chapter 8

active immunity _____
AIDS _____
antibody _____
antibody-mediated response _____
antigen _____
antigen epitope _____
antigen presenting _____
antigen-binding immunoglobulin _____
antigen-presenting cell _____
B cell _____
bone marrow _____
cell-mediated response _____
Class I MHC molecules _____
cytotoxic T cell _____
helper T cell _____
histamine _____
Human Immunodeficiency Virus (HIV) _____
humoral immune response _____
immune system _____

inflammation _____
interferon _____
lymphocyte _____
major histocompatibility complex (MHC) molecule _____
memory cell _____
nonspecific _____
passive immunity _____
pathogen _____
perforin _____
phagocyte _____
primary immune response _____
secondary immune response _____
specific _____
specific immune response _____
T cell _____
thymus _____
tumor antigen _____
vaccination _____
vaccine _____

Chapter 9

abiotic _____
average conversion efficiency _____
biotic _____
carrying capacity _____
carnivore _____
climax community _____
commensalism _____
community _____
community succession _____
consumer _____
decomposer _____
density-independent _____
desert _____
ecological niche _____
ecological pyramid _____
ecosystem _____
energy flow _____
energy pyramid _____
estuary _____
exponential curve _____
food chain _____
food pyramid _____
food web _____
freshwater biome _____
grassland _____
gross production _____
herbivore _____
interspecific competition _____

intraspecific competition _____
K-selection _____
K-strategist _____
logistic curve _____
matter cycling _____
mutualism _____
net primary productivity (NPP) _____
net production _____
ocean _____
omnivore _____
parasitism _____
population _____
predator _____
prey _____
primary succession _____
producer _____
pyramid of numbers _____
r-selection _____
r-strategist _____
secondary succession _____
shrubland _____
symbiosis _____
taiga _____
temperate forest _____
trophic level _____
tropical rain forest _____
tundra _____

Answers for Practices

Chapter 2   Chemistry of Life

1. d   2. a   3. a   4. c   5. c   6. d   7. d   8. d   9. d   10. b

Chapter 3   Cell

1. d   2. a   3. b   4. b   5. d   6. d   7. b   8. a   9. d   10. d   11. c   12. b   13. c   14. a   15. a

Chapter 4   Genetics

1. d   2. c   3. a   4. d   5. b   6. b   7. c   8. a   9. c   10. a   11. d   12. a   13. d   14. b   15. b   16. c   17. a   18. d   19. d   20. b   21. a

Chapter 5   Evolution

1. a   2. c   3. d   4. b   5. d   6. c   7. c   8. a   9. d   10. c   11. b   12. d   13. b   14. a   15. d   16. a

Chapter 6   Biological Diversity and Classification

1. c   2. c   3. b   4. d   5. c   6. d   7. d   8. d   9. d   10. c   11. d   12. d

Chapter 7   Responding to Environment and Maintaining Homeostasis

1. b   2. c   3. b   4. d   5. a   6. a   7. b   8. d   9. a   10. c   11. d   12. a   13. c   14. c

Chapter 8   Defense against Disease

1. d   2. c   3. c   4. c   5. a   6. b   7. d

Chapter 9   Ecology

1. d   2. d   3. d   4. a   5. c   6. c   7. b   8. d   9. b   10. c   11. c   12. d   13. d